Rita's
WORLD

Books by Frank DeMarco

Nonfiction
A Place to Stand
Imagine Yourself Well
Afterlife Conversations with Hemingway
The Cosmic Internet
The Sphere and the Hologram
Chasing Smallwood
Muddy Tracks

Fiction
Babe in the Woods
Messenger

WORLD

A View from the
NonPhysical

FRANK DeMARCO

RAINBOW RIDGE
BOOKS

Cover and interior design by Frame25 Productions
Cover photo © Elena Schweitzer c/o Shutterstock.com

Published by:
Rainbow Ridge Books, LLC
140 Rainbow Ridge Road
Faber, Virginia 22938
www.rainbowridgebooks.com
434-361-1723

If you are unable to order this book from your local
bookseller, you may order directly from the distributor.

Square One Publishers, Inc.
115 Herricks Road
Garden City Park, NY 11040
Phone: (516) 535-2010
Fax: (516) 535-2014
Toll-free: 877-900-BOOK

Visit the author at:
www.hologrambooks.com

Library of Congress Cataloging-in-Publication Data applied for.

ISBN 978-1-937907-37-2

10 9 8 7 6 5 4 3 2 1

Printed on acid-free recycled paper in the Canada

Dedication

Of course, to the memory of
Rita Q. Warren
As I knew her in her last years,
the wise old woman on the hill,
the soft-spoken friend to explorers,
the teacher so beloved by so many students,
the scholar still quietly, doggedly,
pursuing her research.

But dedicated, equally,
to Rita
as I experience her now,
wiser and young again, with wider horizons,
still a loyal friend to explorers,
still the beloved, skillful teacher,
now living what she said would be her ideal life—
endless research and no reports to write up!

Contents

Introduction

This is the record of a series of conversations between two old friends, one of them no longer in the body. Rita and I were beginning again where we had left off, still looking for clarity about life, and the afterlife, and the reality behind appearances.

That needs explaining.

Rita Warren was the first director of the consciousness laboratory at The Monroe Institute (TMI). Over a period of four years, she and her husband, Martin, conducted hundreds of sessions on volunteers in the Institute's isolation booth, or black box, using Monroe's sonic technology to assist them into altered states of consciousness. During those sessions, Rita had sometimes asked the volunteers about the afterlife and other aspects of reality, but when she retired after directing the lab for four years, her curiosity remained unsatisfied.

She and I met shortly after I moved to the New Land community (adjacent to the Institute) in 1998, but we didn't really get to know each other until after Martin died in April 2000. After that, she and I made a point of having Saturday evening supper together at a certain restaurant in nearby Lovingston. We were very different. At age 80, she was 26 years my senior and she had had a distinguished academic career, as opposed to my background in journalism and book publishing. But we had had similar experiences with TMI residential programs, and we were equally interested in the hidden nature of things. The many months of weekly dinners, and emails and phone calls, and shared stories and jokes, all served to build a comfortable relationship between us, based on trust. This would become important.

In the autumn of 2000, I did a series of ten exploratory sessions in the black box and posted the transcripts to a group of email friends, naturally including Rita. Our Saturday evening dinners often centered on discussion of that information. A few months later, at her suggestion, she and I began to do weekly sessions together in her home after I had gotten home from work and had had supper. And that is how, on Tuesday night, August 8, 2001, she began looking for answers to the questions that had long interested her.

Over the course of many months of weekly sessions with "the guys upstairs," Rita and I were given a new way (1) to see the world, (2) to change our lives and, as you will see, (3) to thereby change the world. This promise is not overstated but is, if anything, an understatement.

Anyone who does any serious exploring into the question of "what is real and what is not" is soon presented with difficulties. It is difficult to envision life on "the other side." How do beings there spend their time? What is it they do, and why do they do it? What if anything is their relationship to us? For that matter, what is our life all about? Could such questions be answered? Well yes, as it turned out, they could be.

Rita later told me that neither she nor Martin had ever gotten answers equal in clarity and consistency to what we got from what I called "the guys upstairs." Session by session, week upon week, the guys introduced certain themes, and built upon them, until after a few months Rita and I were living in a very different world. I started to edit the sessions for publication and got Rita to write an introduction, but by the time *The Sphere and the Hologram* came out, she had already made her transition. She died March 19, 2008 and came to me in a dream to assure me that she was fine, and then for six and a half years I assumed our work together was over.

So when, in December 2014, I dreamed of her saying she was ready for us to work together again, I was surprised, but pleased. The next morning, I sat down with my journal and announced myself ready. I was prepared for anything or nothing, as usual in this business of communicating.

∽

What makes me think that I can talk to the dead, or that the dead could talk to me—or would want to? Common sense certainly suggests otherwise.

The trouble is, "common sense" depends upon unstated assumptions:

1. That the past is gone and the future is not yet created, and that the present is all that exists;

2. That the dead either cease to exist or exist beyond the range of the living.

Neither assumption is true. Centuries of recorded experience, including the world's scriptures, testifies to people seeing the future and communicating with the dead. We think of the dead as gone; but in fact, their souls live on, as alive as when they were here, but outside of time and space. *Being* outside of time and space, *all* times and *all* spaces are available to them. This is how, when we communicate with them, they can know what we know (interacting with our minds "from the inside" so to speak) and can react to that knowledge. This is why we can communicate with them about the things in our life.

So who is it are we interacting with? It isn't always possible to know, and it isn't always necessary to know. A message has to stand on its own, to resonate or not, rather than lean on someone's presumed authority. Sometimes I think I recognize the presence of this or that specific individual, but I try to remain aware that what I think I know may or may not be true. I proceed on that understanding, and so should you. The Rita I connect to is not the entire person, any more than anyone is the entire person to anyone, ever. We relate to each other according to who we each are. Some traits and interests are shared, some are not. There never has been and never will be a relationship without mystery. How could there be?

But can we at least prove that when we think we are talking to the dead, we aren't just making it up as we go along? The short answer is no, we can't. There's very little we can *prove* about the source of any kind of knowledge, be it ever so conventional. No matter what we think we know, it can never be absolutely true, and what is true in one context may be untrue in another. Our scientific outlook, our religious outlook, our anti-scientific or anti-religious outlook, whatever, can *only* be provisional. That's just the way it is, and you might as well get used to it.

Instead, the question that matters is, "Does the information resonate? Is it helpful?" If so, what difference does it make if it comes from another life or from another part of your own mind unsuspected by you? You just need to be careful about what you're ready to believe.

Explorers by definition move into poorly mapped or unmapped territory, and by their own experience help fill in the map for those who follow. All that can be required is that they be resolute, honest, and a bit skeptical even of the maps they themselves help to draw. It cannot be required of them that they always know what they are doing or where they are going. If you were to stick to "respectable" or "commonsense" explanations and pathways, what kind of exploring would that be? Sometimes you have to just keep on going and trust that eventually things will sort out. Exploring is the only alternative to either taking things on faith or refusing to think about them at all.

Any culture's scriptures deal with interaction between the physical and the nonphysical aspects of the world. The problems, the techniques, the models are, after all, just so many varieties of packaging. The reality remains the same. But old words go dead on new generations, and so old truths have to be restated to be heard. In our time, neither science nor religion is conveying a picture of the afterlife that we can relate to. Neither the believers nor the materialists provide us with a credible picture of the meaning and nature of life. So where can we find one? Direct communication with the other side of life, the nonphysical side, is as close to firsthand information as we can get, at least until we ourselves drop the body and cross over.

In the course of these conversations, I received information that builds an intellectually respectable model of our lives in the physical and nonphysical world. It has been a-building for fifteen years, but my sessions with Rita are the clearest exposition so far.

⬿⬾

At some point in December, it occurred to me that we should proceed more carefully, and I proposed a collaboration to my friend Charles Sides. I have easy access, and years of practice, talking to people who are not in the physical, and Rita and I were emotionally close for the last eight years of her life, so clearly I would be the right guy to get the information. But

I knew Charles to be the right guy to structure the questions and follow-up questions and to outline the resulting material. He has spent a lifetime formulating the questions and examining the answers that have come out of the East. All that background knowledge would inform his questions, because a lifetime's research had formed his mind and his way of seeing the world. It seemed to me that together we might be able to do what neither of us could do alone.

I asked him to pose questions one by one, and then either pose other questions, or ask follow-ups, whichever seemed appropriate. He agreed with some enthusiasm, so I decided to begin again in the new year. After a short hiatus, Rita and I began again in January, and the information came fast and furious for several weeks, then tapered off, until, by mid-May, we had reached a natural place to pause. This volume carries the conversation through the month of February. Our talks from March into May will comprise volume 2. Rita and I still communicate, and perhaps we will accumulate enough material for books beyond these two, but in any case what you have in your hand is quite enough material to change your life.

The Sessions

December 2014

Saturday, December 6, 2014

Correcting the picture

7:30 a.m. Well, Miss Rita, a dream tells me that you are ready to communicate—or maybe that you have been, and I am now ready. It would be a pleasure.

You have had an effect on my life here, you know. Letting people in body know of our work together results in some of them contacting me, not necessarily being aware of it, which of course affects me here.

> [I took this to refer to *The Sphere and the Hologram*,
> and my talks to Guidelines groups at TMI.]

Not an unwelcome development, I hope.

Not unwelcome. Unanticipated during my time in the body, certainly!

I suppose so. I seem to remember hearing that Bob Monroe was concerned about people trying to contact him being a problem—though come to think of it, that may have been people just talking. So, Rita, open for business. Those lovely months

*communicating nearly every day with Papa [Hemingway] came only after you were
gone, so we never had a chance to discuss any of the process or contents.*

You needed to do it on your own anyway. It had to be your process.

*I guess. So—did you have something in particular you wanted to start with? Or
did you already?*

That's as good a place to start as any—the continuing interaction
between those in and those out of the body, not necessarily known to those
in body, but real nonetheless. There is a tendency to think of life in the body
as an interruption of life outside it, as though we come into form, have a
lifetime's worth of experiences, and then report. But it doesn't work that
way. I'd like to correct the picture, but it can't be done in a hurry.

*Well, I got the sense, the other day, that I was being primed for a new set of lessons.
Didn't guess that it was going to come via an old friend rather than anonymous "guys
upstairs."*

You did get, by "accidentally" coming across that passage in the
Hemingway book you brought forth, that your understanding to date was
merely provisional unless you lost your nerve or your appetite for further
refinement and redefinition.

Continuous communication

Then let's begin. We're going to begin in a place that will perhaps surprise
you, telling you what you think you already know, but hang on for the ride
and see. The first statement:

"This side" and "the other side" are in continuous unbroken communication, regardless what it feels like to those in body.

Some, like you, won't find anything to object to in that statement;
but in fact, in day-to-day living, in ideas as expressed in action, few if any
live that reality. In fact, in actual living, you live as though communication
exists only when you intend it, or are aware of it.

This is not "good" or "bad"; it is how the separation of 3D life leads you to experience (or not experience) that aspect of life. But your life is bounded by your expectations of life, and we're interested in expanding these expectations.

The idea that there can be a separation between physical and nonphysical stems from the idea that different substance is involved in either realm. As you were told pretty much right away [in our 2001-2002 sessions], there is no difference between beings in the physical and in the nonphysical except the conditions of the terrain each is on.

In other words, although it is convenient to talk of different beings, in truth we are all part of one thing—the "everything"—in a way you can't yet imagine, which I am going to try to help you with. Many of the contradictions between systems disappear if you see that all is one.

"All is one"—it is a New Age cliché—but what does it mean in practice? Next time.

Sunday, December 7, 2014

9:15 a.m. So, Rita, here I am—hopefully here we are—and I'm more nervous than when I first started talking to Ernest Hemingway (at your suggestion). On the one hand, I feel like we're at the beginning of something, maybe something big. On the other hand I'm worried, trying not to be, but worried lest the material not be there, you not be there, nothing make sense—you know the litany. But I don't know anything else to do but to open shop and see. So, over to you.

I think you will find things different now, because the landscape is different. You have now had so many years of doing this, and you have seen so many reassuring results of the material, that continued nervousness or apprehension is more like a nervous tic than any real apprehension that might cripple your ability to interact.

Let's hope. Okay.

Communities and distinctions

Yesterday was "continuous communication," and I said today's would be "all is one," so let's look at that.

Material given to you when you and I were doing sessions, and in fact before, tell you that it is a mistake to think that there is any such thing as an individual in the way the "modern world" thinks of individuals. But, as you were also told, neither is the other side shapeless jello. Rather, one productive way to see things is as an endless cascade of communities, each of which—anywhere up or down the scale—could be experienced or conceptualized as an individual.

You sort of got that, and sort of didn't, so let's look at it a little closer.

You need to expand your focus sideways, so to speak. Not only do you need to try to keep in mind the great chain of being, you need to remember that every link of that great chain also extends to the nonphysical, because everything is one thing, as said. There can be no absolute separations in a fabric, and all reality is one fabric.

I feel like we're beating a dead horse, restating this, but different people will require different ways of seeing it, and the same people will require different ways at different times—partly because different people are in charge at each different time. (That is, a person, being a community, will find that community dominated now by one, now by another, member.)

Beating the horse or not, here goes again:

Any division is only provisional and for the sake of convenience. Buddha said when you start to make distinctions, you start making errors. I don't think he meant that a snake and a bowl of rice are the same thing (after all, "all is one," right?)—he meant, the snake and the bowl of rice do not exist in isolation regardless what the senses report.

It is certainly true that we must make and observe distinctions in life— and that, by the way, means nonphysical life no less than physical life, for here, too, although the strands that connect everything are obvious, so are the individual communities, which is why I am communicating with you and not [communicating with] a rock. But it is equally true that we misunderstand the nature of reality if we forget that nothing exists unconnected to the whole.

Now, so far so good. What I've said is still New Age cliché. But you have to build on something, and if you don't have the foundation agreed upon, some people's castles, at least, are going to be built in the air.

So, all is one; let's look closer.

A molecule, an atom, radioactivity, anything you can name—it all has its nonphysical component, however little obvious it is.

Dimensions

These two ideas are often held in different compartments of people's minds—the great chain of being, the connection between physical and nonphysical. The lack of connection between the two concepts makes for distortion.

Perhaps this is enough for today, though less than I had hoped. It may be as well—given that you are broadcasting these sessions live, so to speak—to let people ponder on that connection before building on it. Everything is all connected—on the physical side. It is all connected on the nonphysical side, as well. And it is connected at every level between physical and non-physical. This is an important concept, much more important than it seems at first blush. If it is kept in mind, gradually it changes everything.

Here's a way of thinking about it, building upon a thought you have had more than once. It is obvious that however many dimensions exist, anything that exists, exists in all of them, by necessity. You could not live in height and width but not in depth. You could not live in height, width, and depth but not in time. If a dimension exists, you exist within it, regardless how you misperceive it, or fail to perceive it. As you have been told, reality has more dimensions than people typically experience, and all the dimensions they do not experience, or they misperceive, are crammed into their experience of [the nature of] time. As they learn to distinguish elements of other dimensions, the nature of time, as they perceive it, correspondingly changes, for it then reflects less of the misperceptions that it previously had reflected.

The nature of time doesn't change. The experience of the nature of time does.

It might be worth your while to start to think about the nonphysical as additional dimensions of reality, rather than to make a distinction between physical and nonphysical. The advantage of reconceptualizing in this way is that it will gradually entice you to remove that seemingly impermeable barrier—the "veil"—between physical and nonphysical.

That's the theme anyway, isn't it? Cease regarding the nonphysical as something separate from the physical, something awe-inspiring and—well, something other than part of normal life.

That's right. You've laid good groundwork for that, by seeing your guys upstairs—of whom I am now one, you'll notice!—as *people* rather than demigods or statues. More another day.

Monday, December 8, 2014

8:50 a.m. Miss Rita, you're on. I just reread the first two sessions—and I will recommend to others that they do so as we go along, because they aren't long, and it will help to keep the argument and the trend of the thought in mind.

If people are receiving this on their computers, they can perhaps save them as files and strip out extraneous material such as remarks like this so as to have a smaller file to review—a smaller file to which the gist of each day's entries will be added.

Good idea. I think I'll do that too, though I'll keep the originals as well.

Everything lives

So. Both "sides" communicate; all is one; it turns out there are not two "sides" at all, but one undivided reality in which perceptions determine characteristics. That is, as your perception clarifies, you become able to differentiate characteristics that had been lumped together as characteristics of "time" or had been missed entirely.

Now add this—another *huge* jump for some, especially those rooted in the scientific tradition. And trust me, I sympathize, because I lived my life in that tradition even to the end. Everything is alive, and sentient, and, of course, interacting.

Doesn't seem like much of a jump? Well, consider. You have just left the world of dead objects floating in empty space and have, you might say, reentered the medieval or ancient worldview through a different door.

To find the blindest spots of the worldview you have grown up with, look precisely to those things it condemns as superstition. That isn't to say that every superstition is a legitimate way of seeing things; it is to say that the ways of seeing things that are most antithetical to the prevailing world-view are going to be condemned as superstition because they are going to seem obviously nonsense.

You, Frank, will find this a small step, not only because of your Catholic background that you learned to appreciate, but because of your own experiences and reading. But trust me, some will find this a terrific obstacle.

All the world is alive. All of what is called the physical world partakes of the dimensions usually called nonphysical. This can mean only that either everything is "spiritual" in nature, or nothing is. There is no separation into spiritual and non-spiritual, any more than into living and dead, or sentient and nonsentient.

Now, obviously, this isn't how it appears in the three-dimensionally experienced world. It is only when one escapes the limitations either by dropping the body or by achieving mental clarity that the truth of what I'm telling you emerges.

It must be understood: Life in the 3D world is one of deliberate structured limitation. While functioning in a world with a body, blindness to a greater reality is possible and, in fact, likely. But it isn't necessary, and can easily be overcome by a movement of mind, or shall we say spirit.

And this will be another fact to be addressed. Things you see as separate are usually the same thing seen in different contexts, or experienced in different ways. Thus, "mind" and "spirit." Same thing, in a way—a continuum with mind on one end and spirit on the other, if that's any easier to visualize. Just as color is a continuum, with any given color being one stop on the dial, so mind and spirit are more like two ways of conceptualizing than like two different things.

Let me try that again. Orange is not necessarily an absolute, distinct from yellow on one end and red on the other. It could be described, and experienced, either way, and each way would be relatively true except insofar as each explanation tended to exclude the other.

This is a rule of thumb to keep in mind: Any explanation may have value, but it will have the inherent shortcoming of seeming to exclude contradictory explanations. *Logically*, it follows that any one thing excludes its opposite. But in real life, as opposed to two-value logic, exclusions function mostly as strait-jackets, preventing you from turning to see the same thing from another point of view.

To return to the main point and proceed: If everything is alive—and it is—and everything is sentient, and connected, and partakes of the nature of all dimensions regardless of 3D appearance—then perhaps you can see why the ancient and medieval worldviews understood the world to be peopled with spiritual energies. It is. And the modern world's blindness to those energies served the purpose of creating a new way of seeing, but the usefulness of the limitation has been outlived. A new spiritual scientific view is possible that would not have been possible but for the scientific view of the past 500 years, and won't be possible until that older view is heavily amended.

Only a little more than half an hour, but it feels like you've provided a lot in a small space. I'd say we stop here and I transcribe and broadcast.

That's fine; this is not a bad place to pause.

Till next time, then.

[Rereading this, I see that perhaps I should add that Russell Targ told me years ago that two-value logic is not as accurate as four-value logic. Two-value logic says either A=B or A<>B. Four-value logic recognizes two additional intermediate conditions, one in which A is both B and not B, and one in which A is neither B nor not B. I predict that this, too, will be an obstacle for some people. We'll see.]

Tuesday, December 09, 2014

Redefinition

5 a.m. I realized, suddenly—well, let's put it this way—

Lying in bed, sort of daydreaming about various things, I was remembering that I had intended to furnish a series of sketches for The Sphere and the Hologram, *and I was wondering if I should make the effort to do it now, when I realized that perhaps the material Rita was facilitating would render that view of things obsolete, as indeed they had said would happen unless I was unable or unwilling to leave what had become familiar and continue exploring. All the concepts that have become so familiar these past years—the guys upstairs, the veil, the other side, etc.—if we really reconceptualize, it all goes, or remains as a sort of halfway house, a safe clearing in the forest that allows you to move deeper.*

So. Miss Rita, is that what is up?

It is if you want it to be.

I'm willing.

Then let's continue. Reread what you've gotten so far—just skim it—as preparation, to put it into active memory, so to speak.

All right. So far:

This side and the other side are in continuous communication.

"All is one" means there is no separate "spiritual" world or life.

Reality seems to change as we perceive differently.

Ways of perceiving and conceptualizing that contradict whatever we believe are experienced as nonsense or superstition.

Close enough. Naturally this is not anything new in itself; it is a clearing of the path for something new.

Understood.

You were asked once—by me when I was in the body—what we do on this side. How we spend our time.

I remember. The answer given was, "We relate," which I took to mean, relate to one another, but did not find tremendously illuminative.

No, but now perhaps I can help answer my question; but to do so is going to take a long time, I'm afraid, mostly because so much site-clearing and demolition of old structures must come before anything new can be constructed.

So many silent assumptions to deal with. That there are different souls (or minds); that they relate to one another; that the nature of their "daily" existence is inherently different from daily existence in the body; conversely that there can be any similarity. So many religious beliefs—and anti-religious beliefs. Not least, so many incorrect beliefs about the nature of life in the physical world.

Not so productive to try to tear down beliefs or systems of beliefs. Better to construct alternative ways of seeing that can gently replace them. But of course, this will only help those willing to provisionally adopt them— that is, consider them fairly.

The guys always said—and I can see I'm going to have some trouble even learning how to talk about all this again—I was always told that one strength I brought to this work was my ability to deal with ambiguity, my tolerance for not knowing, my willing- ness to discard past beliefs in light of new experience.

It isn't very easy to move while staying in one place. It's easier to move if you don't demand guarantees in advance that you will like or even remain in the new place.

Perhaps—if I can steer this by way of suggestion—it would help if you give us another way of thinking about what I have called my relationship to the guys upstairs; what others (and I, in other moods) call guidance.

Yes, that is on the agenda, but as I say, it isn't necessarily going to be simple or quick to redefine any of it, because any set of understandings is really a web of mutually reinforcing concepts. I say mutually reinforcing—but some may reinforce, some may contradict; still, they coexist, and changing any will, to a larger or smaller degree, change all. That is what I said earlier.

Guidance

So, perhaps begin here. If you have learned to experience guidance, however you conceptualize it, you recognize firsthand that it is a source of material, or of judgments, or of knowings, other than your more commonly available mental processes. That doesn't make this source "other than" yourself. It doesn't inherently make it anything. All you know about it is that it is not your ordinary mental process at work, or at least is not apparently your ordinary process.

So what happens when your life accommodates this new source of information and judgments to the point that it becomes normal? What then?

One conceptualization is—it was always part of yourself; you just integrated it more closely.

Fine. What does that mean? When you look at it, what does it mean, to say "you" integrated "it" more closely? What defines you? What defines integrated?

This is not playing with words. If it seems so, you may take this as a signpost marking concepts that may be resisting being reexamined. (I am aware that this phrasing will seem strange. This will make more sense after a while.)

Another conceptualization is that it was "the guys" (or any transpersonal being or group of beings). But again, as your access increases to the point that it becomes as normal to you as what you had already considered normal—in other words as your range increases to incorporate what have been "altered" states as part of your normal state—what has happened?

If you talk to past lives, and other individuals, and your own past or future selves, or—on another scale (seemingly)—as you talk to components of your body and/or mind as if they were separate individuals, what is happening?

The rings and threads analogy that was provided in our sessions were given as a step toward loosening our idea that in the body we are individual and thus toward loosening the idea that *out* of body (postbody) we are individual.

All of that was in The Sphere and the Hologram *and sort of digested in* The Cosmic Internet. *Even then—and more so as time went on and I explained it to groups and thought about it—I saw that it couldn't be the complete story. Is any of it going to be left by the time we get through with whatever you're bringing?*

Yes, but it will be modified. You might provisionally look at it this way: Previously you saw the rings and not the threads. The information we received in 2001–2002 revealed the existence of the threads, at the cost of somewhat exaggerating their importance relative to the rings. This will return emphasis more to the rings *in a way* without disregarding or defining out of existence the threads that are so important in the process of redefinition. However, remember that you never had a very clear idea of what those threads were, or were like, or how they functioned, or came into existence, or changed. You played with threads, strings, ropes, cables, and combinations of the concepts. You thought of them as traits, and said rings had millions of them, and then found yourself a little at a loss when you came to consider the world from the question of reincarnation, souls' progress, etc.

But it is almost 6 a.m., enough for this time.

Thanks, and I'll pass it along.

Thursday, December 11, 2014

7 a.m. Feeling a little stretched, Rita. So, missed yesterday deliberately to concentrate on Papa's Trial [a novel in process]. Shall we continue? I'll glance back at the material first unless you don't think I need to.

Always a good idea to give yourself a reminder on an extended topic. Some need it, some don't. Jane Roberts and other trance mediums, didn't need to, and in fact, who knows, perhaps it would have interfered with their getting out of the way. But people who are going to be part of the ongoing process, as you are, may or may not want to bolster their own confidence by taking a sneak-peek at the material.

Then I will. Back before you know it. [A fast look.] But, I see I hardly have the energy to absorb anything. Maybe just as well. So, over to you.

Resonance and proof

You will notice, Michael [Langevin]'s suggestion that you try for something tangible that could be proven does not appeal to you.

No. And I'll explain when I transcribe. [Michael suggested I ask Rita for information that she would know and we would not until we checked, as a demonstration that it was really her I was in contact with.]

There is a reason why it doesn't appeal, and it is more than a matter of lack of self-confidence. It is a terrible example to set, to set oneself up to be judged on anything but the intrinsic resonance of the material for this or that individual. You'll notice this resonance subject came up in your comment to the TMI Explorers list.

It is important for beginners to build their own—shall we call it "provisional confidence?" You have to try it, treating it as if confident of the process and result, then let it sit and go back and judge later. As you have told people in groups [such as Guidelines programs], information received is usually going to appear to be from yourself *while you are receiving it*; if you try to judge too soon, you are likely to dismiss valid material without weighing it properly, because of how the process felt to you. It is only later that you will be able to have enough distance on it. Well, setting yourself up to produce verifiable material "or else" only puts you under more pressure and increases the temptation to abandon the whole process. That's one objection. A deeper objection is that it results in your trying to direct the process from your end rather than accepting what comes through.

Well, I don't know—how different is that from our asking questions? Doesn't that direct the process?

There's a subtle difference. Asking for information on a given topic isn't the same as asking for information that will provide confirmation. The one is asking for the sake of knowing; the other is asking for the sake of demonstrating.

Can't say I really see the difference. I'd love to know from you or from anybody where my lost set of keys is.

No doubt. And if this were only a product of your subconscious mind, the information would surely be there, would it not?

The whole thing is a mystery to me. I concluded long ago that there is a knack or orientation that others may have, but I don't, that might produce such things.

Pray to St. Anthony.

It's funny you should mention that; my friend Michael Grosso mentioned that practice—in a different context—the other day. How different is the tradition of praying for assistance from a saint, on the one hand, and seeking assistance from any other disembodied source?

The difference would be in the person making the request, of course. Whatever you believe, it will tend to work, or at least work better.

This has taken us far afield.

Has it?

Well, come to think of it, it was you that mentioned Michael's suggestion.

And you who made a semiconscious decision to glance at your emails before opening the journal. You would not have seen the message otherwise, and it might have been more difficult to steer the subject this way.

Proceed, I'm listening.

Individuals as flames

It is a simple everyday example of the fact that individuals are individuals only so far. At a deeper level, that both is and is not a valid way to look at it.

Jung saw an individual consciousness surrounded by the unconscious. In other words, what we are aware of in the body is like a flame, a small flame like a candle flame, in the middle of a great external darkness. At least, *that's how the exterior appears to the flame*, relatively darker. "Flame" is not a bad analogy, if you will bring the image to mind. The boundaries and shape of a flame are ever-changing, and it doesn't look the same very long at a time. Even disregarding its coming into existence and its being snuffed out, its lifetime is perpetual change with an overall continuing identity.

A flame. Not a bad analogy for a consciousness in body.

But when you look to see what is outside the flame, it gets more interesting. Jung's thought was of conscious minds as a more or less stable thing sitting atop the things in their lives that had not come to the conscious mind's attention, or had fallen out by inattention, or had been repressed for whatever reason; and beneath the personal layer, deeper connections such as family, ethnicity, race, humanity and still broader connection to other parts of reality, but parts too far removed from the immediate problem of the living to be explored in his short lifetime. (That is, any one lifetime is short.)

But let us change the analogy and see the individual as one flame, say sitting on a twig of a campfire. Maybe the fire has a hundred such flames. They could all be considered part of the greater flame or could be looked at individually as a hundred twigs burning.

Either way, you will see that the flames at some level are the result of the conditions for fire: heat, air, and fuel. So, although the flame could be considered only in itself, to do so without remaining aware of the conditions of

its existence is to misinterpret what you see. A flame *is* the twig it is burning; *is* the air it is transforming; *is* (because equally dependent upon) the
heat beneath which it cannot operate.

So is there an individual flame at all? Even taking that campfire as one
thing—which is another arbitrary division—can it be said to exist in and
of itself? Only if you disregard the air, fuel, and heat that are absolutely a
part of its existence. But how often do flames think to include twigs in their
genealogy?

*I'd add, how often are they even aware of them, being concentrated as they are on
flame-dom, fire-hood?*

That's right. That's the point. It is all well and good to assent intellectually to the proposition that all is one, and the individual is a convenient
fiction—as the guys told us—or a provisional hypothesis. It is a more emotionally stable thing to have an image such as a flame, to bring the idea home.

And this is the direction we must go. Is it any wonder that materialists
can't see how the individual survives the conditions of death? The flame has
no more twig to burn! There may or may not be air and heat, but the twig is
demonstrably gone! So how can life continue?

*That's very striking. It gives me for the first time the emotional sense behind the
idea of death as the end. That may not be news to others, but I never quite saw that
before.*

Yes, because it hasn't occurred to them that the heat is provided not by
physical conditions of existence but what we have been calling nonphysical. Heat and air both. But we'll get to that later. You will notice that when
Nancy [Ford] asked about physical and nonphysical, she got the word and
concept "density," and that—although an entirely different analogy—gives
the sense of it very well. Again, a continuum, not an either/or.

Well, as Car Talk *used to say, we've done it again, we've wasted a perfectly good
hour—*

We're ready to waste another, whenever you make the opportunity for us.

That reminds me, here's an idea. You, Rita, will be familiar with the idea of cross-correspondences. Why couldn't we bring your material forth that way—centering on the TMI Explorers list, say—and thus bring it quicker, with less wear and tear on one particular scribe and in the process providing a real demonstration of what you're talking about?

The only obstacles to such a process would be among you individual-ists. (A smile.)

If you can persuade yourselves it is possible, and

If you allow yourselves to think yourself inherently worthy, and

If you take the results as *provisionally true*—that is, neither Gospel nor evident fraud or error—

You may surprise yourselves.

Well, I'm willing if anyone else is. I guess we'll see. Thanks, Rita. More another time.

Friday, December 12, 2014

Continuity and individuality

7 a.m. I woke up suddenly, thinking of the question I'm really trying to get to. The two ways of looking at consciousness don't cohere, and I think if we are on the right track, it should make sense of things. We haven't done that yet.

On the one hand—The analogy of the flame is very nice, and clearly we aren't as separate from others as we sometimes think.

On the other hand—If there is a continuing Ernest Hemingway presence, say— or a Rita presence!—how does this square? How can we be both separate and not separate? I can't even phrase the question very well. What was clear in my mind does not come out clear in words.

Miss Rita, that is as good an attempt as I can make. I hope it's good enough for you to run with—and of course, I am well aware that, chances are, the question was planted.

Let's start with homely analogies. You live in a place—the house you lived in when you rented from me, say. While you are there, that is your life's center. Your body lives there, and that is where you do your work. You think, you read and write, you communicate, and all your activities, mundane and mental both, take for granted your existence there, on Roberts Mountain Road. You don't think you *are* the house, or the community where the house is, but you take for granted that this is your context.

You move to another house, another community. Your memories are the continuity with the consciousness on Roberts Mountain Road, but your new surroundings are your new life's center. You are the same person as before, yet you are also *not* the same person. You today know things, have experienced things, have perhaps suffered and enjoyed things, have forgotten things, that the "you" living on Roberts Mountain Road had not. Yet obviously you are a continuity.

So if you look at things as flow, you have to say you changed, time passed, that earlier version of you no longer exists, and no one can say that this is an incorrect summary of the situation.

But if you look at things as a series of situations—snapshots instead of movies, or perhaps better, stills from a movie—it's different. If every moment of time exists, and does not cease to exist, the snapshots, or stills, are as accurate a description as the movie.

So—are you a continuity? Yes. Are you a definite defined being? Also yes. The confusion about reincarnation and about life in general is rooted in a misperception of time that is rooted in a misperception of reality due, as I indicated earlier, to imperfect apprehension of higher dimensions of reality, collapsing and confusing them into one's perception of time. As one clarifies one's perceptions, the nature of things changes. In effect, one lives in a different world.

All right, and this ties in to the nature of us as communities.

Yes, because it both is and isn't a mistake to think of continuity in terms of continuity of a given unit. The "you" who lived in my house for those few years did not continue as a unit to move to a new dwelling in another place. As I said, the "you" writing this is not precisely the same "you" as the one of a few years ago. You couldn't be the same and still experience, for experience alters. And such sequential alteration is the purpose of 3D life, after all. The physical end of things is the hothouse, forcing plants.

But if we leave off thinking of the individual as a unit and think instead of each person as being a community, it may be easier to conceptualize how different members of that community may be more activated or less activated by changes in circumstance. If you cease to live in the woods and move to the city, the part of your community that loved to walk in the woods may become quiescent, and the energy of the overall unit flows elsewhere, to social interactions or libraries or whatever.

Two ways of seeing things, both true, neither the whole story.

As I was writing that, the thought came to me, each of the pieces of that individual's community were themselves individuals at some point.

Again, both yes and no, but that will advance the argument. Take an historical figure: Thoreau, say, or Abraham Lincoln, to take two of your favorites.

Or Ernest Hemingway.

Or Ernest Hemingway, but also anyone else who has ever lived, known to history or not. That bundle becomes a strand available to other communities downstream—but not upstream—in the formation of new individuals. That is, *after* Lincoln lives, his life as a whole provides material to be a strand in a person, as for instance he is in you. *Before* he lived, he was not available except by reflection.

You'll need to say more about that.

Oh, I know it! But, you see, we're getting somewhere. As I told you a few years back, sometimes, in order to understand A you have to understand B, but to understand B you have to understand A; and in such cases, all you can do is keep inching closer by continually refining your understanding of either, then reconsidering the other in the new light, and continuing the process.

Stepwise refinement, in metaphysics.

Did you think your time as a computer programmer was wasted? You learned certain skills, learned certain concepts and ways of thinking.

Time and change

So next we need to look at the nature of time. It is true that time *exists*. It does not flow; consciousness flows, and in the body it is experienced as flowing one way and one way only. There is a reason for that. It is experienced in a way that echoes the reality of change.

Consider the pyramids, to use your old example. You cannot tear them down before they were built. You cannot write on the walls of a building before it is erected. You can't marry a person before he or she is born. There is a *sequence* to things, and it is not arbitrary. It has its inherent logic.

Just because time is not what it appears does not mean it can be anything and everything someone can imagine it to be. Every moment of time exists, but it exists, as you exist, as the sum of what preceded it, and as the seed of what will follow it. The fact that the movie may be viewed out of order, and the stills considered separately and at random, does not mean that the movie itself is out of order, separate or random.

So, to return to Lincoln, he is available *as a package, as a new unit, as a new strand,* for individuals downstream from his life. But prior to 1809, there was no Lincoln. (Thank you for the date, which I plucked from your memories.) Prior to 1809, the strands that went into the making of Lincoln existed, but the net result of his life—the container as it was frozen by the end of new 3D experience by death—did not. After 1865, it did.

When you and I got this material a dozen years ago, that part was never spelled out clearly. The guys—as I thought of them (and still think of them, pending a new way of thinking about them)—talked about patterns, and they said some patterns were worth keeping and others weren't; and at the time, that seemed to you like they were saying some were worthy and some people weren't.

You [as conduit of the responses] weren't able to give us a very clear picture at that point, because the concept was too unfamiliar, and your mind couldn't help trying to make sense of what you were getting in light of where you were, what you knew. What would have been clearer would be to say that some people's lives create a new pattern that can be used as one strand in a new bundle, and many people's are not sufficiently different to serve in that way. That doesn't mean the ones that are not different enough to serve as patterns were failures, or were discarded. It means *from the point of view considering flow,* they can be disregarded. Remember, at the time, the guys were working on giving us a new way to see the world. Side trails would have confused the issue, so they often ignored them. Besides, side-trails lead in all directions, and anyway there's not really a difference between the main trail and a side trail. It all depends on where you feel like going. If you want to go explore some bright object you see out of the corner of your eye, there's nothing to prevent you from doing so.

Thank you, Rita. This really does bring some clarity to things.

Whose mouth was it that told me, "the better the question, the better the answer"?

A lot of consequences from that meeting at the hospital elevator, Rita! [She and I met at UVA Hospital in 1998 while visiting our mutual friend Dave Wallis.]

And they don't end—downstream.

I hear that. Thanks, and until later.
8 a.m. That was pretty good. More than pretty good. That really began clarifying things.

Saturday, December 13, 2014

Continuity by intent

5:45 p.m. Okay, Rita, how do we get memories of past lives, when we do? The Leininger boy, for instance, remembering his very short life that ended in 1945. [Young James Leininger's story was told by his father, Bruce, in Soul Survivor.] What is the mechanism? If a given life is only a strand in our present life, how is it that some people can read life after life a person has led?

A thread may be very thick, or I would say, better, may be very *solid*, very much made more permanent by the living of that life, and so it may be more prominent in its expression; it may also be clearer, more accessible; and it may be a good transmission medium for the predominant lives that shaped it.

I hear—like the successive Dalai Lamas.

Yes, that is a good example, for several reasons. It is transmission by intent. It is foreshadowing by clarity and intent. It is continuity through intent and prior achievement. This is a potential for anyone to begin, if one is wishing to do the work.

Perhaps it would be as well for you to unpack those statements you made.

It is transmission by intent. That is, the continuation of the line of awareness and internal access is a priority during life. A Dalai Lama *works* at self-development continually, and that work enables the continuity in a way that would not follow if he spent time at racetracks, or stock exchanges, or mundane family life. Nothing in life is achieved without an exchange of effort and attention.

It is foreshadowing by clarity and intent. The dying Dalai Lama hints to his followers where they will find his next incarnation. This he can do because he can look among futures and choose, and because he chooses by weighing what will be desirable.

It is continuity through intent and prior achievement. The perpetuation of the Dalai Lama line through fourteen incarnations is a project, an intergenerational agreement to provide a people with a living symbol. This could not be done if the Dalai Lama spirit (call him) was unable to continue unbroken intent. Even when young Dalai Lamas were killed by power-hungry and treacherous assistants, the intent to preserve the embodiment of the same consciousness was maintained. You will notice that the present incarnation has his doubts as to whether the long experiment/demonstration/gift should continue, because it is not intended to exalt the bearer of the office, but to serve the people; and if that purpose seems permanently lost or altered, there would perhaps be no need to continue.

The Dalai Lama serves as an example, because everyone knows the name, but not because he is the only example of such enterprise; far from it. He is perhaps the best known, the longest known, but other spirits are doing the same thing, silently, unknown, and not to be known.

So there is your answer in brief. People sometimes remember past lives if they have strands sufficiently active that they are manifest, *and* if it is in their own interest that they be exposed to such evidence. Many experience what you call the resonance, and never suspect it. Some experience it and do suspect it, or define it in one way or another. And for some, the clarity approaches normal consciousness.

It feels like I should continue, but no new questions occur to me. Do you have more you want to say now?

Keep pondering. It helps me to come through with concepts. It is a sort of stirring up the river bottom so I can arrange the sand clouds.

Helps you arrange the tea leaves?

That's a good analogy too. More whenever you are so inclined.

All right; thanks as always.

Sunday, December 14, 2014

6:15 a.m. Miss Rita, our friend Charles Sides emailed me some questions, which I will reread to stir up your tea leaves, and then hope for answers to one or more of them. As always, I am leaving myself open to the possibility that the questions were planted—in this case by Charles, or upstairs through Charles. And as I phrase that, I see again that it is going to require some mental refashioning if I am to get beyond the language—TGU and all—I have been using for more than twenty years. Not complaining, just noting. I realize that you can't sail to new places by remaining in sight of the place you started.

[Charles's email: "Cindi Dale says there are vibrational levels where one rests, reviews, heals, seeks knowledge and then the wisdom to share. These are what she calls the first Five Planes after one dies. Then she describes seven 'higher' planes where a 'soul' goes about 'life' after death. You see, I would be curious to know what Rita experienced. Did she review her life? Did she go back and 'relive' any moments experiencing them from the perspective of others involved? Is there time? What does she do? Where is she? What about reincarnation? Is she thinking about it? Who or what comes back?"]

For the record, I don't know who Cindi Dale is. Someone Charles is reading or has read, presumably.

Those are two different sets of questions. The first [set] asks theory; the second asks experience. Or rather, that is how the answers would sort out.

Reality as net

Bear in mind that the term "vibrational levels" is a concept formed by taking a higher-dimensional reality and forcing it into sequential 3D experience. It is unavoidable, but it is necessary that you remember that it *is* analogy. Everything you can be told is a translation. Thus, the spatial analogy sneaks in—as you and I were told in our sessions—and makes it seem as though one would have to go through territory A, B, C, and D to get to E. As you will remember, TMI participants tended to think in the same way about Focus levels, as though Focus 21 could be reached only by traversing levels 10, 12, and 15.

I well remember when I thought that way myself. The numbers seemed to make it obvious. Only with experience did it become clearer that it wasn't sequential unless you conceptualized it that way.

Bob [Monroe] did try to undercut that assumption by introducing the one-breath technique, but perhaps he didn't want to rearrange people's concepts too much, given that what he had given them was so useful for practical exploration.

In any case, Charles quotes this woman as describing these states of acceptance as if they were sequentially laid out, as if they were stops on a railroad line. A better analogy would be short hops by airplane, with the destination depending more on the intent of the pilot than upon a necessary traversing of terrain. Not everybody touches on each of these stops; not everybody touches on them in the same order.

A continuing source of confusion in these matters is the question of who we're talking about, for this is something as misperceived as focus levels. Are we talking about the personality-essence that was formed in that lifetime and has just emerged into what is its new life? Or are we talking about the underlying continuity from which the personality was formed? And that will take some examining.

I imagine so. And some definition (and yes, I will bear in mind that all definitions are provisional).

The safest way to go about this is to recapitulate what you yourself were told long ago. It will be new to some, and it will develop into new concepts.

Souls come into existence; or, they have existed since the beginning of time. It depends on how you look at it.

Think about that for a moment; don't just breeze past it. New souls exist, or all souls are equally eternal on both ends (that is, they have no beginning as well as no end). Both ways of seeing it more or less true, neither way truer than the other. How can that be?

This seems to me to go well with Peter Novak's scheme in The Division of Consciousness: *people are conscious and unconscious minds, inhabiting the same body, either separating at death or, more rarely, continuing, and this duality caused mankind's two opinions of the afterlife, reincarnation or judgment followed by heaven or hell. What you see depends on what you focus on. [Rather than conscious and*

unconscious minds, I should have said spirit and soul, but I won't go into that, as Peter's
book is not the focus but merely a by-product of the theme.]

The analogy with Peter Novak's scheme holds insofar as us discussing
changing points of view. It does not hold otherwise, given that his starting
point is the individual and mine is the larger community of which the individual is one part. This will become clearer as we progress. The key to this
work of perception and analysis is the willingness to hold two contradictory
views provisionally—not with the intent of eventually deciding between
them, but with the intent of seeing a higher level at which they can be rec-
onciled as partial views each with its own validity. And of course, "higher
level"—and any other way to say it that you could think of—brings in the
spatial analogy. It can't be helped, only noticed, just as the sequential nature
of writing cannot be helped, only kept in mind as an inherent distortion.

We keep coming back to this fact: If you examine a net, it will appear
to be one consistent unit when examined at one level, and a series of knots,
at another, and even may appear to be a confusion of knots and spaces and
strands, when seen at another level. And of course, if the net is examined
folded over itself, or full of fishes—

Existence is a net. I didn't say *physical* existence, for as I said, what you
call and think of as the nonphysical is a part of the one inseparable reality.
That net is alive, and the strands and knots are not more or less alive than
the spaces, which, after all, are only nothingness *when seen from the view*
that sees strands and knots and cannot see what shares the overall form.

Ether, holding together the heavens. A similar example.

Not so much holding together as comprising, but yes, not a bad analogy. Materialist science looks between planets and sees empty space, or did
until recently. The medievals envisioned the planets connected by a matrix
they called aether, or the heavens. Invisible to one way of looking, obvious
to another. So, similarly, the question of what the world is. Take the knots
to be analogous to what you see as individuals. Examine a knot and you
see that it is not actually a thing in itself, but an intersection of strands. Or,
examine a strand and you will see it as nowhere an independent element,

but as inextricably bound to other strands by way of knots, or it could not be part of a net. And, examine the net as a whole (assuming we could envision the whole) and you will see that it is a holder of pattern, that it holds strands and knots in a particular way so as to involve what appears to be space; it binds the three elements that are in fact one element—it all depends on what you examine, how you focus, and what your mental concepts allow you to see.

But of course, like anything else I can say, it is only an analogy. Its use is to remind you and others that concentrating on "the nature of the afterlife"—or "the nature and meaning of life," for that matter—produces answers geared to the focus you bring to the question. If you remain fixated on the individual—as if a net were only knots, and no strands and patterns and spacing—you are going to get a different picture than if you examine the individual knowing, holding in mind, that this is only one way of seeing a more complex reality.

When you have a microscope and a slide being examined, what you see will depend upon how you focus the lens. What disappears in a given focus does not cease to exist; it only disappears from view. The trick is to refocus, remembering.

This [about alternating focus] is very much what I got in the guys' epilogue to Muddy Tracks.

Should that surprise you?

I don't know that it does surprise me. I've tried to look at things from more than one viewpoint for a long while now. But it has been over an hour, and I'm afraid we must quit before you've just gotten started—as usual.

Slow and steady wins the race.

Next time.

Monday, December 15, 2014

Past-life review?

7:40 a.m., Okay, Rita, I'm ready if you are ready. I will bear in mind that anything you describe can be looked at more than one way, which will mean it may look entirely different without the thing itself changing. I will plug in Charles's questions.

> [Charles had written: "You see, I would be curious to know what Rita experienced. Did she review her life? Did she go back and 'relive' any moments experiencing them from the perspective of others involved? Is there time? What does she do? Where is she? What about reincarnation? Is she thinking about it? Who or what comes back?"]

These questions, notice, all are from the point of view of Rita the individual. As you say, seen from other points, the same answers will look like contradictions.

I suspect my saying that was planted. Not sure if it was "my" thought, though of course I agree with it. However—

"What Rita experienced." While still in the body, I was in a coma for the final few days, using my embodiment as a stable reference while I explored options—so, when I dropped the body, I was not disoriented or shocked—I passed over consciously.

Now, listen to that language. I "passed over"—and there is that spatial analogy again. You know, "moving" from the physical to the nonphysical. "Moving" across the "veil." It's all right to use the language, if you can remember that it is *sequential, partial,* and *metaphorical.* I'll go into the implications of those conditions for receiving undistorted information some other time.

Since I "passed over" consciously, my experience was more than tranquil. It was seamless. One minute I was waiting for my body to release, the next moment it was gone (so to speak), but that transition did not in my case involve a transference of self-identification from one side to the other.

I think you are saying, in your case, you were already identifying with your time-less aspects, so you didn't have to jump from identifying with your time-bound aspect to your timeless aspect. You had already crossed the river Styx, but you remembered.

That's one way to put it. But let us say merely that I did not need to reorient myself; not about "where" I was; not about who and what I was (am).

So, that is what I experienced. "Did she review her life?" From the viewpoint of a newly conscious, or newly arrived (however you want to put it) soul, it is a life review. But if you are already conscious, you don't need to do that. *Or rather*, you don't experience it that way.

Descriptions of the life-review process are usually sequential, usually from the point of view of the time-and-space-bound soul, so it can come out looking like you read a book or watch a movie or get a course of instruction. A better way to put it would be, merely, that as soon as I was free of the body, I was free of restrictions on my consciousness, and then I knew.

I didn't have to *learn*, you see; I knew. I always had known, but the part of me in time and space was somewhat insulated from that knowledge, and with time I will try to describe why—the shorthand reason is that conscious minds in time and space can hold only so much at a time (not speaking of brain capacity, here).

So—see it how you please. No, I didn't go through a life review process in the sense of a tutorial. Yes, I received the understanding that would result from a life review process, merely by regaining access. Another thread to follow up on at another time: how we build in meaning as we go along, in the same way and as part of the same process as we shape ourselves by choosing.

Which reminds me that I want to ask about the various versions of various realities and how that fits in.

In time. You have noted the question. Remember it another time and it will be a fruitful topic of discussion.

As to reliving moments, the answer is included in the previous answer. *Access* to these moments is there; a sequential visit or series of visits is not necessary.

Let me clarify that. Someone returning [to the physical] could easily describe what they had experienced as access to information they had never had, from viewpoints outside their own—as if seeing a movie, or reliving with wider understanding and perception. But I would say, again, those perceptions and understandings were intrinsic to the moment, to the situation, and it is only when viewed from outside time and space sequence that they appear to change. Sometime we should talk about the Akashic record.

I can see I'll have to start a list of topics of opportunity, and I will do so.

Good. That will let me continue in a straight line even though I know that all these branches would elucidate and clarify.

But in sequential description you can't go in several directions at once.

Precisely. That's what "the guys" meant when they said the physical is the needle that determines which part of the nonphysical record would be played. *That is relative to life in time and space,* of course.

Translation

So, in your answer to Charles, as you describe your experience, would the same experience be described differently by someone who only gradually woke up to the new life?

To the new conditions of life, you mean. Such a one would have a different experience depending entirely on who and what he or she was. The higher the level of self-development, the easier and clearer the readjustment. But this is a much more complicated question than you realize, and this doesn't answer it. Add it to your list.

Charles's next questions move us off into deeper waters, which is good. With deeper questions—and your riding herd on my answers—we will have a chance of staying focused so that our translation of multidimensional reality into 3D terms may make some sense. But be aware, it isn't ever going to make strict logical sense, because its essence (which does not conform to 3D rules) is always going to have to be *intuited* by the listener. It is the old story; what can't be said, can't be said. It isn't from lack of willingness or skill but from lack of ability to bring more dimensions into representation in fewer. It can be done, in the way that perspective can seem to represent three dimensions in a drawing of two, but perspective only works if the experiencer has already seen three dimensions. That is, if the viewer can translate the two-dimensional representation back into three—and that can only be done by intuition, not by sensory apparatus.

I think you mean, can only be done by imaginative faculties rather than logical operations.

That will do also. However you look at it, the important thing to remember is the presence—the necessary presence—of translation, and translation could be described as the process of deliberate distortion for the sake of creating a useful analogy.

The nature of time

I think we have time to begin [that next question]. It has been fifty minutes. I am on my eighth [journal] page and I used to be able to get ten before my energy flagged. So—"is there time?"

Is there time? A literal answer would be yes, but what good would that do anybody? So, we'll go into it, knowing that Charles has a more sophisticated understanding but knowing, too, that this may be read by others at many different levels of understanding, experience, and theoretical knowledge (that is, reading).

A multi-layered answer:

Time exists, in the sense of a separation of states. But as said previously, time itself, as opposed to time intermingled with various vaguely perceived or unperceived or misperceived aspects of higher dimensions, is not the same thing.

Remember and apply if you can—there is no "here" and "there"; "this side" and "the other side." Reality is *whole* and undivided. Remembering this will help you fight the mental temptation to create fantasies of life "over there." Logic and emotion both, but in different forms, will try to build defensible models. If you but remember that "this world" *is* "that world," that "this side" *is* "the other side," you will see that you are not dealing with two realms with different rules, so much as different perceptions depending on the state of being of the perceiver. *As a rule,* dropping the body marks a significant shift in perception. Therefore it appears as an all-but-absolute boundary between two realms. If you can remember that it is *not* two realms but one, things will gradually clarify.

I feel like I am beating this to death, and I'm sure some people will agree, but it is one thing to intellectually assent, and a very different thing to *get it.* Some time pondering, free-associating, daydreaming about the ramifications if there is only one world, rather than two, will help seat the concept.

We aren't quite finished with "is there time," but your hour is up and you are getting tired.

And here we are toward the bottom of page ten. As Nero Wolfe would say, "satisfactory." Thanks, Rita, and I look forward to more.

Tuesday, December 16, 2014

Our experience of time

8 a.m. So, Miss Rita, as we were saying, "Is there time?"

Separation of states, rather, as I said. Let me explain.

Well, I should hope so!

You are familiar with the humorously stated "Time is what stops everything from happening at once." There is truth to that, said indirectly, which is pretty nearly the only way it can be said. An analogous statement is, "Space is what keeps everything from happening in the same place," which may make it easier for some people to understand the previous statement.

The conditions of 3D life make it easier to intuitively understand the nature of time by comparing it to the nature of space, because space does not include the element of compulsion that time does when experienced in 3D. Unless you are in a vehicle being driven by someone else who is inflexible in sticking to a route you have had no say in determining, you never experience space in the way you always experience time. That is one reason why people who have an experience of life on the other side return reporting that, "On the other side, there is no time." It would be a bit more accurate to say, "On the other side there is no compulsion, no compulsory movement of time in a given direction."

I could feel myself bucking, as I tried to bring that through. I want to know what you mean, but a part of my mind is trying to edit, to be sure the message "makes sense." So, since I'm not sure if I interfered with the message, I'm going to ask it again, or rather, I'll merely ask, did anything you meant get distorted in the process?

More than the whole process normally does, you mean?

Very funny. I have never figured out how to express that feeling of amusement from the other side. I used to put in (or hear, or experience), "We smile."

Nothing wrong with doing that. I suggest that we continue even when you doubt yourself or when you struggle with an answer, and rely on consistency over time. Just as in any cross-examination, apparent contradictions will either reveal themselves or will be resolved by context. You remember how often "the guys" did that for us. Now the roles are reversed, and it is up to you to object and up to me to provide feed to explain. I say this mostly for the benefit of those who are beginning to experiment. As you know, at the beginning of the learning process, it would be easy to become discouraged by what seems like self-deception.

To resume: In 3D life there is no compulsion to proceed in one geographical direction, at an invariant pace. Instead, you have freedom to move around, change directions, hurry or lag or stay still. Time in 3D offers you none of these freedoms, and so referring to your experience of spatial movement may be an easy way to hint at the nature of life within time when time does not have the element of silent remorseless compulsion.

Again, remember. There is no "other side" per se. There is one reality, the same reality you partake of when in the body, but perceived differently.

It isn't that the nature of time changes; it is that the way we live in time changes. It is that our *experience of* time changes.

Suddenly for the first time, I get something I was told a long time ago. The guys told me—us, maybe; I can't remember when it was—to think of successive moments in time as existing next to one another. They were not only telling us that all moments of time exist; they were saying why!

That's right. If you could envision moments of time arrayed like any geographical analogy you care to use—city blocks, one leading to the next, say, or trees in a woods—you could see that moving from one street or tree to another doesn't destroy the one you left, or bring into being the next one you come to. But if something were forcing you along a straight-line route, with no return possible, it would seem like it.

And—this may be important to some—the first step in overcoming the illusion that past time ceases to exist and future time comes into being is to envision the possibility. In our day—your day now, I suppose I should say—it no longer serves to say "on the other side there is no time" because it provides no image or even concept for the busy mind to grasp and gnaw. New explanations for new circumstances, and new times are always providing these new circumstances.

And of course your explanation is shot through with shorthand expressions like "the guys," "the other side," and can't help being so.

Again, to force a picture into fewer dimensions is to either distort it or—with luck and application—invent or employ the equivalent of the technique of perspective.

So—to go back a few paragraphs—separation of states. Envision all moments of time as snapshots, arrayed in the order they were experienced. If that is *my* world now, it is *your* world now. In other words, for it to be true where the distortions of physical existence are removed, it must have been true all along, regardless how it was perceived at the time.

Even that last sentence, "at the time," should make it more obvious that life isn't the way it is experienced, because if it were, —

Sorry, got tangled.

The difficulty—*one* difficulty of many!—is that what I am asking you to do contains a contradiction. I say, envision an array of snapshots, yet each "snapshot" is not a snapshot but is itself a movie, or so it has to appear to you in the body ("within time" as they say) because otherwise you can't get a sense of movement. If life is a series of still photos, how can any of the photos differ? In other words, where does the possibility of movement come in?

Yes, I have felt that question, not quite so clearly.

Zeno the stoic posed it long ago in his conundrum about Achilles being unable to pass the turtle because at any moment in time he is still x amount behind it, even if a diminishing amount.

I never could look at that as any more than playing with words and with logic.

He wasn't attempting to persuade you that a man can't catch a turtle, but that the way we perceive time must be faulty.

So how do you resolve that paradox? I can sense time as a series of stills that do not go out of existence. I can't quite see how—in that analogy or description—anything can change.

The answer is that the pictures don't change, the observer brings the perception of change by movement over the pictures.

Oh!

Connects a couple of dots, does it?

Can I try? Let's say that when all-that-is sprang into existence (a puzzle in itself, but we'll look at that later, I hope) all possibilities exist, as I have often parroted, thinking I understood. Let's say they exist as an array of cards, each a slightly different situation. The observer/experiencer/person-in-3D chooses to hop from card to card in whatever direction he or she chooses at any given moment—any given subjective moment choosing among objective moments, I guess, which is how we "create our own reality." It is how we choose what we will become. It is how we can create the mind or soul that can become a strand in another later on—that is, next in line subjectively. This implies different levels of—

Whew, too much to hold.

Yet it was easier for you to put that out without having to ascribe it to me or to any external mind, thus removing one layer of difficulty.

Would you sum it up and/or correct it, then?

The critical insight is the realization that there are two pieces to the puzzle. One is the "objective" situation—the endless array of potential moments, or, to be more careful, the endless array of moments that may potentially be experienced. The other is the "subjective" experiencer. Without the two, it can only be static, not dynamic. It is the ability to choose that creates the unique pattern, and that *must be* at a different level, or it would be enmeshed in whatever moment.

Take that, Zeno!

Nonetheless, you owe him a debt, or would if his paradox had been the factor that enlightened you to the situation. You haven't really grasped the nature of it, nor need you. But a certain kind of logic-driven mind may find it a potential exit from the trap of appearances.

Enough for the moment?

It's always your choice.

Thanks, as always.

Thursday, December 18, 2014

One reality, not two

7:20 a.m. All right, let's see where we go today. Miss Rita? I have received a couple more questions to address after we finish with the group Charles sent, but I haven't gathered them into a list yet, and won't have time or leisure to do so today. Shall we postpone, or can we continue?

It would be worth your while to find a simple way to chart out what I'm saying so that in one page, or one drawing—in some compact form—you have a précis of the circumstances I describe, so as to help you draw your own connections as you go. If I describe something and you are forgetting that there are not two realms (physical and nonphysical) but one which *appears* to be two, you will be unable to properly fit the new piece into context.

Well, I was thinking, the other day, that we need to figure out some new language to replace "the guys" and all the other shorthand we have used up to now. I'm open to suggestion.

It is a bigger project than you might think, for of course it entirely reorganizes your thinking on the subject. But—

—*One* world, inhabited in common by physical and nonphysical alike, because of course any being must inhabit all and not [only] some dimensions of reality.

But inhabiting a dimension is not the same as being *aware* of it. What seems shadowy or nonexistent to one set of awareness will be firm and obvious to another, and vice-versa. The physical world as you experience it—the densest part of reality—is but shadow to those whose awareness centers in more rarified dimensions. Similarly, the nonphysical world as I am experiencing it is solid and definite to us, shadowy to you.

The fact that it is *one* reality, not two, helps explain—or will when you consider it—why those in the physical can "visit" nonphysical reality and vice-versa. Have you ever thought that, in a sense, nonphysical presences on the denser plane are ghostly—and so are physical presences on the nonphysical?

No, it's getting tangled up in language, as I said.

Just that much is enough to show you the problem and the opportunity. For as long as you can remember "one reality, not two," you can hear the space between the words. But to the degree that language brings you back to two worlds, the new almost-felt perception slips away.

I was thinking you were going to give me the new language to use. But you want me to devise it.

Not devise it as much as feel it. Because, you are still connected with a physical body holding you in a stable material place; you are still in a mind with certain constraints on the breadth of connection it can hold in physical consciousness at any given time; and you live among others in the same conditions, which makes it far easier to know how and why things will be perceived in a given way.

My turf, for the moment, not yours.

Yes. Because of the links between us, we can communicate. Because of your links there, you can communicate among the embodied—now and anyone who comes across it later.

Communicating

My sister Margaret and I visited the Fine Arts Museum in Richmond yesterday, and in one of the rooms they had Egyptian exhibits. I was trying to feel back so many centuries, and failing. I spent time looking at a mosaic tile from the Romans, maybe 1800 years old, and tried to remember that those stones had been fitted by a living breathing alive-to-the-moment person, and could do it mostly intellectually, very little by any emotional process. The characters in a TV show or movie or novel are almost more real to me than these departed souls. Time is an enormous barrier.

No bigger than space, but you can traverse space. And you can learn to traverse time/space by way of the higher dimensions—what do you think you are doing here? Communicating with me is communicating *beyond* time-space; it is *transcending* time-space. And yet it is but little different from communicating with yourself.

Because we are all one.

Yes, all one. The shorthand description is that all the strands ultimately interconnect. It's just a matter of—well, actually, that is yet another long topic, though a fascinating one. I could never quite see it, in the body; too many concepts to unlearn. But we'll get to it, only not today.

Anything more to be said about "is there time?" before we move on?

The "more" will emerge in the course of the discussion, for everything changes with each new brush stroke, just as any painting, whether by judgment or words or ways of thinking.

I get that I need to organize your talking-points into compact size before we continue with Charles's questions and go on to others. Why is that?

Because a reference to continually refer to—a reference that will grow and change as your background and structure change—will color everything new that is said. I can't *give* it to you, but it will be a powerful tool, trust that. Your devising it will make it yours in the way that coloring a complicated diagram, or drawing a reproduction of an elaborate network of things, would do. And as you are to be the translator to others, it is well to have it in your mind as *yours* rather than as something you feel obliged to represent faithfully (which might make you less intuitive and overly logical in your approach).

So I gather that is a hint to any who are following the discussion to do the same for themselves, rather than waiting for me to produce it for them.

Modern technology makes certain ways of proceeding possible that never have been possible before. So today you can communicate daily, or hourly if you were to choose to do so, and can convey vast amounts of changed and changing materials easily. So the method of transmitting knowledge and even wisdom has changed. Rather than one person or that person's scribes writing down an invariant text to be transmitted, today the material can be sent and received piecemeal, and constructed by each recipient on the fly. Thus, instead of you being the wise man coming down from the heavens with the tablets, *each* person is tasked and is able to open to the wisdom according to his or her own circumstances.

I set out hints, and encouragements, and it is up to each person what to do with it, how to connect thought to life, how much to accept, how much to modify or reject.

And it never has been any different; it is just faster now.

I predict not everybody will like the idea.

Not everybody will like anything. But these are the conditions for the explorers. Reading a map is not the same thing as occupying or even traversing the territory.

And this way will seem ponderously slow and repetitive as long as people are attempting to absorb the material quickly, judge it, and move on.

Something new—or perhaps I should say the newness within the familiar—is never really understood all at once. It is more a process of ripening with time.

I can see that we don't have time enough now to proceed on the other questions Charles posed, let alone others. But there's always tomorrow. At least, until there isn't.

It is for you as it is for everybody. Nobody is obliged to do tomorrow's work today any more than they are obliged (or even able) to be elsewhere while being wherever they are. Diligence is the best one can do, and all one need do.

I always got from the I Ching, "righteous persistence brings reward." I take it as admonition. More tomorrow, I hope. Thanks, Rita.

Saturday, December 20, 2014

A change in consciousness

7 a.m. Charles asked, "What does she do?" What can you say to that?

[pause]

I gave you a minute to remember how blank you feel about the question, before I try to answer it. You can't imagine. Not really. You were told [years ago, in a session with "the guys"] "we relate" and accepted it, but it did not really answer anything.

You have to admit, that's pretty vague.

It is a complicated answer actually brilliantly compacted into two words. The reason it is difficult to explicate is the number of hidden assumptions it needs to respond to. We have started to look at them, but only started. If you try to impose (silently, unaware that you are doing it) 3D qualities to the explanation, you will only get that much more confused. But to remove those unstated assumptions, you have to be aware that they exist. That awareness is the first piece of the puzzle. Nothing can be done without accomplishing it first. Or—it can be done, but the resulting picture will be unnecessarily misleading.

What do I do? Remember what we have to keep in mind: Who is "I"? Not the apparent unit you (and I!) knew in the body, but more like a community of reaction-systems bound by a will that was formed and exercised during the lifetime, which may be said to be the real accomplishment of the lifetime. That is, the components existed separately before the incarnation. It was the controller of the newly assembled bundle that was added, and what was that controller but the will, the ring that bound them? But outside of the very specific 3D conditions of existence, the relationship changes. The various strands, though continuing to be associated, function more autonomously (because not tightly bound by one controlling con-sciousness in a limiting environment). The extensions in all directions—

Let's begin that sentence again. While in the body, the community making up the individual functioned more as one individual, isolated from everybody else, than it does outside 3D, where consciousness no longer limits.

Let me try to rephrase that. I think I know what you want to say, and you can correct whatever I get wrong. I think you mean, all the strands always connect to their previous lives (put it that way) whether in body or not, but while in the body, they can function only in the background unless called to consciousness. Once you are outside of time-space, without having to deal with the constrictions of 3D, those strands and their extensions in many directions increase in relative strength—that is, they are more prominent in your new consciousness. [Typing this up, it occurs to me that what I said was only from the point of view of the former individual. Those strands, viewed from other points of view, may seem entirely different.]

That's all right. Now let me rephrase it, not to correct—for it is a cor-rect statement as far as it goes—but to provide triangulation. "I" being now outside the body, need not exist, as I did in 3D, with a limited intense field of consciousness. *Need* not, *can* not. Conditions do not allow it. Instead I inhabit a far wider consciousness, correspondingly less intense except under stimulation from 3D contact or other things that we cannot go into now. Therefore my self-definition is different. "I" am not the same as the Rita you knew, or, no, put it this way—I, as I experience myself, am not the same as I experienced myself in 3D. Therefore I am aware of things I didn't know in the body, and I react differently. Remember when you were told that what Jung called the unconscious was in many ways a definition of the guys upstairs?

Not specifically. I remember having had the thought.

Well, it would be closer to say his unconscious—be it the personal unconscious or the racial unconscious or other levels we can't discuss here without going off-track—are more or less the strands that connect us in all directions.

So when you think you are talking to Rita, you are and you aren't. You are, because everything you know of her is here; you aren't, because the vast bulk of the iceberg that was hidden from you in life—"past-life" connections, etc.—is actively participating.

Can you see why you were told (well, Rita was told, through your voice) that "we relate"? We relate on so many levels—

We relate to all levels of ourselves, and that can stand some explication.

Consider the levels involved. First, of course—or maybe not "of course"; perhaps you never thought of it—

Let's put it this way. Think in terms of ever-widening spheres of influence. First is the specific bundle of strands that was "assembled" to create Rita. (And by the way, I see that we didn't have the threads and traits description quite right, mingling two different kinds of things. Later we can untangle that.) Those strands, that spent a lifetime functioning as part of a community functioning as a unit, continue to relate to one another as they did, but, as I said, under changed circumstances. They are less constrained, more equal now that there is not the inherent bias provided by a limited field of consciousness.

Meaning only so much could be held in mind at any given time.

Meaning much more than that. But let me briefly finish the sketch of spheres of influence. First, those that were the most active strands in the lifetime; then, those plus the strands that were relatively or entirely inactive during the lifetime. Then, all that plus—gradually, as fast as one can absorb it or as fast as one *chooses* to absorb it—wider and wider ripples, because of course every strand that had a life connects thereby to other strands with which it is in intimate unbreakable connection. And so on and so forth, for no matter how far you extend the chains, there is more beyond, and who can absorb all the connections available to creation?

Not all those strands were human. Not all were even the kind of animal life as, say, whales. Some lived in other places, for Earth is not the only field.

So, consider what an unending research project, or extended foreign travel, or pen-pal correspondence, it is to be outside of 3D's constrictions but still aware of what they were.

I knew you were on extended research, which you once told me was your idea of endless fun.

I don't believe I said "endless fun" in so many words—but it is!

I think that is as much as I can do today, but, a nice start on the subject.

Small bites may ultimately prove more digestible anyway. Don't forget to compile questions and, for that matter, compile answers. You will possess new material only to the extent that you chew on it. Merely reading it once will not make it yours.

Thanks, as usual, and I look forward to a continuation.

Sunday, December 21, 2014

Bridges, not monuments

5 a.m. Rita, your tutorial is meeting response. Charles is summarizing the points you have made already, and I have begun a file of questions people ask. Whenever we exhaust any one topic, apparently we'll have more.
So, do we continue on "what does she do?"

We have hardly gotten started on that one. Let's continue with the first set of definitions to be held in mind—who is the "I" or the "you" being considered? I provided you a hint about our consciousnesses as connectors, able to follow links to other communities of experience (which is how an individual may seem to us). But now let's return to the part of me that more closely resembles the Rita you knew—the bundle that was born, lived, made connections, developed habits, interacted, thought, studied, daydreamed, did a million practical day-by-day things, and died. We have said that that part of me survives, and I suspect that this is what Charles, for one, expected to hear about.

I think I'm with you so far. You could be considered in your most expanded form—all the network that was used to fashion the nucleus of your Rita-mind and life—or in that Rita aspect considered as if separate.

Not quite "as if" separate. It *is* separate—only separation isn't what it seems in 3D. It is a way of looking at things, not an actual barrier. Other than that caveat, though, close enough.

When you consider the unit of consciousness that knew itself as Rita, you are closer to what you used to hear as "in-process Rita," to be distinguished from "completed Rita."

I understood that to be a distinction between our consciousness at any given moment age 35, say—and the overall view the consciousness attained once it had gotten the complete picture.

Remember, the concepts we were given then—like the concepts I hope to provide now—are not designed as monuments but as bridges. They are to help you move from wherever you are at the beginning to a more sophisticated understanding.

Edging toward understanding A by understanding B, and vice-versa.

Yes. You may find it inspiring or depressing, depending upon your temperament, but there is always more to learn, always redefinition of what you had previously made yours. Always, unless and until you choose stability over growth, at which time learning ceases until you are ready to proceed once again.

And I'm getting the feeling that neither choice is somehow wrong.

Not at all. Eternal life is a marathon, not a sprint, to use one of your analogies. Different people need to take breathers at different times.

So, your previous understandings are to be refined—some of them, to the point that you may feel them being overthrown, rather than refined. But that is the way to new understanding.

I'm not going to worry about it.

No, that's your strength.

Orientations

All right, "in-process" versus "completed." Those concepts were put into place as place-holders, you might say. They allowed us to save the phenomena without having to delve into labyrinthine complexities. But now that your base of understanding has jelled and matured, we can go back and redefine what served.

It is true that every moment—and thus every moment's mind, consciousness, experience, awareness, state of being, interim status—continues to exist forever. That is what the Akashic record *is*. It isn't the annals of what happened year by year, though it would serve as such. It is, rather, the *substance* of the life of every moment. You appreciate the distinction? It isn't *merely* a record; it is the actual moment. All of them, from every viewpoint (or rather—well, that's too long a digression. Maybe another time.)

To use another of your analogies. Reality is a CD-ROM, recording all possibilities as it is created. No. Let's start again, that has too many misleading nuances.

It is a common mistake to think that reality came into being and is created moment by moment. Rather, it came into being and is *experienced* moment by moment, decision by decision. Your decisions participate in the creation of the version of reality you will live. The unchosen paths exist equally as those chosen, but in the version you experience they aren't *activated*, let us say. In effect, they might as well not exist. You see them not, nor experience them and their unchosen consequences.

Nonetheless, they exist, and another path through the same reality, making different choices, will experience a different reality. Different in *effect*, not intrinsically.

So, people's past-life reviews show them the life they created by their choices and the effects that followed. It shows, sometimes (depending on the person's receptivity) the life they *might have* created by different choices.

And now you will ask, why don't these people also experience their extended being? The answer is, who are you talking about? If you refer to the extended being from which they were created in the first place, certainly it is no less aware than it has ever been. But if you refer to the specific mind created during that life-experience, it may or may not be aware—it depends upon the level of awareness it attained. And this is not to be taken as a "greater than" or "lesser than" comparison. It is more a matter of the composition of elements, that render the mind more aware, or less, of any particular phase of existence. After all, none of us comprehend the whole. (And I mean to use the word "comprehend" to mean "extend to" as well as "understand.") There may be no particular advantage in Davy Crockett being a mystic, for example, or, say, Lucretia Mott.

Small side-trail. You tend to think of these laboriously created minds as if their primary purpose were to relate to 3D life. But in a way, it would be more accurate to say that 3D life is created to allow for the formation of such minds *which then are available for interaction on* "higher planes," or "the other side," or "heaven and hell."

So, to return, if you were to contact a mind in its 3D-orientation (that is, without conscious connection to the rest of itself) you would be told of it experiencing eternal life one way; another, equally 3D-oriented but with that orientation containing an active link to the "nonphysical"—such as you, such as myself, such as anyone whose life included that dimension—would report an entirely different experience. The difference is not in the reporting nor in the terrain, of course; it is in the mind doing the experiencing.

Regardless of the nature and extent of the mind you contact, the answer to "what are you doing?" is going to be—relating. If I am experiencing my afterlife only from within the mind I created, and that mind has no wider, deeper connections because I did not concern myself with such matters, maybe I will report that I have been to Sunday School at my accustomed church; or perhaps I have been attending classes or teaching class, at my accustomed university; or I am having Sunday dinner with the family

I grew up in, or the family I formed. You get the idea. Whatever interested that mind in its 3D lifetime will probably interest it afterward, until it is interested no longer. (Topic for another time: How do people cease to be interested? Clue: They are still connected "upstairs" as you say, and that connection still gives hints.)

And this is not mere putting-in-time. Real, constructive, work is being done by people continuing their living in different circumstances. They were fashioned—to some degree self-fashioned—to do just that, after all. Someone fascinated with mechanics doesn't have to lose the fascination just because the limited 3D framework has been suddenly (or gradually) experienced as wider and deeper than had been thought. There is nothing more (or less) important about metaphysical speculation than about an appreciation of leverage and inertia and the other phenomena of 3D existence. After all, you have Hemingway going fishing in his afterlife, do you not? He knows he is creating, he creates in such a way as to allow a wide range of outcomes, and he continues to experience *as if* he were still in 3D, only by his choice and according to parameters he sets. And still he continues to function on other levels, as he did in life. (I might *almost* say, "*because* he did in life.")

That's going to have to do it for this morning, I'm afraid. I always feel like we barely get started and the hour is gone.

Righteous persistence brings reward.

So I've heard. Thanks.

Saturday, December 27, 2014

Cooperation

7:30 a.m. So, Miss Rita, let's try again. I presume you will be working with Charles on this project, not just me. And perhaps others?

If you will all bear in mind that a group project on "your side" implies a group project on "our side," it will be easier to see that these kind of projects are neither uncommon nor particularly difficult. Only, usually the collaboration from the nonphysical end of things isn't as obvious—isn't conceivable—because of the assumption that thinking occurs in the brain, that brains are not connected to each other, and that the surface appearance of individuals cooperating as if they were playing poker or some other card game was the reality.

Poker?

A useful analogy. If people don't participate, by sitting with the others, by anteing in, by drawing cards and playing them, there can be no game. But poker assumes that each brain is unconnected to the others, that concealment and deception are possible, that only physical clues [to the other players' minds] exist. So—a joint endeavor, but one that assumes a coming together of physically separated individuals. This is the model for nearly all cooperative activities "on Earth." But a deeper look will show you that the cooperation is deeper than appearances suggest. The minds interconnect, creating what we could call the field of cooperation. (This is another subject, too, but cooperation and competition are inextricably linked, are in fact the same continuum on different points. They are not opposites.)

I've often tried to explain that to people.

Your bias is more toward the connections between things than the separations. You see a net where others see mostly holes.

All right—so, this project?

You and Charles do your best and relax about it. You funnel questions to him as they come to you from others or from your own mind (not *quite* a meaningless distinction) and let him build the scaffolding, a skill he has been perfecting this whole lifetime. When he gets something wrong, misplaces an emphasis, say, we will be there to help. And he will have to juggle two equally important attitudes: He will need to trust his own intuitions, yet he will need to trust yours, or the material's (it won't always be clear to either of you which is which). You will also have continued or intermittent input from others, to act as beacons.

It really feels like this one should be by Charles Sides and Frank DeMarco rather than the other way around.

No, wait and see. Besides, it keeps your name sorted with others you wrote in what might be considered a series. [That is, books with Frank DeMarco as first-named author will sort together.]

In computer searches it doesn't matter any more, but anyway he and I are content to see what happens.

Yes, you'll make as good a team as you and I did. You should remember always—trust between questioner and receiver is essential; without it, you can't get past a certain guarded-ness.

Me in particular?

You in particular but it is no less a general rule. Any barrier to trust is a barrier to free communication.

I look forward to see how we do, when we begin in a couple of weeks. Meanwhile I'll try to finish Papa's Trial.

Righteous persistence—

I know, that's my only hope, sometimes.

January 2015

Saturday, January 17, 2015

Past-life reviews

7 a.m. Time to get started. Miss Rita, care to take a shot at Charles's first question?

[Discussing the matter with my friend Charles Sides, I proposed that he ask one question at a time, and I would ask Rita.
After reading her response, he will then provide another question for the next day, either a follow-up, such as a request for
clarification (which as far as I am concerned can include quar-
reling with the answer if need be) or an entirely new question.
This takes advantage of his decades of study of metaphysics
and metaphysical questions and frees me from having to
alternate between roles, first talk-show host, then guest, so to
speak. His first question, sent the night before:

["Rita said she did not go through a life review but she regained access. She said this would be another thread to follow up on at another time. So . . . what does she mean by regaining access?"]

I think the question may be based on a misapprehension. I meant merely, the same process looks different depending upon the context from which it is considered.

What looks like a past-life review, when seen as an extension of physical conditions as you have always experienced them, will look like a *process*, a sequential process: First you look at this, then this, then this. NDE reports can be read that way without either the experiencer or the reader realizing that such a report is a reinterpretation into familiar sequential-time terms of a process that did not actually occur in that way.

What I myself experienced was the same thing *in effect*, but I realize that it is more accurate to say that rather than my being shown something, I regained access to something I had never been separated from.

Let's put it this way. We are put into an Earth-life, and we are both a continuing entity and, at the same time, a *new* entity. Beginning from a pool of potential elements, a relative few are selected to live together in one body, fusing themselves into a new soul, or a new mind, or a new center of localized consciousness.

If you examine that life from the point of view of the elements that comprised it, you will see a long string of "past lives" (not necessarily on Earth) and a long evolution of the soul.

If you examine it from the point of view of the particular mixture that became a new element, you will see a beginning of consciousness, a growth of a sense of self, and a living-out of life in relative isolation from all the other elements that are equally part of it, but that did not manifest with it as part of its particular mixture whose 3D experience was to fuse a new center, a new mind or soul.

The circumstances are the same. It is the appearances that are different. It is the conscious and unconscious context of the viewing (and the report) that may make it appear like two different things.

Now, when we come to die—when we come to move beyond the internal division between things known to the earthbound portion and things known to the entire being of which the earthbound portion is one part—our own assumptions at the time we pass over may color how we experience the transition, in the same way that assumptions color any experience, mostly unconsciously, so that to us it seems we get an objective report. If you expect to cross the River Jordan and see Jesus, you will, and that perception won't be "wrong," it won't be "nonobjective." It will be an interpretation shaped by expectations—*and this is always so.* That's why, incidentally, people who believe in nothing [that is, believe that nothing follows 3D life] sometimes initially meet blankness. For as long as their soul-perspective governs their perception, they get what they expect to get. Only when the overall being, what you have called the "larger being," feeds its perspective does the returning new soul have its horizons broadened.

By the way, that is the retrieval process, though we never thought of it that way. When we in the physical extended to others no longer in the body who were "stuck" or bewildered, what we were doing was getting their attention, true enough, so that they could break out of their unconscious self-imposed isolation. What we didn't realize was that the "helpers" or the unnamed forces behind our scenarios were actually that person's own larger community opening the person's perceptions. What we saw was a soul reacting to a scenario and responding—"seeing the light," in a word. But what we didn't necessarily see—*I* never did, anyway—was that the person wasn't "going somewhere new," even metaphorically, but was handing over perception to a broader consciousness of which they were a part. Establishing diplomatic relations with the previously unsuspected rest of themselves, so to speak.

I did not go over expecting to see Jesus, or needing to see relatives or friends. My few days of coma provided me with a smooth transition of consciousness. But whether it had been smooth or not, my transition would have been the same process of moving from a limited to a less-limited perspective. As I knew what was coming, I didn't have to experience it in sequential fashion. I had been relatively closed off and then I was not.

I think you are meaning that this is the same for everybody, not that you were relatively closed off as opposed to relatively open during your life.

Correct. I am explaining as clearly as I can—even a bit pedantically, I am afraid—that my "past- life review," like anyone's, was merely a matter of greater awareness as I moved beyond the constrictions of the physical part of the universe.

But bear in mind that this is still a simplified picture that does not convey various differences in effective consciousness caused by the change of terrain. Our new circumstances lead us to experience ourselves in very different ways, and it is this usually unspoken context that leads to so many misinterpretations.

For instance, while in the body, perhaps mostly unaware of "past-life" connections or nonphysical connections of any kind, one may live thinking oneself a unit comprising only 3D elements. *But our opinions about ourselves do not change who we are, what we are.* It doesn't matter that you think yourself an orphan in the universe. You aren't and couldn't be. You were created, you came into being, as a unique combination of elements that were to learn to live together, you were continually affected by internal adjustments among various elements, you expressed inherited traits not only from your physical heredity but from your nonphysical heredity as well. You were less a unit than a family learning to become a unit, and each member of that family brought along its own heritage, which is why your life was a unique window into existence.

Well, you need to keep this unvarying fact in mind when you consider any other aspect of life, either physical or nonphysical. To the degree that you keep it in your mind as background, your perception of new aspects will be clarified. And this gradual process of clarification, incidentally, is why these things take time and perseverance to sink in.

It is, yet again, that old "to understand A, you have to understand B, but to understand B you have to understand A."

Yes it is. Coming to truth is a continuing process of refinement [of understanding]. You don't leap toward a greater truth; you edge toward it, clarifying our perception. (That doesn't mean you don't suddenly make a great stride. It merely means that becoming clearer is a process rather than a destination or event.)

In the past, I have noticed that some people thought my reference to the larger being of which we are a part meant that I was finding a new way to say "God" without using the word God. I don't know that I was ever able to persuade them that I was saying something different from what they expected, and so they weren't actually hearing what I was saying, but were cramming it into their accustomed ways of thinking.

All you can do is explain as best you can what you are meaning to say. No one can guarantee understanding of what they say; Communication requires two things, expression and reception. Express as carefully as you are able, and leave the rest to your audience. People take what they need, which isn't always the same thing you said or intended to say. Nothing wrong with that—remember, their other elements may be seizing on things as a clue for the person, and so may be very opportunistic.

Lost it.

Enough for now. You are getting tired.

I am, though it has been only a little more than an hour. Very well, I will type this up, send it around, and wait for Charles's next question, whether it be follow-up or even argument. Thanks, Miss Rita.

Sunday, January 18, 2015

Levels of consciousness

6:30 a.m. All right, Miss Rita, here we go again. Would you address Charles's question, please?

Gladly. It is always interesting to see the different "flavor" of different people's minds, and perhaps this manner of proceeding will help you and others to experience the sampling somewhat as we do here.

[Charles's question: "Rita says, 'We' are put into an Earth-life, and we are both a continuing entity and, at the same time, a *new* entity. Beginning from a pool of potential elements, a relative few are selected to live together in one body, fusing themselves into a new soul, or a new mind, or a new center of localized 'consciousness.' I'm realizing much more clearly that any answer depends entirely on which 'level' of consciousness is doing the perceiving. From the perspective of the continuing entity or the strands, how do they communicate, select the few that are chosen, fuse themselves and decide on a body for a 'new entity'?"]

The question is rooted in time, of course. It assumes process and sequence and—most of all—assumes separation in a way that is not quite appropriate. In higher dimensions, or "the other side," we don't have meetings, exactly. Yet it would not be accurate to say we all function as one undifferentiated person. "Person" is a term best confined to discussions of life in the 3D realm.

The short answer—which will be merely cryptic until we can provide the context—is that no level of consciousness decides its own state of being. Our lives are always guided and shaped by the next higher level of consciousness, which is itself shaped by *its* next higher level of consciousness, and so on and so forth.

No one pulls himself up by his own bootstraps.

Now, those few sentences have provided you with material for many a question, if you ponder them, as I encourage you to do. The process of pondering—a combination of active thinking and receptive musing—allows new meanings to suggest themselves. It is a richer means of absorbing new ideas than mere logic and certainly more than mere memorization.

Let me return to the point I made earlier. Life is not divided between the physical and the nonphysical. We do not move from one side to the other. We do not cease to exist in one realm and appear in another, though it certainly appears that way. We live in all existing dimensions, because there is no other way it can be. You can't live in depth but not in width or height.

Ponder the relevance of this statement to the question posed.

Now, return to another statement, the connection but differentiation among different levels of consciousness. You as the controlling consciousness are in charge of your body. You coordinate the society of cells; your central intelligence provides the stability for the system. All the specialized functions that cooperate to continue your life—respiration, elimination, digestion, the electrical and chemical homeostatic systems—all depend upon you as the linchpin, even though your conscious life knows nothing of the everyday functioning and interaction of these subsystems.

You are, in essence, a higher self, or larger being, to all these more specialized intelligences. Your life is of a different order, your everyday concerns are incomprehensible to them.

Why should you expect it to be any different between you as a time-bound, 3D-bound individual element and the next higher level of intelligence that is to you as you are to the parasympathetic system?

Could you read the *New York Times* to your liver or lung intelligence system? Could the mind that filters your blood profit from reading the financial section? Could it even have any idea what it was about?

This sounds whimsical. It is not. It is a statement through which you can better understand the very true statement: "As above, so below." That does not apply only to the relationship between human life and the placement of the stars. It refers to the fact that everything in the universe is *scaled*. Everything is a repetition in miniature or in magnification of every other layer. Levels of being do not change the fact that *all life is one pattern*, scaled differently but scaled to the same pattern.

You may give intellectual assent too quickly. In practice that will have the same effect as instant rejection—it will leave your life untouched. To make these concepts yours, you must *wrestle* with them, argue their ramifications, test whether you can really understand and assent to them *as you see them manifest in your life*. So, go back. Ponder.

Meanwhile, remember the question and try to tie it together with two concepts—connected but different levels of consciousness, and stewardship.

Higher intelligence

What makes you think that at any level, the components decide what comes next? Your experience of life shows you that you are responsible for acting and reacting. They do not show you that you are responsible for producing the events (call them that) that produce the need to choose. It is true that you create yourself moment to moment (and thus cumulatively) by what you choose. It is *somewhat* true that you bring things to your life by what you are. It is wholly *untrue* that you shape the circumstances that are the larger framework of the pattern. You do not cause the sun to rise or set. You do not cause or select the millions of social interactions that shape your world moment by moment.

Yet clearly, life is not chaos. What can all this mean, save that the order in life is provided by a higher intelligence that functions at a different level? I mean to say that the layer of consciousness that produces the conditions among which you live is *essentially* different from yours in the same way that yours is different from the intelligence that directs your lower functions. You cannot read *its New York Times*, either.

Now, in all this, it is important to remember, I am not drawing the distinction people often erroneously make between a layer of consciousness while in 3D and our layer outside 3D. *That is a false distinction.* We in the higher dimensions (and that is a clumsy and misleading way to put it) are at the same layer of consciousness as you who center in the 3D world. *We are the same level of consciousness,* but functioning in different conditions.

You don't become a lung-mind and you don't become a god-mind by dropping the body. You remain what you were, but your sphere of awareness expands. Is that as clear to you as to me?

I know that people describe life planning and past-life review and meetings to decide what to work on next, and, looking in hindsight, the process can look that way. But is that really the most accurate description? Did you enter life knowing your plan, etc.? And—since you didn't—why is it that a 3D life always appears to clarify out of a mist so to speak? Even the children who remember "past lives" themselves merge from a mist, unless they are close continuations of a "previous" intelligence (often one whose life was cut short by design or choice or accident) that carries through, rather than a new mixture of ingredients.

This is somewhat shorter than usual, but it has taken you an hour to bring it through, and I suggest that it will provide fodder for several more questions, so may be a good place to pause.

All right. Very interesting, Rita. We'll see where we go from here.

Monday, January 19, 2015

Soulmaking

7 a.m., All right, Miss Rita, I will put Bob's question here, and I will reread it, and hope-fully off we go.

> [From Bob Friedman: "The material [on Saturday] prompted
> some thought on the transition period. I understand broadly
> what Rita is saying about going from the limited 3D perspec-
> tive to a broader perspective of some sort of collective soul.
> I found myself wondering just how the 'Bob Friedman' per-
> sonality and collection of experiences, beliefs, work, etc., is
> perceived 'over there' in the nonphysical realm. Does one
> maintain all those memories and personality traits as 'Bob,'
> or is one more of a conglomeration of everyone's experiences
> in the so-called 'collective' of past lives, other soul parts and
> their experiences, etc.? In other words, more *specifically*, how
> does one perceive oneself on the other side and how do others
> perceive the former earthbound "you"?]

A good clarifying question, and the answer is just the kind of "yes but no"
answer we used to get, or, not "yes but no," but more like "either and both."

Back in our sessions, early on, we were told that the guys regarded our
minds as little more than habit systems, and I don't remember ever pursuing that very vigorously. So perhaps now is as good a time as any.

The whole point of creating a soul in a given time and place, comprising certain traits and predispositions, is to create an enduring resource; so,
when successful, there would be no point in throwing the elements back
in the soup! A point of view, an accustomed collaboration of elements in a
new container, is an accomplishment. It is valued. Certainly Bob will continue to be Bob as, for instance, I continue to be Rita and all those past
lives people connect to on occasion continue to be themselves. No need to
fear dissolution! However, that isn't the end of the story, because the opposite—or what seems to be an opposite—is also true. In effect, we are all one;
in effect, we are all individuals. So if you ask for some specific information,

it is the equivalent of doing a "search." The information is here, and if it is here, it is available. (The limits on information are on the 3D receptor's end, not on this end.)

I am not yet sure what you mean by "specifically." I recognize that you don't wish to be fobbed off with generalities, but I don't know what else you want. I am of course willing to clarify or expand if you can let me know what you have in mind.

Meanwhile, these thoughts on the subject. Has it occurred to any of you yet that this question, and things I have said already, provide a good deal of clarification into the *process* of soulmaking?

Take the word "traits" and substitute "minds" or "lives" or "past lives" or "other related minds" and see how this sentence reads:

A new soul is created by the combination of many past traits into one time and place and genetic structure.

I am tempted to sit back and say, "Do you see?"—and if I were in a classroom, that is what I would be inclined to do, for anything reasoned out by oneself is more permanent and definite than something presented by another. But—as Frank doesn't like waiting (a joke) and as we want to use his time as best we can, time being a limited resource—here are the implications I want you to get.

Everyone on Earth (that is, in 3D) may be considered a community of certain past individuals.

Everyone is thus a recapitulation of what has gone before. This will need to be filled in.

The mental world *in 3D* as well as beyond it is thus made continually more complex and attains more possibilities because any combination of previous elements has greater potential for complexity.

This is why change is a continually accelerating process. With each iteration, the building blocks are more complex, so the resulting new entity can become yet *more* complex.

As was said earlier, time experienced as chronology matters. You can't tear down the pyramids before they are constructed. You can't use simple lives as building blocks until they have come into existence, nor can you be used until *you* have come into existence.

This, by the way, or perhaps not so "by the way," is the truth behind evolution. It is not that things continually get "better," whatever "better" means. It is that things build on prior things, resulting in ever greater possibilities.

That's quite a lot from one question. I get the impression you want us to rest on our oars, even though it has been only twenty minutes.

No, that is more you panting and gasping for breath because it came out so fluently. Take a moment to recalibrate. Sip your coffee. No rush—but as I said, we must use your time while we have it.

Yes, I heard that, and I didn't take it to be a pre-obit, but a reminder that tempus is continuing to fugit.

Not in the context you are considering it, however, or let's say not *only* in that context. It is true that your time and energy and attention are limited, as is everybody's, but I am not concerned that you won't complete the work. My concern is that it be completed in a timely fashion. People are finally ready for this new understanding (or nearly so, from your perspective), and it will be a shame if we do not provide them with this new utensil.

I look back at my black-box sessions of 2000, and your and my sessions of 2001–2002, which were at your suggestion, and I see suspicious footprints.

How does a footprint entertain suspicion?

Very funny—that isn't the kind of joke I associate with you, Rita.

Remember, I both am and am not the same person.

Yes, need to remember that. Okay, more?

Let me say it explicitly—don't hold all this for eventual polishing into a book. Get the material out as best you can—TMI Explorers list, your

friends, your blog, Facebook—so that it may marinate. If it becomes a
book, all right, and this moment-by-moment dissemination won't hinder
but will help the book. And if it never becomes a book, it will still have
been put out there.

This reminds me to ask about the many-versions idea.

Yes, but not here or now. Let Charles insert it into the flow as he is
moved to.

Your soul's heredity

*You said, "Everyone is thus a recapitulation of what has gone before. This will need to
be filled in."*

Perhaps it is obvious to some. It won't be obvious to all.

Let's put it this way. A moment while I shape an example. [Brief pause]

Let's use you as an example, although the detail isn't right. You were
formed in 1946, of certain materials. (And this will enable me to clarify a
few things left over from our sessions when I was the inquirer rather than
the encyclopedia.)

Your *physical* heredity is from your genetic heritage from your parents
(and, by extension, from their families, emphasized for many previous generations but theoretically including heredity from the first person, that is,
forever).

Your *cultural* heredity is from the environment you are placed in. This
includes not only physical surroundings but intellectual and perceptual and
emotional influences.

But your *soul* heredity, call it, is from the previous souls whose pattern
has been used in order to fashion you.

I know what you mean (I can feel it) but I don't think that last part is yet clear.

I am about to be more specific. For you (silently going along with certain erroneous identifications you have made, such as Joseph Smallwood's
name):

Katrina, the Polish-Jewish girl.

John Cotten, of Virginia in the 1700s.

David Poynter, the Welsh journalist.

Joseph "Smallwood," the transcendentalist.

I'll stop there. You could trace out your spiritual heritage just by examining the qualities of these "past lives" and seeing how they manifest in you. And this is not to mention Bertram the monk or Joseph the Egyptian whose emotional link to the nonphysical shaped you so strongly.

Do you see the point of this? You are shaped not of abstract "traits" but of *lives* that exhibited what we call traits. How could you comprise these lives if the lives weren't yet lived?

Yet—and this is an important clarification—it is *as if* future lives exist within you, as well, because—well, take your example. Joseph Smallwood is one of your strands. That means that he is connected directly to you, a "you" that is *partly* him and mostly other. You comprise *all* of him—and many others. He, and anyone in what we might call the objective past, equally comprises you as one strand, but in a different way.

And I can see that this is a tangled mess, mostly due to linguistic difficulties and considerations of time.

Mostly due to the limitations of sequential presentation in words. A picture would present it instantly—if such a picture could be drawn.

Well, maybe we can go at it again, at another time. I think it's time to quit. See you another time. Thanks as always.

Tuesday, January 20, 2015

Experiencing the nonphysical

Good morning, Rita. Bob [Friedman]'s follow-up questions. Number two I think I could answer from what you've given, but I'll be interested in your response to them all.

[Follow-up questions from Bob: "What I mean by *specific* is more detail about what is *perceived* (both by the former 3D person and others perceiving *them*) when he/she crosses over: 1) Is there a body of some sort resembling the former body? We often read about the "astral body"—is that similar in any way to the physical body, and are others, either parts of the greater entity or other former physical persons, aware of this body/person as 'Bob' or 'Rita'? 2) Do the memories of 'Bob' carry over into a new nonphysical-brain consciousness? 3) Does the 'Bob' life (and presumably other past and future lives), or any former physical entity now on Earth, gradually or ever lose awareness of its memories and traits from the former 3D life?"]

I see. You want to know how the nonphysical part of the world appears to your consciousness when you drop the body. But it seems you really want to know "how is it really" in the afterlife. Is it solid or not, do we have form or not, is it a continuation of this or that aspect of physical life? Believe me, I recognize the question—it is one reason (of many) that led me to suggest to Frank that we do weekly sessions, to explore just that kind of issue. But my agenda got hijacked by what we were calling the guys upstairs, or what I had been instructed years before to call "energies," and I see now why: to answer my questions as posed would have encouraged me in misunderstanding.

1. ["Is there a body of some sort resembling the former body? We often read about the 'astral body'—is that similar in any way to the physical body, and are others, either parts of the greater entity or other former physical persons, aware of this body/person as 'Bob' or 'Rita'?]

Answering what sounds like an easy uncomplicated question in this case is neither easy nor uncomplicated, but we can try. The simplest answer is, people perceive (a) what they need to perceive, or (b) what they are able to perceive—and those two conditions change with time and experience, so their perception also changes; thus, if you are expecting heaven, you may get it, and it may not last! Nor hell, nor nothingness.

But that simple answer does not mean what it appears to mean—that it is all some sort of imagination game. We have to consider two things more: who is the "you," as usual, and who is the other, or *what* is the other.

As to the first, remember, the prime change when you drop the body is that you cease to be unaware of the rest of your being. I put it in that double-negative form purposefully because "cease to be unaware" has a different set of nuances than "become aware" or even "remember again." It is not an act of *will* on the part of the soul departing 3D life, but of *perception*. It is more like opening your eyes than it is like determining to see.

If the newcomers to life unencumbered by the restrictions of life in the physical world are able to become seamlessly aware that they are part of a larger being, that's one thing. If they think themselves the same unit, only now deprived of (or relieved of) the body, that is a second thing. And—more usually—if they are somewhere in between, it is a process, and so "the afterlife" seems to change around them as they change.

If you will go back and look at Bob [Monroe]'s first book, you will see anomalous descriptions of the afterlife, discrepancies he was unable to account for and was unwilling (bless him!) to suppress for the sake of an apparent consistency. This is less a matter of the afterlife's nature changing, or of it having different compartments with different attributes, than it was of his approaching it with different attitudes (mostly unconscious of the difference) at different times.

Consider, too, the experiences of Lifeline retrievers. [Lifeline is a residential program at The Monroe Institute that concentrates on teaching access to what might be called lost souls, with the intent of helping them regain their bearings.] You go to do a retrieval. Your consciousness is inserted into a scenario not of your choosing, you connect to the mind that is lost or stuck, the person has an epiphany and "moves on" as you say. Did the afterlife change, objectively, for that person? It changed *subjectively*—and *in the absence of an anchoring physical body holding you to 3D conditions, the distinction between objective and subjective ceases to exist!*

Reread that, please. It is important. Many of the discrepancies and apparent contradictions in reports from the "afterlife"—including descriptions of heaven and hell among religions—stem from lack of realization of this very important fact. "Objective" reality is only possible in 3D, because of its conditions. We were told that in the past, Frank, but not in so many words, only by implication, and neither of us understood it in that way.

This is why in the "afterlife" there can be no deceit, no concealment. This is why there is perfect justice, and why things automatically sort themselves into perfect order. And it is why the 3D world was created (one reason why): to provide a place with perception of separation, and delayed consequences, and the cohabitation of elements of different types [in one body] so that they may similarly associate in the non-3D world in a way they couldn't otherwise.

The simplest answer to your first question is that there are as many answers as there are experiences, because everyone's subjectivity is the only objectivity. That isn't the end of the subject, but enough on that for now.

2. "Do the memories of 'Bob' carry over into a new nonphysical-brain consciousness?]

Your second question is easily disposed of. Not only your memories but everything about you, including facets you have no hint of while you are in the physical world, "go" with you, because you are what you make yourself, and making you was the whole point of your 3D existence. In addition, as I said earlier, the non-3D mind is accessible to all. (However, this is true while you are still in 3D, as well, only you may or may not realize it.)

3. ["Does the 'Bob' life (and presumably other past and future lives), or any former physical entity now on Earth, gradually or ever lose awareness of its memories and traits from the former 3D life?]

Your third question leads us into very interesting territory, via one of those "yes but no" answers we became so familiar with.

First, no, because why should it? But this answer has two caveats that amount to "yes, in a way."

First caveat: As you digest experience, you change. That is what absorbing experience *means*. And something that has been assimilated has no reason to continue to exist as a separate piece of data. So—the larger being of which Bob is a part holds his memories as it holds everything about him, but the better it assimilates his life, the less prominent any specific item in that life—such as memories—becomes. Why should your larger being remember your old telephone numbers or ZIP codes? They are still there; they are so little needed or consulted that they might be considered to have been forgotten. And this says by inference that the most important things in your life sort out to the top, which is only what you would expect.

Second caveat, a more interesting one: The interaction with the 3D world helps determine what is forgotten or remembered.

This one bears thinking about, and requires background, and then we're done for the moment.

All minds exist in "the nonphysical" and interact according to non-physical rather than physical rules, as we have said. In 3D, you access your mind primarily through your brain; nonetheless the mind, which cannot be destroyed, exists beyond the confines and accidents of the 3D world.

Your consciousness in 3D is limited and bright—the comparison the guys gave us is apt: the difference between star-glow that is all-extensive but relatively dim and a flashlight that is narrow but intense. That your 3D consciousness is narrow but intense is the result of 3D conditions. (Your mind itself remains unaffected, but its expression is focused.)

Therefore, your attention from 3D to someone not in 3D has the effect of lighting up their consciousness. In effect, you provide an energy boost that results in their seeming more "there." An example is just what we are doing now. This process focuses your attention on me, and so I am more aware, in a way. This is what we outside of 3D get out of this process, over and above what else we want to accomplish. You have heard of the "hungry ghosts" concept, perhaps. That energy boost is what fuels it.

So, you can see that as you are forgotten by those on Earth, you *in effect* lose awareness. Not really, for nothing is ever lost, but in effect. Nor is this necessarily a bad thing. An adult is not necessarily dependent upon being able to remember the details of childhood, and what advantage would it provide?

So, that's our morning's work, and thank you for the interesting questions.

Thanks, Rita, and we'll talk again whenever we do.

Wednesday, January 21, 2015

Visualizing the afterlife

5:40 a.m. Rita? Charles's question?

[Charles's question, given to me the night before as usual, was phrased this way: "I know that a misunderstanding could

occur if everyone believed all death experiences would be
the same. I also know that everything, including 3D life, is
subjective. With that in mind, Rita, would you please tell us
your 'subjective' experiences? The 'specifics' that Bob and I
would like to know pertain to how you, Rita, are perceiving
your 'existence' now. Most, if not all, of the readers knew you
as Rita here in 3D. Most of us have read that in the afterlife
beings take on a body, continue learning, help others make
the adjustment, act as guides, as well as other 'activities.' So,
bearing in mind the question does come from a 3D mindset,
would you tell us what 'life' is like for you now, maybe as you
might write a letter describing your new environment and
activities to someone after you've moved?"]

I know what they would like me to provide. It is what I wanted, too,
when I was in their situation. It is what you would like as well. But how
many contradictory stories would you like? How many will be enough to
satisfy that need? Will one more definite story delivered with or without
nuance and caveats help anybody to understand anything? No, it won't. It
would only force or encourage people to choose among visions.

No such story will accomplish what is needed, which—I say it again
although it seems to me I have said it continually—is to replace the unconscious and conscious assumptions with new ones.

What good is it to describe an afterlife or a version of the afterlife or a
specific of "the afterlife"—when the entire preliminary point is that *there is
no separate afterlife?*

What use is it to describe "the other side" when we are trying to accus-
tom you to the idea that there is no division in the way you have been thinking about it?

I don't object to the question—anything that is on your mind will help
clarify the situation—but I will keep coming back to the point that you don't
move into new territory by remaining in old territory. Not that exploration
requires abandoning everything you think you know but that it requires
entertaining an entirely different structure.

Suppose I were to say, I was met by Abraham at the River Jordan? Or I entered the Re-education Center in Focus 27? Or I found myself in Summerland? Or I merged with All-There-Is and live in cosmic bliss? Or I found myself in an analog to physical existence and had to remind myself, from time to time, that I was not "alive" anymore?

I am not mocking the question. I am trying to shake you from the habit of thinking you can hear something new by putting it into accustomed terms. I can draw analogies, and they may be helpful and anyway are needed to bridge the gap between preconception and unsuspected reality—but by definition an analogy is not a photograph. Something that is more or less "like" something else is clearly *not* like it in other respects, or it would be not an analogy but an identity.

Now please *move* from where you started. To get any benefit from this or any communication, you have to do more than be open to hearing; you need to prepare the ground. And that means be *actively* aware, while you read what I or others have to say, that at least some of what you have constructed as a mental framework is *wrong*. At least some things you may have discarded or may never have considered are *right*, or more right than you have considered. Thus, in Christian theology you will find many glimpses of another way to see things, just as Frank always insisted and I resisted. This is *not* to say the Christian theologies (for there are more than one) are right, or that I see things in those terms. It is to say, merely, that here as elsewhere you may find valid hints.

As for instance, angels. Have you thought of angels as "beings" who have not had and will not have the 3D experience? Have you thought of the relationship between such beings and the other beings—the larger selves of 3D beings—who have had it? *That* is the kind of thinking you will need to do, if you wish to follow me to the new ground I hope to bring you to.

Rita's experience

I have not forgotten the question, and I don't intend to dance around it. I am trying hard to assure that you put yourselves into a place where you can actually hear something new and not cram it into accustomed ideas.

Remember.

No "other side," but only additional dimensions not clearly perceived from 3D, and hence crammed into attributes of time.

No afterlife separate from physical life, but one continual life that always partakes of all dimensions.

No separate self that dies and goes on to a nonphysical experience, but a seemingly separate part of a larger being that moves from relative isolation to recovery of its awareness of unbroken connection.

No external objective environment outside of 3D, no subjective shell, but *one* undivided reality. (This does not mean no relative separation into units—what am I if not that? It means you realize that you are a part of everything in a way that will require some extended discussion, another time. Make note of this as another question, perhaps.)

I have to say, I am afraid that as soon as I move to the next part of this, you will immediately forget what I have just said, and will busily pack everything new into your accustomed containers, thus preserving your comfort at the expense of your potential growth in understanding. I know, from personal experience! There is nothing harder than realizing, all the way down, that you are hearing something new. That's why so much report-age from "the afterlife" is so contradictory. I used to wonder if "the guys upstairs" ever got frustrated in their attempt to communicate. I think now, the answer is yes and no. Yes, because so little gets through the mental fil-ters. No, because it is a worthwhile effort, and every communication that does get done is worthwhile and satisfying.

Now, you will think I am only now getting to answering your ques-tion. If so, that will serve as a sign to yourself that you haven't *really* heard anything I've said so far, but have been impatiently (or perhaps patiently) waiting for me to "get to the point." Well, I have put out the signs; it is up to each of you, whether you follow them.

I spent my last days in a coma. That meant my body was abandoned in terms of my conscious supervision. I could maintain a form of focused consciousness that is possible only in the body, yet not have to focus it on keeping the body safe and functioning. *Thus*, I could experience "the after-life" in a way impossible after dropping the body.

I see that I must explain that. Bearing in mind that we extend to all dimensions (because there is no other way it can be) and that the conditions of 3D life result in our consciousness being intense, focused, and narrow in extent, you can see that it is a greatly different viewpoint of the higher dimensions than is afforded when our consciousness is centered in the higher dimensions *without* the focusing effect. In a sense, the coma was the best of both worlds when it came to exploration. But this was only because I was ready for it. An unprepared mind would not be able to comprehend, though it might observe. Another way to say it is that our backgrounds and biases form the limits to what we can comprehend, which is why reports and scriptures differ.

As I lay in a coma, as I went exploring possibilities, I saw things still in my accustomed manner—and why should we expect anything else? We do not suddenly (nor gradually) become someone else just because we distance ourselves from, and eventually drop, the body. So, I saw research projects, you might say. I saw continuities rather than new departures. The differences I saw I attributed to new conditions, the similarities I attributed to my remaining me.

Then, I finally was finished with that tethered form of existence. I released the body and hence released my connection to the factor that centered my attention in one 3D focus. That does *not* mean I left 3D. How could I? If we are always in all dimensions, how can we leave any of them? Instead, it means my consciousness was released from 3D conditions. I was no longer constrained, and, in effect, the barriers between my consciousness and the conscious presence of my larger being were removed. (This is analogy, remember. Not barriers of any kind, really, more an accustomed focus.)

Now what situation did I step into? (And here you hope for a description of day-to-day reality, forgetting or disregarding everything I said at length earlier. Try to get beyond that.)

I saw that I was part of a being—one being among uncounted others, by the way. The larger being is not a code-word for God, nor for The Human Race. That being, that in a way could be looked upon as my creator, or perhaps like my parents, or like the soil from which I as a newly formed separate intelligence had sprung—that being always exists regardless of sojourns of any part of it into 3D. The 3D experience—*each* 3D experience, I should say—only adds to the total. It is valued, but it is not the central focus of the being.

So my consciousness remained, and it also transformed, or I should say acquired an alternate way to experience itself. And, parenthetically, I think that may be the simplest explanation of what people call the past-life review: It is their sudden seeing of their life from the point of view of the larger being. Because they return to 3D, they naturally report the experience in 3D terms, which is not *wrong* but is radically *incomplete*, as if you were to describe a person as seen only from the right-hand side and not from front, back, and left, not to say and from above and below, inside and outside.

I suddenly realized (that's how it would appear from the 3D point of view) that "Rita" and Rita's whole life were (a) only a small part of my being's life, (b)

Phooey, lost it.

It has been over an hour. Not surprising.

Well, let's try to get through what you were saying.

When my consciousness was released from its 3D-centered existence, I saw all the unsuspected background of my life—all the non-3D activity that was going on while I graded papers, so to speak—and I realized that neither my 3D life nor the non-3D life centered on 3D. It *seemed* to, while I was there, or was focused there, I should say, but in fact it did not. 3D life is in support of the larger life, not vice-versa. But I'm afraid we will have to pause here, because it can't be expressed as an addendum.

Thanks, Rita. I can feel the effort you are exerting to try to make a true statement, and I appreciate it. I can say, I wondered how you would respond to the question. It is still true, isn't it, the better the question, the better the answer.

Still true. That's our hope here.

Till next time, then.

Thursday, January 22, 2015

3D and non-3D

6:30 a.m. Rita, you said 3D life is in support of non-3D life, just about the time I ran out of gas. Is that where you want to pick up?

I am continuing to answer the question of how I spend my time here, as part of what I experienced as I moved my consciousness from a 3D focus. It isn't a question that can be answered in twenty words or less.

If you bear in mind the conditions I described "yesterday" (to you), you will see that nearly all descriptions of the afterlife you have ever received have been analogies, conscious or unconscious, designed to motivate, to encourage, 3D consciousness to—

Dammit, went wool-gathering. Again?

There is no hurry. Just stay with the process and we'll get there.

Descriptions of the afterlife are *analogies*, for one simple reason. Describing additional dimensions (or rather the effect of awareness of additional dimensions) in terms comprehensible to fewer dimensions can only be analogy. So what's the solution? Twofold: (1) work hard remembering (on both sides) that it is analogy and (2) work hard (on the receiver's end) to stretch to try to *feel* the meaning rather than to read it as a logical exercise or a travel story.

Any such description is provided in the hope of encouraging the reader or listener to make just such a stretch of comprehension, because the very process of stretching will open new possibilities. What did our *The Sphere and the Hologram* book do, after all, but put into words new ways of seeing things, for the purpose of helping people to stretch? What did Seth do, and intend to do, but the same thing? But it does no good to read something intended to change you by making you aware of unknown parts of yourself as if it were merely a travel diary that assumes (and leaves) the accustomed 3D life as if it were a stable, fixed, immutable reference point.

Prime among distorting background assumptions is the one that thinks 3D and non-3D are two different things. They *are* in that they are *relatively* different. They *are not* in that they are points on a bell curve rather than either-or.

That's why I started with my experience while in a coma. When I was ready and able to drop the body, I moved pretty seamlessly to a new awareness because I had been moving toward it for eight years, not to say my entire lifetime. After all, who suggested to me that I suggest to you that we do weekly sessions to follow up your new information obtained in 2000 and shared with me and others?

So what happened? *Because* I refocused from 3D to non-3D consciously, I had no need to reorient myself. That is part of what I meant in saying my past-life review was merely a process of seeing my 3D life from the point of view of my non-3D component.

Because I didn't need orientation, I didn't need analogies or scenarios. Hence, no past-life review, no crossing the river of no return, no white light, etc. All that is a 3D-oriented description of a change in consciousness, and the process that enables or smooths the change.

So, seamlessly, I was "there," or "here." But what did that mean?

Immediately, it meant a sort of reorientation, as I remembered that my non-3D self experienced my 3D life as I lived it. Then I knew that I had been in the higher dimensions all along, regardless how oblivious to them I was.

But at the same time, I realized that *I was still in the 3D dimensions* even though not focused there—because, again, how can there be any dimensions we are *not* in? If reality is six-dimensional, you can't be only in three nonphysical dimensions, any more than you can be only in three physical dimensions. In either case, you can be *aware* only of some and not of others, but in no case can you not actually *be* there.

Think about that!

Really, think about it. You always were in the non-3D dimensions, but your awareness of them differed at different times, and certainly differed by different individuals. It isn't any different from "the other side," from the higher dimensions. We remain in 3D, though our awareness varies both in time and between people.

Now, if you move over thinking you are exchanging the physical world for the nonphysical world, what you experience (at least internally) will differ from what you experience if you realize that you remain in the one, undivided, reality, moving only your focus. And between the two extremes may be found every description of "the afterlife" ever expressed. By the way, can you see the assumptions hidden within the word "afterlife"? You might taste what it is like to think of it, instead, as the "non-3D life" or "life beyond 3D"—assuming you can hold in mind that you always did live in non-3D, regardless of your focus.

Now, if you are still with me, you may begin to see why contradictory accounts of the non-3D initiation and continuation are all expressing any one aspect of a huge and simultaneous experience. Words are too slow and sequential to show it easily, but I will try to give it in word-sketches, and maybe Frank can come up with a line-drawing to express it as he did with TGU's self-portrait.

Hmm, let me try that right now. I get what you intend to say. Let me fool with pencil and paper, and if I get something, I'll sketch it here, and if not, I can always continue. My assumption is that you will help provide the sketch.

Well—I will try to keep the point to be illustrated clear in your mind. But the actual work of translating it will be up to you.

All right, let's see.

[Six sketches. See page 79.]

All right, that didn't take long. I don't know how I will reproduce sketching on the computer, though.

As an interim measure, merely scan the page and include the scan as an attachment. Meanwhile, say a few words on the six sketches.

All right. I drew a vertical line with a sort of tripod at the bottom. The tripod represents the three physical dimensions; the vertical, the extension of ourselves to the other dimensions, however many of them there are.

Our awareness after death may remain in the 3D, in which case we are "stuck" and may benefit from a retrieval.

Or, it may move entirely to the non-3D, forgetting Earth (that is, the 3D dimensions).

Or, it may alternate between the two.

Or, it may expand to incorporate the whole.

I think you will find that even this description of these very simple stick diagrams makes more comprehensible what I am going to say.

I think so, too, just as our earlier sketch in 2001.

In my particular case, I experienced the fourth possibility, after a relatively brief period of concentrating on the new non-3D dimensions. But a description of all this must wait till you are recharged, as your hour is about up.

Interesting to have to participate in a more active way. Thanks for your continued efforts here, Rita.

You're welcome, and I now understand what "the guys"—our non-3D dimensions—meant when they expressed equal gratitude for 3D attention to the problem. Only in 3D can you act, as you were always told. That doesn't mean quite what it appears to mean, but close to it.

All right, till next time.

Friday, January 23, 2015

How to receive new material

6:40 a.m. All right, Miss Rita, ready on this end. I just reread the past two days' information, to try to keep it fresh in my mind, and I notice how hard it is to stay focused, rather than have a part of my mind—the larger part, it sometimes seems—wander off on tangents suggested by the material. And that doesn't even count the tangents that have nothing to do with the material, but refer to my life in other aspects. Still, reviewing seems to help on this end, so I assume it helps on your end.

Th 1.22

3D
answers   non 3D   or beyond 3D
               answers

Different possible positions after [Transition]:

continued   [forgetting] 3D
fixation
on 3D

alternation   [expanding] to
or [intensity]   include all

All right, that didn't take long. I
don't know how I will reproduce
sketching on the computer, though.

[As an interim measure, merely scan
the page and include the ——— as an
attachment. Meanwhile, say a few
words on the ——— sketches.]

* All right. I draw a vertical line with
a sort of tripod at the bottom. The
tripod represents the three physical
dimensions, the vertical, the extension
of ————— to the other dimensions,
however many of them there are.

It does, but wouldn't if you attempted to keep what you just read front and center, rather than as recent background. That would amount to *clutching* at it, and how can you actively clutch and, at the same time, be receptive to new material? I know you would think you were trying to keep it where the new material could actively associate with it, thus conglomerating them, but it doesn't work that way. It would be a more subtle form of clinging to the familiar (even though only familiar for one or two days) while trying to move into new territory. So let this note serve as a guide as to how to absorb the recent while receiving the new. It is a valuable hint, or will be to some.

All right. So how do you want to continue? Or have you said all you wish about Charles's question?

Look at where we have been (assemble it by making note of the two sessions' transcripts).

All right:
No "other side" or separate afterlife or absolutely separate individual (i.e., not separate from the larger being of which it was formed).
All of us, physical or non, in all dimensions regardless where we are focused.
Once free of the body, four possible orientations: on 3D, or on non-3D, or alternating, or expanded to include awareness of both.

Yes, very good. All this is standard pedagogical technique, you see. Present something new, connect it to previous material, set forth a recapitulation of the material, and do it all over again with new materials. The first mention requires many words, but each reminder serves only to bring into awareness what has been absorbed, so requires only a shorthand allusion to it. It is, in a way, a process of creating shorthand descriptions so that many more things may be held in consciousness together. Slow starting, but ultimately greater potential for communication. And that is why those without patience can only be taught by hard experience.

I know the old saying—"Experience is a hard school, but fools will learn in no other."

Fools, but also people who are not fools but are crippling themselves by impatience, or what you could call spiritual greed, or those who cannot rouse themselves from their accustomed formulations, but rather try to fit new material in prematurely. I say prematurely because, after all, at some point new ways of seeing the world have to be meshed with everything else that you are—but you can't mesh something new unless you have it, and you can't have it unless you first consider it *in itself* (as best you can) *without* forcing it prematurely into agreement with what you are used to thinking.

You can't explore by staying home. Same old story.

Same old story. So—look back at that capsule summary and we'll go on.

Okay.

Experiencing the larger being

I experienced the fourth option: having been prepared by my present (that is, immediately past) life, and by other lives that were comprised in my being, and by the larger being itself, which, in sum, has its own characteristics, I was able to expand my consciousness to what I truly was, rather than only the 3D representation I had just emerged from, or any non-3D models I might have had, or an alternation of the two. And, I'm sorry, but that warrants what will seem a lengthy digression.

Go ahead.

Several digressions possible, in fact, because of course they are not digressions but additional equally important facets of the situation.

1. Past lives. If our beings—our 3D personas, perhaps I should say—are composed of many strands, and those strands are not really traits, as we deduced when talking to "the guys" in 2001, but are each previous individual lived-out-in-3D minds (as well as other factors that more truly could be called traits), you can see that each of them will have its own biases that will enter into the total. Indeed, how else

can it be? Creation of the bias is the *point* of physical existence! Still, it can add up to many internal contradictions
that may be more obvious once we are no longer confined
(and, somewhat, protected) by the limits of consciousness
in 3D life.

2. Remember that the larger being is not a code-word for God.
   A much closer analogy would be a family or group. That is,
   any ten larger beings would seem to each other as individual
   as any ten people in 3D. They don't have an uncountable
   number of 3D-lives within them, and neither are they the
   35.6 they used to tease me with when I used to ask how
   many I was talking to. Like ourselves reading this, they are
   societies that function as individuals. As above, so below.
   The world—the universe, call it what you will—is *scaled*.

Actually, that will do, as far as digressions, because the third point is not
a digression at all, but a continuation: Expanding my awareness changed
me, in effect, yet left me what I always was.

It *changed* me in the way that any new way of seeing things amounts to
a new experience, which, integrated, amounts to a slightly or significantly
altered being.

It *left me unaffected* in the sense that the particular individual consciousness that I had just laboriously fashioned in nearly 90 years of Earth-
life was not altered or expunged (which would defeat the purpose, would it
not?) but remained a resource.

It depends on which one we contact.

So to speak, yes. I am the same old Rita you knew, and that is our connection (or, more properly, *one* of our connections, but I throw that in only
for the sake of completeness, and to serve as a reminder later that what you
are getting does not contradict this shorthand statement). But I am also so
much more than the Rita you or I knew because I am the being of which I
only partially and occasionally partook.

Both, not one or the other. And I am aware of this because my consciousness expanded, rather than choosing or alternating, once free of the confines of 3D time.

So now, consider what this means, in terms of my immediate perceptions upon dropping the body, and in terms of my "day to day" existence here, which—I have not forgotten—is the nub of the question.

When I transitioned, or "went over," or dropped the body—think of it as you prefer—the fact that I was able to expand meant that I had no need of analogies to serve as a bridge, as I mentioned earlier. Therefore, after the brief moment of reorientation, my life here assumed the pattern it has maintained since.

And—here is the nub of it—that meant that I ceased to function as an autonomous individual in the way I thought myself to be while in 3D, and resumed functioning—or rather, assumed my position for the first time, "Rita" not having been previously in existence before the life that created and shaped her—as a *part* of the larger being.

In other words, don't think that you, "coming over to this side" (as you persist in thinking about it) will set your own priorities and busy yourselves with your own projects and, perhaps, find yourself at a loss as to what comes next. Such reports as you have had of people in that fix are reports of 3D individuals who are fixed entirely on non-3D but are not yet aware of their proper place as part of the larger being. You could consider them victims of amnesia, in a way. They don't know who they are beyond the self they grew and became accustomed to in 3D.

This should be a tremendously encouraging fact! You aren't in charge of the agenda; you don't have to figure out what to do; you aren't in any way lost; and nothing you became is lost or unemployed. It is a state the very opposite of stagnation.

And—our starting place for next time, I hope—you as an individual element within the larger being are a specialized function, a specialized organ, for you came out of 3D, and hence are the larger being's window on the 3D world, or one of them.

And there is your hour.

Thanks, Rita. You remain a brilliant teacher. Till next time.

Saturday, January 24, 2015

Compound beings and unitary beings

6 a.m. Ready if you are, Rita.

Still working on Charles's question, trying to convey my own experience, as he asked. It feels like describing how to make a watch, in response to someone asking what time it is, but I don't see what else is to be done.

I always told him, we're in the position of a fish at the bottom of the ocean trying to envision a man at the top of a mountain watching television—to say nothing of trying to imagine the TV show.

Yes, it is a lot of translation, even for an ascended fish looking over the man's shoulder.

Now, I said that the 3D dimensions are a part of the general reality that includes the higher dimensions. And I left off last time promising to begin with the function of partially-3D beings such as ourselves in the greater scheme of things. So here goes.

First, realize that one way to classify—

Well, I suppose I'll have to backtrack first. I need you to realize actively that the higher dimensions are well populated, and most of the inhabitants have *not* had the 3D experience. That is, among various larger beings, some include 3D elements and some do not.

Did I get that right? Something didn't feel quite right, like I slurred something.

Very good. Probably I wouldn't have stopped to correct you, because I don't like to interrupt the flow unnecessarily, preferring to go back later and correct. You heard, "some larger beings have, and some have not, had the 3D experience." But in fact the *only* beings to incorporate 3D elements (as far as I know) are what I am calling larger beings. The others appear more unitary, though in this I may be mistaken.

That is, larger beings appear to be more composites than unitary—more like compounds than like elements, if you will. As far as appears to me—and to the larger being of which I am a part, and to whose knowledge I have access, you understand—we are communities of individuals which are themselves communities of individuals—*ad infinitum*, practically. This is so of necessity because we are units formed (deliberately, and for a purpose) of heterogeneous elements that otherwise never would have fused, because outside of 3D conditions they never *could* have fused.

So a more correct statement would be (picking up where I was), the higher dimensions are filled with larger beings at least partially shaped by the 3D experience, and by another type (or, probably, types) of being that are unitary in nature because they are not formed by the close association of elements in 3D conditions.

So, less Earth School than Earth Blast-Furnace.

Or Earth Smelter, yes.

And between the lines, I've been having a struggle that makes me smile. I keep wanting to write "the heavens" and I keep forcing myself to stick to "the higher dimensions," thinking how it would have grated on you, in life, to have used such an expression with its religious connotations.

You may use either translation, provided it is understood that "the heavens" does not exactly mean whatever comes to the reader's mind because of an association with the word "heaven." At the same time, I acknowledge that in turning my back on Christian tradition *as an indicator of spiritual realities seen and described in the past,* I missed something. The problem is that too much of religion is dead repetition without understanding, as if following rules and forcing what is thought of as belief could lead to any growth of understanding, or any valid experience that which, in turn, might lead to a growth of understanding. However, if that problem can be overcome, there is much value in it. Whatever your tradition — Christian, Jewish, Muslim, Buddhist, whatever—delve into its mystical component and you will find very valuable indicators. Only, don't throw out the baby. It is of no advantage to swap beliefs in the hope that a *new* belief system (including one based on what I am telling you) can advance your understanding more rapidly. The best such a switch could do would be to clear the field of misunderstandings, but perhaps at the expense of allowing the same mental habits that constructed the first misunderstandings to busily start constructing *new* misunderstandings.

So, to return to the point, the heavens are filled with at least two kinds of beings—those who have been shaped by the 3D experience and those who have not. We *are* different, we *perceive* differently, and in the larger scheme of things, we serve different functions.

I have said, if there are six dimensions (or twelve, or however many; I am not writing a physics textbook, and I cannot say how many, first, because I do not know and second, because I suspect "how many" would turn out to be a matter of interpretation, in the way that any different scale of measurement produces different results because of including or excluding different levels of detail)—if there are x number of dimensions, we must be in all.

That is a true statement. However, it is an equally true statement that one could be not in all, but in none. Or, more closely, that one could be in a *different set* of dimensions, that either overlap with those we know, or touch them tangentially, or are entirely separate. These other beings who have never been in (or should I say were not formed by) 3D appear to me to live in a universe that has overlap with ours (or how could I perceive them?) but does not entirely or even largely overlap ours. And so, one function of the larger being of which we are a part is that of interpreting 3D to those who have not experienced it and never can.

And where do you suppose the larger beings derive the knowledge they pass along? Where if not at least partially from us? And we, of course, are part of them, and so you must see that our function is to be one part of beings that *change*. They change continually, by preference but also because that is their nature.

As far as I can tell, beings who have not part of their being in 3D do not and cannot change—which makes our larger beings unique and, thus, uniquely valuable. Is this much clear?

I seem to remember stuff from our sessions [in 2001 and 2002, which were published as The Sphere and the Hologram*] that might have been trying to say* *something like this, but it has been a long time, and I'd have to look it up. Humans were the trickster factor in the world, as I remember.*

That was a somewhat different context. That described humanity as the species that deliberately and continuously changed its environment, often unconsciously.

I used to wonder why beavers couldn't be considered to be doing the same thing.

The response, you may remember, was that beavers were transforming in a regular way, within limits. They cut down trees and dammed rivers, but they don't mine ore, for instance.

No, I'm saying something different. In the heavens, there are our larger beings, and there are others, and we are a unique factor among them because of our origins, our nature, and our effect on everything else. But bear in mind, for all I know, the heavens are filled with other kinds of beings equally unique. But this is beyond my first-hand knowledge, even drawing on the memory banks (so to speak) of the larger being I am within.

A research project

Our unique function includes successively modifying 3D conditions partly by creating new beings—creating new souls—on a regular basis, and partly by other interventions. Obviously, if you are going to modify, you are going to monitor. And such monitoring in a way is a good description of my "daily" life now.

But what does that mean? Am I continually watching the news, so to speak? Am I fixated on the 3D world I just left? Well, as so often—yes but no.

Yes, in that I preserve my awareness of the 3D dimensions (or how could I be interacting with you, even though your mind itself extends to the higher dimensions?), but no, in that I am equally interacting with others here as we share information and thus refine our understanding.

Your perpetual research project!

In a sense, yes. And our mutual interaction "up here" is not without purpose, any more than my interaction with 3D is without purpose. But remember, *the purpose is not merely whatever I might want it to be.* As any subsystem serves the larger mechanism, and as any organ serves the body it is a part of, so I serve the larger being, and in that is no flavor of subservience or coercion. I am doing what is natural, and how can that not be comfortable and fitting? All beings strive to fulfill their nature.

Hmm. A lot to chew on, there. Do we go on to another question, or do you care to say more next time?

Perhaps it would be best to leave this question and answer for a while—to marinate, as you like to say—and move to other things. They will illumine aspects of this answer, and it will illumine them.

All right, well thanks very much. I'm getting feedback that says people are enjoying and profiting from this, and on their behalf as well as mine, again thanks.

You're welcome, and as you've heard before (and I heard when I was in 3D) our thanks from "over here" for your attention.

Sunday, January 25, 2015

Consciousness as a condition of life

6:45 a.m. So, Rita, Bob asks what consciousness is.

[Bob Friedman's question: "What is consciousness, what is it made of, and how does it work, that allows it access to all six dimensions (or however many there are) at once? Is this 3D consciousness a piece of that larger consciousness, and if so, can she describe that?

["From what she says, we are all part of that larger being that Frank draws. And this larger being is part of even larger beings, and presumably it all is part of what Seth calls All That Is, which is the totality of consciousness (which some call God) and all it 'creates.' It's well-known that all our materialist scientists together can't explain the nature of consciousness. Maybe Rita can give it a go, with information that some of these more open-minded materialists can explore further. What would they look for? Is it ever 'provable' or even *describable* in 3D, since it is so much more than 3D and the physical brain?"]

I don't suppose that will take you more than a couple of minutes to explain.

Every language describes the world differently. In effect, each one describes a different world, psychologically, because the assumptions of the language are built into it, and then they feed these assumptions right back to the users. Some are better at describing these things than others, because of the level of the people who developed them to express their view of the world.

We aren't going to explore linguistics here, but I want you to be aware that language makes you, or tempts you to, consider some things as real and definite, which in fact belong to an entirely different order of things.

Thus, the word "consciousness." It is natural (at least in English and in many Western languages) to think of consciousness as a condition rather than a relationship; or even as an object (if a nonphysical one) rather than either a condition or a relationship. This is inappropriately concrete.

I need you to understand this point, or anything I say about it, will be a waste of words, time, and effort. Those of you who are familiar with other definitions, please, suspend what you know and consider this as if you had never pondered the problem. After all, if previous answers satisfied you, why continue to look; but if you keep looking, why bother if you are only going to say, "That isn't what I read here, or was taught there"? *After* you ponder this, is the time to relate it to previously absorbed ideas. Otherwise, you are just going through the motions. Sorry to sound so directive, but I need you *here, now* (whenever you read this) if you are to get anything at all from this work.

I understand that. It can be a problem, not letting some background programs in our minds run while we try to concentrate on one thing.

I well remember it! That's why I am reminding you in advance. And, parenthetically, that is the value of our minds once we have left the body—we can serve to translate 3D experience accurately because we know first-hand what it is like to function in those conditions. You also find it hard to remember the context we have been creating, which—if you disregard it—results in your attempting to cram new explanations into old, inadequate, contexts.

Aha. New wine in old wineskins!

One aspect of what Jesus meant, yes. There was more, but that is not our subject today.

Suppose—this is not a diversion—suppose you were to ask me what gravity is, what it is made of, how it works. Or love. Suppose we tried to find a way to make it provable to those who doubt what it is or *that* it is. Suppose we tried to do so for the aether.

You know the story of the man who was looking for his lost keys where the light was brightest rather than where he dropped them. *One* point of the story is that you can't look for something where it is not, no matter how favorable the conditions. That is, you can *look*, but you will not *find*!

Consciousness is a condition of life, no less than gravity is a condition of life on Earth or than love is a condition of separated elements feeling their essential unity. You won't find life without consciousness any more than you will find anything in creation that is somehow not alive. The *form* of the consciousness will vary according to condition, just as the form of life varies according to condition, but the one is as universal as the other.

It might be theoretically possible for a fish to scientifically investigate what water is, but it isn't very likely. And even this is an inadequate analogy, because water is to a fish what air is to a scientist, and scientists can study air. But how can scientists study consciousness when they cannot see it in contradistinction to unconsciousness, because nothing exists without con-sciousness any more than anything exists without gravity?

They don't understand this, of course, but that is the nub of their diffi-culty. Not realizing that everything is alive and conscious, they cannot realize that there is no place for them to stand *outside of* consciousness to measure it.

The world is made up of certain essentials and cannot in any way, at any place, for any time, exist without them. We keep coming back to it—you can't have height and depth without width. You *can't*, any more than you can have a system of numbers with a gap in it (regardless of nomenclature; I am speaking of the unbroken unity of the reality).

Can you see that all the background you have been given to this point is not only invisible to your hypothetical scientist but actually antithetical to the context of everything he has been taught? You cannot expect very many of them to welcome such an upheaval, any more than medieval scientists welcomed Copernicus, Kepler, and Galileo, and for the same reason. *Their* system had been worked out in great detail and had great precision within its range of competence, and the new system seemed to them a flight of fancy.

If a scientist were to examine this question of consciousness from the starting point of a 3D world created out of the non-3D, however, he or she would quickly see that consciousness, love, and other essentials were the framework on which 3D reality was constructed, hence were built into it, hence could nowhere *not* be there, hence could not be studied in any way that assumed it as an element that could be studied from the outside. *Qualities* of consciousness, yes. *Conditions* of consciousness, *manifestations* of consciousness. Not consciousness itself. The best anyone could do would be to . . .

Sorry. Lost it.

It was, perhaps, a bridge too far. Let it stand: The study of how consciousness manifests in different conditions (among plants and minerals, for instance) is possible. The contraposition of consciousness and a hypothetical unconsciousness is not, because the hypothesized conditions contradict the conditions of existence. Again, try to imagine the world without love, or without gravity. You can *sort of* do it, in a science-fiction-y way, but not really, because it can't hold together.

I know readers will pose the question, so I'll do it for them. Love?

You see cruelty or indifference, and you think, "we know what absence of love looks like," but you don't, because it (that is, absence of love) does not, and can not, exist in the 3D world. What you observe is love restricted to too small a circle by various people—at an extreme, the circle being confined to themselves only. But even here, and even when they also hate themselves, without love there could be no existence, because it is the air you breathe, know it or not, approve of it or not, conceive of it as even a possibility, or not.

Perhaps this answers the question, and if not, I am open to follow-up questions as always, but your hour is up.

I was always told that teachers get into the habit of speaking fluently for fifty minutes and then dry up. I see the habit persists.

You were also told, or read, that Edgar Cayce did fine bringing through messages when he confined it to once or twice a day, but rapidly depleted his body when he tried to do it too often, too long.

Point taken. I think today's material will start a lot of rabbits running, and it should be interesting to watch you run them down. Our thanks as always, and I'll see you hopefully tomorrow.

Don't count on *seeing* me.

[Smiling.] I still can't get used to hearing that sly humor. Okay.

Monday, January 26, 2015

Consciousness and awareness

6 a.m. Good Morning, Miss Rita. Bob asks a couple of questions that I have more than an inkling of the answers to. Seems to me these are more or less what you were asking in 2001-2002.

[Bob Friedman asked: "1) How is consciousness, which is nonphysical, connected to a physical brain? Scientists have

demonstrated that when certain parts of the brain are stimulated, images and words and events may appear (memories, I
suppose). I have always thought that memories were part of
what we physicals call consciousness, as our 'awareness' can
call them up (pre-Alzheimer's of course) as part of what we
call 'thinking.' How can consciousness manipulate the brain
to 'park' those memories—through a chemical process or
something else?

["2) When 'Rita' was in 3D, she spoke and thought in
English. She is communicating to us now, through Frank,
in English (or does she just stimulate Frank's language so he
writes the words in English)? It's hard for us in 3D to imagine anything without use of whatever language we use on this
planet, so how does the use of English, French, Swahili, etc.,
'translate' over to the non-3D consciousness? Do you 'think'
and communicate in a language over there, or is there an
entirely different way to communicate?"]

Care to comment? Or do I have to make up something?

You may make up something, if you wish. The distinction between
people "making up something" and "receiving information" is less than
people suppose. It isn't like it is a game of one pitching and another catching. (I omit consideration of situations in which the intent is to deceive;
I am talking about any person's process of idea-reception. Bookmark this
topic, if you wish; it would be productive. It is the difference between thinking something through and following chains of association. It involves the
temporary group mind as an active if rarely suspected aspect of a person's
consciousness.)

Now, to these specific questions. The first question, I am afraid I have
to say, indicates that Bob has not absorbed, or is not taking into consideration, what has been said so far. Either that, or he silently means "insofar
as humans are concerned," but it doesn't look like this latter is this case. At
any rate, here is my attempt to clarify the subject. I will answer the question

as posed, and you each may proceed to apply the general answer to human consciousness in particular.

I am engaged in a silent argument here, Rita. Doesn't Bob's first sentence show that he means humans, or at least humans and anything else that has a brain?

Well, let us proceed, and we'll see. He asks, you see, how consciousness connects to a brain. I understand your thinking he is asking a special case of connection, but I cannot accept the question as posed without seeming to agree silently with several assumptions included equally silently.

This reminds me of your asking the guys, in our first session, how many we were speaking to, and their throwing out the assumptions behind the question rather than giving you an answer that would have been approximately true but would have reinforced assumptions you didn't even know you were incorporating.

I have more sympathy now with their predicament then.

I'll bet! So—?

Perhaps my objection would become clearer if I were to repeat the question substituting the word "gravity" for "consciousness," or using "love." Can you see that this question as posed is as if we had not had yesterday's discussion? It treats consciousness as a specific rather than a universal precondition of life—indeed of the existence of the world. I will answer the question as posed, but not in such a way as to lose the ground we gained so far.

So let me parse the question. In the first place, it would be truer to say that consciousness is nonphysical *and* physical in nature. It is not bound by physical rules; however, it *shapes* physical rules. It is not so much *found* in the physical world as *comprises* the physical world. It is not a thing or a condition; it is a piece of what the world is made of. That is why, as I said "yesterday," Bob's question can't be answered in the way he would have wanted—scientists cannot examine what they cannot isolate—at least, they can't understand what they are dealing with as long as they misdefine it.

So, consciousness doesn't *connect to* a brain; it *comprises* it. The brain—and all of physical existence—is *made* of consciousness. And that was my initial hesitation that you picked up on, Frank. Consciousness has no necessary connection to a brain. Not even within humans, but more broadly not to clouds or soil or radioactive waste or orlon fibers. You tend to think of things *having* consciousness when it would be more useful to think of them as *expressions* of consciousness. They are all coordinated—the world is held together—by the fact that *one* factor holding it together is this undivided consciousness.

It is in God that we live and move and have our being, it says somewhere.

That is one way to phrase it, and one way to look at it. But it jumps a few levels, let's put it that way. It is as *relatively* true as any other way of seeing the connectedness of all things.

Now, there is a difference between consciousness and human awareness, and I realize that this is closer to what Bob means. But again, the question seems to exist without reference to previous answers, which is not good. I mean, it leads nowhere to consider these questions as if in isolation from previous answers. It is in the drawing of connections that a new way of seeing the world will emerge for you. If you do not draw the connection—it cannot be done on your behalf; it requires that you work at it—if you do not draw the connections and feel your way to inferences, this will be not an exploration but, in effect, idle speculation that nowhere touches your real life. For, if you *do* work to absorb the material and thus change how you see the world, even if you wind up rejecting the new construct, it will have moved you to a new understanding. *But first you must have worked with the material.* That is your safety valve, you see; it is less the specific information than the general reorientation that is being presented, and less the reorientation than the temporary or permanent expansion of the ideas that, for you, comprise the world. This can only take place if you work. This is not a science fiction story to be enjoyed and forgotten.

I well remember how your life and mine were transformed by the material we brought forth in our sessions.

Yes, and as it turned out, even the things that unsettled me and left me wondering if I knew anything, were of great value. In fact, I might almost say that *was* the value. But, to continue.

There is a demonstrable link, of course, between the physical matter of the brain and access to any particular memory. But it is just as was explained to us, the difference between access and location, although actually I need to say more about that, more than "the guys" were able to get across to us because we were only in the first stages of absorbing their concept of access points.

I am going to recommend—in fact, I am doing it now—that people find that part in The Sphere and the Hologram. *Maybe I will look it up, and if I can find it, I will insert it here.*

The switching mechanism

[And here it is, from material received in Rita's and my 2001-2002 sessions. First of two transcripts:]

I've been wanting to ask the guys about this. We understand that there's now quite good scientific evidence that our consciousness does not seem to reside in the brain or in the physical body. There's now interest in the same question with respect to memory. Do you have any comment you'd like to make about that?

TGU: Well it's all the same thing. You're looking in matter for things that are not material, and you're not going to find them. Given that the organizing principle for the whole body is outside of the physical, and the physical is laid down on energy patterns that are set from beyond the physical, it would be foolish for us to then entrust a vital part of the mechanism to a physical place, when it's already in a nonphysical place.

The circulation of your blood is a physical function. The storing of your memories is not *entirely* a physical function. The accessing of the memories is more physical than anything else, but the actual storing of them is not. Just as with your consciousness, the accessing of your consciousness is *partly* physical. If you have a brain injury (even though that's also an energetic injury), you could look at it as a physical injury that may make it impossible for you to access memories or abilities that you had prior to the injury. But when you drop the body, you'll find that all of those abilities and memories are still there on call, because they weren't destroyed. They were never in the physical in the first place. Your *access* to them was destroyed, or damaged, but not the actual abilities or memories. This is why some of you have been surprised that people with extensive head injuries who were given sympathetic and loving attention over long periods of time regained abilities that had been thought to be lost. They learned new pathways to something which was invulnerable because it wasn't in the physical.

All right, can you talk about the process—it's important to some of us, these days—about losing memories as we age.

TGU: Well again, you aren't losing the memories, you're losing the access to the memories. The memories are as they are, as you would find were you to have an operation and have them open your brain and touch portions of the brain with the needles. They've done that for years, they know that they are there. But it isn't that that particular piece of the brain is exactly the memory; it's more like that particular piece of the brain is the doorkeeper to the memory. A subtle difference, but it is a big one.

So something has happened with respect to the antenna that picks up the external information?

TGU: The switching mechanism, we would say. Like a telephone exchange. It could be that portions of the lobes that are the gateways no longer function, and it's as if the memories are gone. But ordinarily it's that the switching function is inhibited, and can be restored sometimes; and when the switching function is restored, it's found that, lo and behold, the memories were there all along. You see, there are two things going on. The switching function, on the one hand, that enables you to access the places in the physical gateways, which then access the memories, and on the other hand, the gateways themselves.

So if the gateway cell, shall we say, is destroyed, then there may not be any access to memory, although perhaps another one can be developed.

Or, if the switching system fails to access the cell that's perfectly good, still you've lost your access. In neither case has the memory been lost absolutely; it's all there, as you would say, in the Akashic record—which ought to tell you that it's there in the first place. It hasn't been so much transferred from the physical as stored, in the first place, in the nonphysical.

[End first transcript.]

[Second transcript, which, I notice, uses the word "consciousness" more in the way we use it every day, from a session in the black box in which Rita was acting as monitor while Skip Atwater worked the machinery:]

Skip has a question here for me to ask. He's asking, what is the equivalent of the switching system when you leave the body?

TGU: Well, you see, when you leave the body, you don't need that switching system in just that way, because that switching system is necessary because you're living in time-slices. You're going blip, blip, blip, blip, and so there is a sequence. There's a limitation on your consciousness, which is that it can only hold so many things in consciousness at the same time, and your consciousness really does sort of have to move moment to moment, to stay in the same place. Once you're outside of the time-slice problem; and once you're outside of moving, moment to moment, to stay with a sliding present, you don't have that same situation, and then it's more like the crystal analogy that we gave you a long time ago, in which we said that the volume of the crystal has innumerable places in it, all of which interconnect. They don't move; it just depends on which way you shine your flashlight.

Did that answer the question? Your switching system is because your consciousness is required to hold things together while you're moving from moment to moment in the present. That is to say, while the present is moving around you and you are staying up with it.

[End of transcript from *The Sphere and the Hologram*]

[Rita, resuming:] "The guys" were making an incomplete and only approximately accurate statement because often—especially with new material—that is the best that can be done. The actual memories reside in what people call the Akashic record, in that everything that occurs—whether seemingly physical or seemingly mental or seemingly emotional (as if any of those could exist in isolation)—is automatically recorded there. In a sense it could be said to *occur* there, because that "record" is not separate from life but *is* life.

However, that last point aside, our brains . . .

Wow, that was different! First it was you forming the sentence, then it was me, as I realized when I had written the word "our."

Mark that subject "to be continued." It is a sign, by the way, that this process is continuing to refine your perceptions. For your comfort, *I* will continue the sentence. Human brain tissue contains access points that allow us to access the memory, but those access points are more like local copies of the original than like independent replications.

I don't understand that last statement.

If you consider the brain tissue that connects to the memory, realize that if it were quite that simple—

Hmm, this requires a longer discussion than we should begin toward the end of a session. I will resume with that in our next meeting. Meanwhile, let me wrap up other aspects of that first question by saying, again, that consciousness is not a quality, to be included or not included depending on what we're considering. Consciousness is part of everything.

Note: I did not say everything is a part of consciousness, but consciousness is part of everything, in the same way one might say either "humans are spiritual in nature" or "spirits have human experiences" and come up with a different meaning.

I feel like I muddled that last.

You're tired. Leave it at that, and we'll come back to the subject.

Doesn't feel like we've come very far today.

It's hard for you to judge when you can't see things as a whole, because you are within a life of time-slices. Clearing away misconceptions is valuable work, and implicitly constructive.

All right, till next time, and I trust you are enjoying the process.

I always loved to teach. Thank you for your effort and attention.

Tuesday, January 27, 2015

5:30 a.m. All right, Rita, I have reread yesterday's transcript, including the excerpts from The Sphere and the Hologram, *and I must say that as always it is a weird feeling to know more or less what subject you are going to address, and have no idea what's coming, yet at the same time have confidence that something is coming. I'll paste Bob's questions in here, along with your bookmark, and then over to you.*

> [Bob Friedman: "Rita said yesterday that she would start with this thought that she did not want to begin at the end of a session: 'Human brain tissue contains access points that allow us to access the memory, but those access points are more like local copies of the original than like independent replications. If you consider the brain tissue that connects to the memory, realize that if it were quite that simple—]
>   [pause]

[Rita:] Notice that I gave you a few seconds to realize that you aren't making it up. The worry that you are making it up is, as you well know, an inhibiting factor in developing the ability to receive material. Note, I said in "developing," not in "discovering" or in "creating" such an ability. As you also well know.

But maybe we never get fully beyond that worry.

Maybe you do, maybe you don't, it is a matter of personality and experiences. But "called or not called, God will be here," Carl Jung says.

"Called or not called ..."

Now that is weird. I heard that last sentence as loud and clear as if I had spoken it internally myself, so I wrote it even though it did not belong and I doubt if it was you, Rita, who said it. It is utterly unlike anything you would have said in 3D—even to the use of the word God, if my memory serves. So what is going on?

You know full well what is going on, but you intend something different and so you say, "This cannot be, I refuse to acknowledge what I know."

Very well. Welcome, Dr. Jung.

This is not an either/or situation over here, you know. You have said and written for many years that separation is a quality of physical life rather than nonphysical life, and yet when that quality manifests, you do not expect it. You silently assume that we over here will follow the rules. But they are not our rules, and this is not our game, or yours, but, shall we say, a compromise between the two, a translation between worlds.

I see you are using the terms that Rita has been moving us beyond—here and there, physical and nonphysical, etc.

Consider any scheme of things to be less a description than a metaphor meant to be instructive and helpful. If

Dammit, I have a bad habit of going wool-gathering if I let myself pause in this process.

Not so much if you let yourself pause; more if you let yourself entertain two trains of thoughts, or if you worry over what you are receiving.

Can you continue where you were going when I lost the connection?

Merely, *use* alternative explanatory schemes. Do not allow yourselves to be *enmeshed* in them. There is no advantage to changing denominations within the church, save to be more comfortable! The exchange per se does not bring you closer to the truth, although the *experience* of it, may.

Viewpoint

However, I entered the discussion to do two things. One, to make you aware that this process has listeners on the nonphysical side, no less than on the physical side, and two, to say something on the subject of consciousness.

Someone on the TMI Explorers list had suggested I ask you, I think.

Called or not called, those you connect to by your nature, your interests, your sympathies, and your tasks will *also* be there. But more strongly so if we are called.

An example of how we are continuously more connected than we realize we are—

Go back to the beginning of this new series of conversations and see for yourself. Rita began by saying the communication is without beginning or end, by the nature of things, regardless of whether the interaction is observed consciously, and certainly regardless of whether it is reflected upon by the 3D experiencer.

Well, it is an honor to connect with you. Am I mistaken in believing that where Jung is (at least, in relation to me) Robert Clarke cannot be far behind?

That is correct, and the clustering of souls relative to any given individual might be a subject for you to explore at some point, although perhaps not now.

Well, I remember being told years ago that anyone who reads a book connects—not metaphorically but truly, though of course nonphysically—to the author and to everybody else who reads or did read or will read that book.

Yes, an approximate statement of the process of clustering. You shouldn't carry the statement too far, but it may remind you of the value in choosing good companions. However, to return to the matter in hand—

Remember, as this process continues, that any discussion of any topic may or may not resonate, may or may not prove productive of new connections, new insights, but will not produce absolute statements that may be accurately taken only one way. The key to anyone's understanding is that each mind, each soul, is *a point of view*. That is, each 3D-created mind is a particular window not only on the 3D part of the world, but on everything that mind ponders. The bias incorporated into a more or less permanent habit-system (as you once heard the human mind described) is valued precisely because it *is* a bias; it *is* a particular way of seeing things, a particular slant on life. Far from such nonobjective bias being seen as a detriment, it is recognized as *the point* of 3D experience.

But—any given viewpoint is just that—*one* viewpoint. Even if the viewpoint is itself an incorporation of the habit of always seeing things in many ways, that viewpoint is itself only one way of experiencing things.

In other words, we mustn't expect to receive any final answers, here.

No. And you—yourself, Frank, as transducer of energies—should rejoice that this is so, as it removes the impossible burden of the need for omniscience or, more, infallibility. And for the reader it removes the burden of deciding whether to throw over every other system of thought and follow whatever you derive. Not that anyone would do it anyway, but that they might criticize themselves for being unable to do so. They should *work with* this material, not be captured by it. The same words will seem to mean different things to different people at different times and in different contexts.

You said you came today to say something on the nature of consciousness. My hour is nearly gone—can you still get it in?

I am smiling, my friend. I have said it already. The point I made is the point I wanted to make. And now I will let you end with Rita, only now knowing to remember that this conversation is wider on both sides of the veil—I use the older idea purposely, to reassure you that you need not confine yourselves to carefully censored language—and that your own community (that is said for anyone who ever reads this) is more extensive than you usually realize or dare realize. You are none of you isolated, no matter how it may feel. You are not orphans, nor are you stranded on desert islands.

Thank you. I know that such reassurance will be of great value to many people.

But not you, eh?

All right. Miss Rita, anything else before we close shop for the day?

As you used to say, tomorrow we can resume our regularly scheduled programming.

Okay. Thank you for being the catalyst who started this very interesting enterprise.

As to who started what, that would be an interesting discussion at another time. No need for it now, however.

Okay. See you tomorrow, probably.

Wednesday, January 28, 2015

Brain v. mind

6 a.m. Well, Miss Rita, I'm a little at sea as to how to proceed. The interrupted thought, you said you'd follow up later—is it still available?

[Rita said she would start a session with this thought rather than trying to tackle it at the end of a session:

["Human brain tissue contains access points that allow us to access the memory, but those access points are more like local copies of the original than like independent replications. If you consider the brain tissue that connects to the memory, realize that if it were quite that simple—"]

. . . . your memories would be quite as much at risk as if the memory itself was stored there.

So we are like local CPU's, accessing the cloud?

Don't tie your understanding too closely to physical analogies—particularly not to technological analogies—or what will you do when the technology has become replaced by something else? But in a broad sense, you have the idea of it. Perhaps you could regard your brain as a temporary local copy of the mind you are constructing safely outside of 3D vicissitudes.

I begin to see why you didn't want to start into this at the end of a session.

Yes. Any statement needs to be described as to what it means and what it does *not* mean. Many times the second part of the process is overlooked or omitted because the need is not seen or the implications are unimportant or mostly obvious. But when one makes a certain kind of statement—something seemingly familiar but actually a novel spin on old concepts, or an unfamiliar usage of familiar words—it is well to try to reduce potential misunderstanding.

Thus, the paragraph preceding the previous one contains several ideas.

1. The brain a temporary local copy of your mind

2. Your mind continually being created outside of 3D

3. Implicitly, your mind *already existing* outside of 3D and therefore containing the results of your future choices, as well as your present and your former futures, if we may call them that. And it is this last comment that will require the

most thought, as it will be a readjustment for you, Frank, if not necessarily for anyone who may read this.

As to the first statement, which is only *sort of* true, the important part of it is the thought that your physical existence is not required for the preservation of the active, living, record of your life. Now, language is a problem here, because as soon as you read "record"—even though the word has been preceded by "active, living," you tend to think of it as something fixed, and dead. A record of something is itself not living and vital—or so language tempts you to think. So find a better word than "record," so you don't have to make the continuing effort to remind yourself of the limits of the analogy.

How about ghost, or spirit, or shadow?

That might work if you can remember from usage to usage (i.e., from moment to moment) that *it is the physical that is the ghost of the reality,* and the nonphysical that is the actual thing being considered.

Speaking of making a Copernican Shift—

Yes, and you might as well begin making a habit of doing so. When you place the sun in the center of your mental solar system, many relationships clarify.

The second point is also only approximately true. *From the 3D perspective*, your mind is being created as you go along and is being created not in the physical, as it usually seems to you, but in the nonphysical where it really is because where *you*, or the larger part of you, really is. Remember, we are not talking about physical and nonphysical being separate; we are talking—or trying to, against the silent bias of language—about the physical world being a local area of the whole—three dimensions among many. (And yes, the whole idea of dimensions is itself an approximate term, used for shorthand convenience.)

Not just the *record* of your life; not just the m*ental part* of your life, but the very physical existence you are aware of, all resides in the full set of dimensions because, as I said, everything has to exist in all dimensions if it exists in any. So all this talk about physical or nonphysical is not meaningless, but it is not the absolute dichotomy it appears to be because of the language we employ.

And then we come to the third point, and I suggest you refill your coffee cup.

Yes, the same idea occurred to me!

Uncountable versions

Here is the complexity that required a fresh mind.

> [Typing this, the sentence stopped me. Then I realized she meant, a mind fresh to the task rather than at the end of a session. The meaning was clear when I brought it in, but had blurred by the time I came to transcribe it.]

I know what you are intending to relate it to, and if you can clear up the tangle of half-understood concepts that we reported in The Sphere and the Hologram, *but couldn't untangle, I'd be very glad.*

Summarize the problem, if you would.

Well, the guys told us that the results of every decision constitute an alternate version of reality, but that the idea of the world splitting with each decision was the result of thinking in terms of a past that ceases to exist, a present in which choices are made, and a future that is determined by the present, in contradistinction to the view of time as existing—every conceivable variation of every conceivable scenario—from the time the world was created, here using "the world" to mean not Earth but the entire material universe.

It seemed to me this meant that some version of every one of us took every possible path—usually unknown to one another, but not invariably, I gather—which sort of defeats the point of "choosing, choosing, choosing" as the purpose of life, it seems to me.

Again, put the sun rather than the Earth in the center, and things clarify. If you stop thinking of physical life as "real" and start seeing it as a set of projections of nonphysical life, you aren't faced with the question of—oh, where do those uncounted number of alternate worlds exist? Which version of your life—of your soul—is real? How can all this make sense in terms of *one* individual (yes, *relatively* individual, but you understand what I'm getting at) being shaped and then functioning?

I could never get a good handle on it. I brought it through and had confidence that my translation wasn't very wrong, but I couldn't really make sense of it, though I tried. I mean, I could sort of wrap my head around it, but I couldn't really connect it to the life I experience myself leading day by day. And relating it is the point, isn't it?

It is. Here is one clarification that may bring you far—again, provided that you make the Copernican Shift in your mind.

Start with the idea that the larger being selected this and that combination of elements to be you, inserting you in a certain place and time. That is well and good as a working statement, but, in fact, it describes the situation only approximately *and from a 3D-based perspective.* Alter the perspective and you see that reality is actually a projection of inherent possibilities rather than a physical reality. Therefore, it costs nothing to explore this or that set of possibilities. One is as real as any other.

I do get what you mean, but I don't think you've said it yet in any way that can not be wildly misrepresented.

Suppose a computer-generated image. Suppose the image is systematically transformed so that every possible combination is displayed. Suppose—harder, I realize—that all these possible variations are on display simultaneously and are simultaneously apprehensible. The possibilities (whatever they may be) were all inherent in the computer program. If they were not inherent, they could not have manifested, clearly. There is no need to decide (or rather, arbitrarily choose to regard) which one is uniquely "real" and the others a copy or a theoretical manifestation, only. Which one is "real" is simple—it is whichever one you are connecting to.

This, minus the sequential-time implications that insert themselves into the analogy, is more or less the situation.

But understanding it depends entirely upon your making the Copernican Shift.

If you try to understand it while trying to think of life as physical, sequential, and "real," you can get only a vague and theoretical understanding that will have no application to your life.

So—I am sure someone will ask—if all possible worlds exist, meaning that all possible choices are made by some aspect of ourselves, what is the point of choosing, what is the point of working to create ourselves?

You are walking the possibilities.

Oh, that explains it! Huh?

We'll start there next time. And we will sooner or later get to the rest of Bob's question, but after all, there is no hurry.

Well, it's an interesting process, and on behalf of those who are reading this or will read it, thanks. See you next time.

Thursday, January 29, 2015

Walking the possibilities

5:45 a.m. Okay, Rita, here we go again. We are walking the possibilities, you said. Meaning—?

Copy the line from yesterday.

If you try to understand it while trying to think of life as physical, sequential, and "real," you can get only a vague and theoretical understanding that will have no application to your life.

That's the one. Writing it out rather than being able to copy it from a computer file engages you in the process, helping mesh our operations. Whenever you get stuck, you can try it; it is a simple tool.

One I've used occasionally in writing, come to think of it, but not for many years.
Okay, so—

Feel your way back to an understanding of life as a unity—no splits,
no physical or nonphysical, no "other side," but *one* thing all together with,
shall we say, specialized locations, or perhaps local specialties. That is, it
isn't at all homogenous, but neither is there any absolute division. And feel
yourselves back to a sense of 3D reality being actually a special condition of
overall reality, one that is projected from, or say *conceived out of,* the larger
reality to produce a test tube's specialized conditions.

When you remember life that way, it is easier to feel how life is lived as
unknowable patterns of energy, presenting themselves as tangible realities,
and you don't have to imagine rocks in your path when you come to move.

I got that, but in case anyone didn't, I take it to mean, if we think of the world as
physical and somehow "realer" than energy, it is hard to really get the idea of so many
realities being equally existent. The idea of physical reality is one of "rocks in our path."

Exactly. Much easier to think of changing channels.
So. Proceeding from the imaginating starting point

That word stopped me.

Well, what word would serve better? Imaginative sounds like "we're
going to play pretend." So does "imagined," only past tense.

I see your point. It just stopped me, is all. Okay, so proceeding from there—

You were one time given a vision of reality as not moving events, but
planes of an unmoving crystal, planes *inside* the crystal—not external facets—that were illuminated alternately depending on how one shined a light
on it, or perhaps we should say *through* it.

I remember. In my sessions with Skip in 2000, I think.

Well, you see, that is a very good metaphor for the underlying situation, if I can explain it.

The world is created. (Not Earth, here; I mean physical reality in general.) As it springs into being, all of its potentialities spring into being in exactly the same way as an individual's potentialities spring into being with his or her conception.

You see? It's all there from the beginning, because outside of 3D—it isn't *process;* it is *being.*

There isn't any "becoming" about it because it isn't filtered through successive time-moments, the way we experience life in 3D. That what you mean?

Yes. Translated into 3D terms, it looks like "becoming," because it is so alien to 3D experience to think of something in a state of *being* rather than *becoming.*

But, of course, "becoming" is precisely what we do experience here.

Of course; that is the intent. It's in the design. But you can't understand things in a new way by continuing to see them only in the accustomed way.

I understand.

Hold that image, of all 3D reality as one giant unmoving and unchanging crystal. (If that is more than you can do comfortably, envisage all aspects of your life as a crystal. The image, not the precision, is the helpful thing here.) The crystal contains all possibilities. By nature, it contains what it is, no more, no less.

Let's call it a transparent crystal, and let's put ourselves outside it, with a laser pointer. Shine that laser at the crystal, and it will illumine a path into it. As far as you are concerned—as far as *you* can tell—only the path illuminated exists; all else is darkness, background. What is illumined is real and everything else is theoretical.

Now change the angle the light strikes the crystal at—ever so slightly or quite a bit different, whichever you prefer. What is illumined changes; what is background includes the path that was previously illumined. What was "real" is now "only theoretical," or is "unknowable." What was unknown, perhaps unsuspected, is now clearly seen as "real."

This, up to this point, is background. Now I move on to what I meant by walking the possibilities, and here I must introduce a complication, though a very clarifying one. The music on a record was only revealed when a needle dragged along the groove of the record. No needle, no perceived sound, although the sound was inherently, latently, *really* there in the composition of the record.

I see where you're going with this!

If what you perceive as 3D reality is the record, your awareness is the needle, even though your awareness is also part of the record (because you and all your experiences are part of it).

The guys told us the record and needle analogy as we being the needle, they the record. You're saying not so simple?

Simple enough if you can remember that you are "the guys" *as well as* your physical existence.

Oh yeah. It's hard to keep that in mind once we sort of move on to other things.

Practice, practice. As you get accustomed to thinking in a new way, more sophisticated levels of understanding become possible precisely because you become more able to hold each new awareness in mind as accepted background.

So, walking the possibilities.

Manifesting possibilities

Well, it should be clear enough now. The *possibilities* are inherent in the creation. But they are not made manifest to the non-3D part of creation until they are experienced in 3D and conveyed.

Which means experiencing them as if each were the only reality.

That is the setup. It adds immediacy, interest, intensity. Mostly it adds clarity.

Pinpoint focus on the flavor of a life led along a path illuminated from a certain angle.

Well, don't get fixated on that image, helpful though it is. Don't let yourself be led to think of your path as straight and strait, just because you imagine a line to be that way. Light can bounce off slight irregularities and take quite a ride—to switch metaphors.

All right, so I gather that—Oh! I think I got it! The point is not us as individuals shaping ourselves (though that is true) but that we experience whatever we experience because of our choices so that the non-3D can experience what until then was only potential.

Close enough. And since different versions of yourself experience different lives because of different choices, we in non-3D (so to speak) get to see all the potential, not any one version alone.

George Bernard Shaw scoffed at what he said was the Englishman's conception of the universe as a "moral gymnasium." This is closer to his point of view, isn't it?

Find the Emerson quote you like and insert it.

[*Emerson in 1828, age 25*: "If you think you came into being for the purpose of taking an important part in the administration of events, to guard a province of the moral creation from ruin, and that its salvation hangs on the success of your single arm, you have wholly mistaken your business."]

Next time we will begin with Bob's question about language, which should be easy to dispose of.

Well, this is extremely interesting, Rita. Thank you on behalf of your audience, whoever they are or may become.

Till next time, then.

Friday, January 30, 2015

Language in the non-3D

6 a.m. So, Miss Rita, here we go again. This is becoming a habit, very like my fond memories of getting up each morning to have coffee with Ernest Hemingway and see the sun come up while sitting at the dining room table—your dining room table, come to think of it—writing. So you said you wanted to begin by disposing of the question about language.

> [Rita had said, "Next time we will begin with Bob's question about language, which should be easy to dispose of."]

That sounds like I'm going to toss it aside, but I'm merely going to clear up a point that many may not have considered. It isn't particularly complicated, but some easy questions are nonetheless worthwhile.

In other words, there are no stupid questions, so people shouldn't worry about asking things.

Yes, but also there isn't any way to tell in advance which question may illuminate something important, and which may not. So—same conclusion: People shouldn't worry that something they really want to know about may not be worthwhile. If we—or you, or I alone—choose not to answer a question for a particular reason, fine, but there isn't any reason for people to hesitate to ask, provided their question is sincere.

You saw me decline to ask you a question that would bring us to ideology or politics.

The real objection is that it would move us from the real work of examining reality from two viewpoints at once (in hopes of seeing it more clearly) and would move people into the easy and unproductive terrain of *opinion*. Opinion has its place, and so does agricultural price reporting or news briefs or economic speculation, but this isn't it.

In any case, to proceed with the question of language.

> [Bob had asked: "When 'Rita' was in 3D, she spoke and thought in English. She is communicating to us now, through Frank, in English (or does she just stimulate Frank's language so he writes the words in English)? It's hard for us in 3D to imagine anything without use of whatever language we use on this planet, so how does the use of English, French, Swahili, etc., 'translate' over to the non-3D consciousness? Do you 'think' and communicate in a language over there, or is there an entirely different way to communicate?"]

This is one of those questions that sounds complicated but is actually rather easily clarified.

I'm remembering the joke about the rural preacher who opposed bilingualism because "if English was good enough for Jesus, it's good enough for me." We don't speak in words at all, do we?

Well, that depends on which "we" you mean. Within 3D rules, everything is sequential. You experience one thing, then the next thing, one at a time like children reciting their ABC's. And that is what language *is*, a sequentially processed code. Written or spoken, it is one word at a time, no matter how quickly the words are said or how simple or complex the words used, or in what language. That is one reason why Bob [Monroe] stressed the use of NVC [non-verbal communication]—it is in simultaneously "grokked" understandings that 3D-accustomed people—meaning, anybody experiencing themselves as in the body—may

Lost it.

Next time don't go back to fix the grammar or dot the i's, etc. until the thought is complete.

Mostly it doesn't matter; this one went on too long, not meaning too many words, but too many turns in the thought. Try again?

[And it occurs to me, typing this, that some will not know what "grokking" means. From a Robert Heinlein novel, *Stranger in a Strange Land*, it describes the instant comprehension of something, rather than the sequential processing of thought.]

Simultaneous v. sequential perceptions

If you (anyone, that is, not just you in particular, Frank) practice experiencing communication in nonsequential ways, you get closer to communication as it is in non-3D. In other words, the way guidance is experienced, the way "psychic" knowing comes in, is always nonsequential, even if it needs to be translated into sequential processing for the individual to accept it. Thus, if you can pick it up without such translation, it is a sudden *knowing*— which is why such knowings are the purest form of such communication. If the information cannot be comfortably processed in that form, it may have to be experienced sequentially, as a vision, or speech, or some variety of dream or dream-like way.

That's very interesting, and puts what I already knew in an enlightening context.

That's the idea here. That's what teaching mostly *is*, the reinterpretation of familiar things in a new context.

So the question was, in essence, what language do we speak in non-3D, or to be fairer to the question, it asked the relation between various kinds of speech experienced in 3D and our communication in non-3D. As you see, you *already* experience non-3D speech, some of you more often or more consistently than others. It is in the simultaneous grokking that accompanies the temporary group mind that true communication occurs. It is in the subsequent "stopping down" of such communication into 3D-sequential speech or thought that communication with minds occurs (and slips). It is in the spoken or written conveyance of one understanding to another 3D-processing-system connected to another mind that 3D communication occurs, usually with huge slippage and, therefore, distortion. Clear?

To me, yes, but I have the benefit of direct communication, so I am grokking things every so often, as you know. Whether clear to others, I guess we'll find out from feedback.

Summarize your understanding?

Okay. In 3D, everything sensory is experienced sequentially—speaking, writing, reading, even watching or hearing or anything sensory, I suppose. Therefore we communicate by codes that are sequential, a faster version of tapping out Morse Code messages. Different people speak different languages, but they are all sequential because everything sensory is sequential.

Or is perceived as sequential, anyway.

Yes, that's what I meant. But in the non-3D, it isn't sequential but simultaneous, though come to think of it, I can't quite imagine it, so non-3D thought is experienced not in sequential systems like language but in bursts, or in—

Well, that's close enough. Your summary made clear to you, and thus to others, something you hadn't yet thought about. It isn't really simultaneous outside of 3D—from the 3D understanding, anyway—but is very, very fast.

A million times faster.

Tell them.

I read somewhere that the conscious mind perceives 42 (I think it was) bits of information per second, and the nonconscious mind 42 million bits per second. This million-to-one disparity tells me that the unconscious mind—which I imagine amounts to us outside of 3D, experiencing life directly as opposed to us experiencing it through sequential processing—is probably the same thing as saying "the guys upstairs." Anyway, anything we experience a million times faster than we can process it is going to appear instant to us.

Yes. And although there is more to be said on the subject, if only because everything connects to everything else, that is enough for now. A delay in saying more will enable people to ponder on just this much, and will give them a firmer ground as we proceed. Saying more now might tend to slur over certain things.

Okay, you're the boss. Do you want to continue by going back to the first question?

There is no supernatural

["How is consciousness, which is nonphysical, connected to a physical brain? Scientists have demonstrated that when certain parts of the brain are stimulated, images and words and events may appear (memories, I suppose). I have always thought that memories were part of what we physicals call consciousness, as our 'awareness' can call them up (pre-Alzheimer's of course) as part of what we call 'thinking.' How can consciousness manipulate the brain to 'park' those memories—through a chemical process or something else?"]

The last sentence assumes something special when there is only life as you know it. That is, biological processes can be well understood in their own terms. No need to try to divide them into "natural" and "supernatural," or, as here, into part physical and part nonphysical *process*.

All physical life is a miracle, viewed one way, or none of it is, viewed another way. Memories are implanted in the brain (or so it seems) by the understood chemical processes. It is in the description of those points as gateways rather than repositories that our view differs from conventional anatomy, nothing more. And, by the way, the fact that stimulated memories (stimulated by a probe touching a neural point, I mean) bring to the person detail and clarity beyond what was experienced at the time, should tell you that the person is experiencing not a record but the original perceptions.

Okay. By the way, writing the date at the top of the page just now, I notice that it is the 30th. Happy birthday, Miss Rita. You'd have been 95 this morning.

I prefer to celebrate it here.

A smile. Very well, more for today, or is that a good place to stop?

Enough for the moment, and we can begin a fresh topic next time. Make a note, though, that we're always ready to answer follow-up questions on anything. They can be very valuable.

Okay, thanks. Blow out the candles.

Saturday, January 31, 2015

Time in non-3D

5:30 a.m. Miss Rita, if you have recovered from your postbirthday hangover, let's go again. [Pause.] No comeback?

The delay wasn't on this end, and perhaps we should say, wasn't on your end either. We just weren't linked for a moment.

So that might have been because I wasn't in the right place—what else might it have been? For this will interest people, I have no doubt, particularly those who are doing the same thing and occasionally meeting frustration in their attempts.

We can go into it sometime; let me think on how to answer it. Meanwhile, we can proceed with the questions you have in queue.

I am always surprised when I hear from the other side—or from non-3D, or I hardly know how to think of it—that time is required to think something through.

That's only because you still have remnants active of the attitude you began the work with—thinking that beings on the other side must be perfect in so many ways as opposed to life in the physical. Thus, they must know everything (including the future). But—that romanticized and fuzzy view was not grounded in the reality described to us over many months.

It is true that I have gradually come to think of the other side—the nonphysical side of life—as having its own form of duration, but I'm not consistent.

It isn't that *you* aren't consistent, so much as that different parts of you have different assumptions, and different helmsmen steer your ship at different times, you usually not noticing the difference.

Correction noted. Do we ever get to the place where our community of comprising strands become a truly consistent unity?

Go reread our book with that question in mind. That is more or less what "the guys" were trying to explain to us about becoming crystallized. But my and your deficits in understanding them led us to misapprehend their meaning somewhat.

Yes, I seem to remember maybe applying logic in trying to shape their answer. Or, put it this way, I would have a vague sense and would put it into words as best I could, but the process of putting it into words was warped by my process of trying to square the latest with the previous. That still doesn't quite say it, but those who have tried this will know what it is to get in their own way by trying too hard.

But I well remember you wrestling with language, unable to really grasp the difference between our 3D experience of time and what they were calling "duration" to differentiate between the two. I think you were really trying—well, rather than put words into your mouth, I'll let you put words into my mouth, or anyway my pen. What were you experiencing?

Like you, I had always read that outside of physical life "time does not exist," so it was an adjustment to have our friends insist that yes it does, but it's different. Now that I am here, I can see the difference and can see why it can be difficult to understand it while in 3D. But if you will remember my insistence that 3D and non-3D are part of the same undivided reality, it may be easier to see that the same conditions apply, only modified according to the constraints of 3D existence or their opposite. [That is, constraints or lack of constraints.] But as this side is not unchanging, clearly something separates the two. I had a hard time seeing it, that's all. [I think "something separates the two" means something separates the before and after states around a change.]

All right, on to this morning's questions? Or do you want to pursue this?

Let's proceed.

Emotions in non-3D

[Jenny Horner's first question: "Do emotions exist in non-3D Reality? Does Rita experience frustration, irritation, joy, happiness?"]

This first one isn't hard, is it? Not if you read our dialogue about it.

Maybe this whole project is going to turn out to be an ongoing plug for The Sphere and the Hologram.

Well, there's a tremendous lot of material there, as well as a sort of guided tour, or call it an escorted journey, from the more common ways of seeing the world to a much less common way.

Plus it was a lot of work to transcribe, assemble, edit, and publish! It would be nice if it wasn't all in vain.

The process itself was not in vain. It helped seal your understanding of much that had been brought forth.

Okay. At any rate, today's first question. Emotion in the non-3D?

As the guys explained to us, the conditions of existence—or I should say of awareness within existence—are different because of differences in terrain. So, in 3D you experience emotion, as you experience everything in your life, as a localized "hot" phenomenon. Here we experience it as a generalized, hence "cool," phenomenon.

Yes, that's very clear to me.

You will find it is less so to those who don't remember what the guys said about it.

Didn't they use the analogy of something hot touching our skin and us maybe getting a burn from it because our skin couldn't conduct the heat away (laterally) fast enough, whereas on the non-3D side, easy and extensive connection means instant and efficient conductance, thus a wider but less intense experience?

They said, "you would find it somewhat chilly emotionally," or words to that effect.

However, I think Jenny is asking something more than that.

Yes, but it has to be understood in terms of *how* it is experienced, if *what* is experienced is to be understood with the minimum of distortion. A yes or no answer—even a "yes but no" answer—would not clarify anything.

So, within that context, I can say that we here experience emotions secondhand as you experience them, say, and first-hand *in a way*, but really, in such a way that it would be better described as a tinge, a flavor, than as a mood or a change of state.

Experiencing what you experience should not require amplification. As we experience anything else, we experience your emotions. We are permanently along for the ride, whether or not we put our hands on the wheel for the moment. But what we ourselves experience is a little harder to convey.

What we do *not* experience are the emotions proceeding from a sense of isolation or from a sense of being helpless captives of a process beyond our control or modification. In other words, we do not experience lack of connection—how could we? We do not feel ourselves to be hurtling toward death, or buffeted by "external" events—how could we? So that is a massive difference right there. If anger is the difference between what is and what is desired, doesn't that depend on a certain sense of time?

I could feel my connection wavering on that last sentence. Again?

Any emotion stemming from the difference between what you want and what *is*, depends on a perception of your being subject to circumstances partially or wholly beyond your control. It would be impossible for us here to feel that, relative to each other. We may be opposed in values and even in perceptions, but that is not the same thing as being able to believe in blame. We can't help knowing better, and not abstractly but practically, with all our being.

If anger stems from fear—what is fear going to stem from, here?

Could you say—what just came into my mind, so maybe it's you saying it, for all I know—could you say that the negative emotions cannot exist outside of 3D, but the positive ones can?

Can and do, but again, subject to the conditions I just reminded you of. Reduce everything to love or fear, and see these two polarities as the experience of oneness or separation, and you can see that while that duality is useful and, in fact, inevitable in a world of duality, it is only slightly applicable outside of 3D. We *know* we are all one thing. The most we experience of separation is a relative difference, in values, in experience, in what color on the spectrum we represent. Can green hate red? They can be seen as opposed to each other; they are certainly different points in the spectrum; they are certainly not interchangeable. But how could they—knowing that they are part of one thing—hate or fear each other? And without hate or fear, the negative emotions are not here to be expressed. You could say that this is why it is said that all is love. All is the awareness of unity, hence love, hence all the positive emotions.

Something of a shock to see that our hour is up. We didn't get very far today.

Far enough, and tomorrow is another day and we can proceed to Jenny's second question.

Very good. Thanks as always.

February 2015

Unlived potential • The shadow • A chat group • Reorientation and faith • Perceiving higher dimensions • Considering good and evil • Language as a problem • Tastes and values • Pure good, and pure evil • Duality in non-3D • Duality and scripture • Maps and explorers • Good and evil in non-3D • Combining scales • Scaling • Three forms of evil • Evil as external • Evil as attractive nuisance • Evil as compulsion • Angels and humans • An undivided reality • Discovering unconscious assumptions • Defining the larger being • Love and fear in duality • No reincarnation? • Memory • Is 3D functioning correctly? • Cruelty and suffering • The justice of the world • Controversy • Delusions of competence • Hidden relationships • Choosing your attitude • A survey cruise • An assumption of separation • A compass • Suffering as by-product • Modes of operation • Pain as feedback • Unsuspected background influences • The real nature of tragedy • What is it for? • Context • Choice and free will • Choice • Mirrors • Cognitive impairment • Autism • Non-3D life and the 3D world • Non-3D's stake • What non-3D cares about • Fishing • "What would I ask?" • Higher dimensions? • Compound and unitary beings • Limitations on communication • Words and the non-3D • Living in communication • Unique windows • The purpose of creation • Manifesting the non-3D being • Openness to guidance • Soulmates and resonance • Spirits contend • Passion • Q&A • Living our values • Aggression • Being and doing • Pole stars • Communication • Authority • Consistency • Preventive maintenance • Paths • Bees and hives • Sexual reproduction • 3D and non-3D

Sunday, February 1, 2015

Unlived potential

6:30 a.m. Rita, you said you'd want to begin with Jenny's second question. Have at it.

[Jenny's second question: "We are born as 'potential' and create a 'linear life' by the linking of experiences chosen and 'bestowed' by life's circumstances. Every step of the journey through a human life, one is 'haunted' by the 'shadow,' the un-lived potential for both positive and negative capabilities. As humans we are challenged to acknowledge this shadow (not repress it,) and find healthy expression for its energies. Is there a 'shadow' aspect to non-3D Reality, and if so, what is its form and function?"]

I hesitate between responding to the description of human life contained in the first part, or answering the direct question. I think I will begin by answering the question, merely noting that the description of human life is at best partial. Maybe we'll come back to saying why, if the question itself does not take too long.

Any way you want to do it.

Taking the definition of the shadow as given—unlived potential—the short answer would be, no, outside of 3D conditions there is no shadow. But explaining what that means, and why it is so, may take a bit of work. And really it would have been easier *in a way* to address the first part of the question first. But—let's see.

Remember the defining conditions of 3D experience:

- A conviction (illusion) of separation

- Separation from others in space

- Separation from all other moments in time

All other distinguishing characteristics, such as delayed consequences, stem from the fact that you experience 3D existence as one moment of time, followed by another moment of time, followed by another moment of time—forever, as long as you are experiencing yourself in 3D.

In such conditions, of course, your awareness is going to be limited, and it is in limitation—in awareness, in choice, in "life unlived because of other choices"—that the shadow is generated.

The shadow, as Jenny rightly notes, is not inherently bad. It is not being repressed so that civilized life may exist, as Freud may be said to have assumed. It is the parts of you that are *better* than you, as well as those that are *worse* than you, that are not actualized. Sometimes this is from lack of opportunity. Sometimes it is because your consciousness rejects them. For whatever reason, this is the gnawing half-knowledge that your self-definition is inadequate.

As in Steppenwolf.

As in *Steppenwolf*, yes. Harry Haller came to see that not only his fears, but even, in a way, his ideals were standing in the way of his proper growth, for it is difficult in life to let something within take you to unknown territory *of its accord* rather than yours.

I have read, and have always been irritated by, the saying that "man is a bourgeois compromise," and have never understood the meaning of it till right now. It means our lives, including our predictability and our experience of ourselves,

Funny, I got tangled up in my own statement. Interesting how the process gets continually less well-defined, so that now I am missing my own thought in the way I sometimes miss yours.

Not that it is happening more, but that you are more aware of it. Others around you see you do this all the time. Finish your thought.

Merely, our lives as we lead them are the result of our own self-limiting "safe" choices. What we think of as normal is, in fact, stunted. I might have gotten the sense of this much earlier, if I had not been so irritated by the word "bourgeois," which in my youth was misused by every half-assed radical to try to show that he (or she, but mostly he) wasn't middle-class, but was deeper than that. When of course that is exactly what he was. However—

The sense of the saying is correct. It is in the self-definitions and definitions of others and of life in general that stability is maintained, often at the expense of growth, but also often as a means of preserving the predictability on which normal life depends.

Such compromises are not possible in situations in which your awareness is not limited.

I see that. And, no limitations, no shadow.

Well, no *unacknowledged* limitations. Everything has limits, even if they are relative rather than absolute. But it is the ignorance of one's existence, or part of one's existence rather, that is the cause of the existence of the shadow.

The shadow

Does this imply that outside of 3D we know exactly what we are, and that we integrate all that previously unacknowledged shadow?

No, we need to look at this a little more slowly. As always, it is the unsuspected assumptions in your thought that lead you in wrong directions. There is a form of duality here that I need to explain.

Jenny's question, I take it, asks if we outside of 3D conditions actively experience a shadow *relative to our non-3D being*. The short answer is no, because outside 3D there cannot be the restrictions on awareness that generated it within 3D. However, do not take that to mean that our component "lives" are somehow changed by now being outside the restrictions that shaped them. If you led a Victorian life, your mind—your soul—remains what it was when you finished making active 3D choices; that is, when you dropped the body. It does not magically change to be everything it might have been and wasn't.

Except—that is true and it isn't true. True insofar as what you might call the in-process life (even though the life is actually ended); not true in terms of the overall view of the life—the completed self, we have been calling it—because that encompasses and incorporates all versions of the life, and therefore by definition can have no unlived potential.

Do you see why I made the distinction? It is merely for completeness, lest anyone think that their choices in 3D do not matter.

They do but they don't.

You're going to find it hard to make absolute statements whose opposites do not also apply. Every statement's truth or falsity depends on the point from which it is viewed. Context is everything.

We have a few minutes. Care to say what was on your mind about the first part of the question?

No, on reflection anything I could say about it is likely to cause confusion rather than clarification.

So you don't want to say why the definition strikes you as partial?

No, I think I'll leave it alone. You can see what her questions meant; the fact that the literal words employed may seem to suggest things beyond what she meant is just a fact of life. I remember "the guys" taking me to task (for that's what it felt like) for the words I would use to pose a question. They knew what I was asking, but they would use the form of the question itself to demonstrate to us assumptions I hadn't known I was including. That is what I would be doing in this instance, and in this instance, upon reconsideration, I decided not to do it.

A chat group

We still have nearly ten minutes, and I'm not too tired, if you want to go on. Charles says there is a different feel about this material from that in The Sphere and the Hologram *and wonders if your guys are in a different group from my guys. At least, that's the sense I get.*

Try to resist this idea of groups as if you were talking about baseball teams or street gangs or professional associations. Think of it more as an on-line chat group organized around a particular topic or set of topics. The composition of the group varies from moment to moment, not only as people drop out or return to it, but as others are drawn in or released.

If you hold in your minds the fact that outside 3D the inherent connections are more obvious than they are in 3D, you will lose the need or the temptation to think of us as a jumble of units, or as marbles in a bag. We are more like drops of water than cubes of ice. Our continuity is as much in evidence as our particular individuality.

So, any given conversation will magnetize a different (and perhaps continually changing) group. You may not even be aware of it, but it changes by the moment.

The *constants* are Frank on the 3D end and Rita on the non-3D end, but this isn't as simple as it sounds, either. And in the old days :) it was Rita on the 3D end—and Frank on the 3D end—and "the guys" on the non-3D end.

The flavor of the exchange depends more on the constants than on the non-3D components which, as I say, fluctuate continually. The complication is that, of course, the person or people on the 3D end themselves extend into non-3D and themselves participate from both extremes to greater or less extent.

Okay, and our hour is up. Anything more you'd like to say today?

Merely that—as "the guys" used to say to us—I am enjoying the process and I trust you are as well.

I was then and I am now. Thanks, Rita.

Monday, February 2, 2015

4 a.m. Good morning, Miss Rita. Charles suggests these questions for today. First, James Austin asks for ways to make your statements practical. To wit:

["I'm requesting Rita's insights on ways of living life that help one turn her words into personal experience. . . . She speaks of having an awareness that made her transition to the nonphysical simple and 'seamless'; are there practices that can help me grow more like that?"]

Let's start with that.

Reorientation and faith

You know, it is less a matter of practices or exercises—certainly not of ritual or mere belief without experience—and more of a reorientation of one's being. Like everything we have to discuss, the explanation of *why* takes considerably more than the easy statement of *that*.

I think I bollixed up that last sentence, my mind half elsewhere. A moment while I refocus.
All right.

The reason I didn't have to be reoriented as I dropped the body is that I had oriented myself while still *in* the body. That is, I did not come to die thinking that it was the end, or that an afterlife in some vaguely less physical body would continue life as though I was still in physical conditions. I knew that I didn't really *know* what awaited, but I also knew that it would be all right. My last years were a process of letting go of much that I had thought I knew, but replacing the *belief that I knew* with a confidence that all was well, all was always well, which "the guys" had repeated to us many times.

In a sense, you could say you died in faith.

That's true. Not faith in a particular Christian way. Not faith in New Age or other beliefs. Not faith in the descriptions "the guys" had given us, nor even in the many evidences they had given us of our own extended abilities, with all that promised. Faith, instead, in that all was well. Faith like a child's faith. All was well, and I could trust: I didn't have to die worrying if I would do it "right" or would need retrieval or would be "saved" in any way.

So, to answer this question simply, I would say, practice living in faith that all is well, all is always well.

Now, maybe your reaction is to say "that is merely abstract, and of no practical value." Or perhaps it will strike you as a platitude, or as no work at all. But I tell you—not you, Frank, obviously; you *heard* it just as I did, and in the same way, but for the sake of any who don't yet feel it—this reorientation will change your life and your being. You will begin to live in a different kind of world, and it will transform everything.

If you live knowing that "all is well, all is always well," can you live in fear and anger? Can you experience that gnawing sense of inadequacy, or the helplessness of someone trying to steer a raft safely through a cataract? Can you look at politics and world affairs in the same way?

I seem to remember you following politics on CNN every day, right to the end. I couldn't understand that.

The *things* you occupy yourself with don't matter nearly as much as the mind you bring to them. I watched CNN, you read about the Civil War or read mystery novels or whatever. The content seems wildly different, but the base from which we operated was very clearly aligned. In just such a way, two sisters might be much alike in their way of seeing the world even if their activities and daily lives did not resemble each other's.

> [At the moment, I thought she was referring to her and her
> sister in that life. Now I wonder if this implied that she and I
> had been sisters once. Or maybe she merely used sisters where
> I would have used brothers, feminist that she was.]

But I interrupted.

Not really. The point is made because it is a simple one. Living in faith that all is well, all is always well is much like making a habit of using the [visualization of a] waterfall to replenish the body's energy and correct its patterns. It isn't the specific exercise that changes you; it's more that the change manifests in your exercises, or—more broadly—in your life.

It is the strangest thing, even after more than twenty years of doing this, to be writing out an answer even while wondering if it makes sense or is a repetition or is chasing its tail. Speaking of living in faith!

In any case, I'm not certain our friends will see your statement as an exercise, as a practical means of change.

Perhaps this will help them see it. You cannot live your life believing that all is well without soon coming to realize that you are trusting your own nonphysical awareness; you are allowing yourself to be guided by the non-3D part of you that has your wisdom and has a broader view of your circumstances than you can [have]. Can a lifetime of living aligned with your non-3D guidance not leave you in a good place when you step off from the raft that was your physical life onto the terra firma of non-3D awareness?

Michael Langevin asked a similar question.

["Has Rita spoken of how she best prepared her mind and spirit? An unprepared mind would not be able to comprehend, though it might observe. I am curious what 3D activities, practices, skills serve our expanded 3D selves most?"]

Have you already answered it?

I am reluctant to prescribe specific practices—I now see why the guys were similarly reluctant—lest the *letter* of it overcome the *spirit* of it. You can each find your own paths, and one person's path will be different from another's—perhaps from *all* others—as your lives and aspirations are different. What is important is the polestar. Fix your orientation on the Copernican Shift from the 3D-self being in control to the larger being, which you participate in via your non-3D-self, and the job is done. Any ritual or habit or practice that appeals to you will serve, if it serves to orient you properly.

Everything I have learned, these past twenty years and more, seems to me to reflect something Jesus is reported to have said, reinterpreted out of the 3D-self understanding through which his words were seen. In this case, the need for a child's faith. I still maintain that someone should be going through the world's scriptures, seeing what will seem different when seen through new eyes.

Well, I can hear that argument with more sympathy now!

I'm smiling.

Perceiving higher dimensions

All right, James Austin also asks about experiencing the underlying aspects of time.

["{Rita} says we misunderstand time because we 'roll' the experience/effect of other 'dimensions' into our perceptions of time. Are there ways I can better experience those dimensions and learn to separate them from my experience of time?"]

I understand the question, and the motivation for the question, but that's addressing the question wrong-end-to. Unpacking the question of higher dimensions from our experience of time is an *effect* more than a *cause*, a consequence of a more vital quest, which is for ever-greater consciousness.

Let me say this carefully. In a way, it doesn't make the slightest difference how you perceive or don't perceive the higher dimensions. In a way, it doesn't matter how you conceptualize them. In a way.

In another way—seen from another viewpoint—unpacking these questions may serve to reorient you so as to loosen 3D's hypnotic effects. But that is all it's good for.

Did St. Francis worry about the higher dimensions versus our experience of them as being part of time? Did Thoreau or Emerson? Did I, for that matter?

I understand; what I don't know is whether others will. Let me paraphrase. If we live our lives as best we can, we don't need to worry about higher dimensions conceptually. Your discussing them was merely to help loosen the mental bonds formed of a less complete scheme. But reorientation per se does not depend on our experiencing dimensions differently. It depends on our seeing ourselves differently.

That is what I said, yes.

So the bottom line is, reorient around "all is well, all is always well" and stop believing in the reality of what is being reported.

Stop believing that things mean what they are reported to mean. An earthquake doesn't nonexist just because you don't hear of it, or you disbelieve in reports of it. But it doesn't necessarily mean that the gods are angry, or that the world is coming apart, or that it was engineered by secret forces physical or otherwise. You understand—the *phenomena* exist. But do they mean what people take them to mean? Are they, in fact, what they seem to be? What is their relevance to *your* life as you fashion it, and what is their relevance as indicator, *if you continue to believe* a priori *that all is well, all is always well*?

That sounds like a place to pause, and that's our hour. Thanks, Rita. Charles tells me that this is our thirty-first session already. You're going to owe me quite a bit of lost sleep.

Yes, but I told you, after Gateway in 1979, I lost all my capacity for being guilt-tripped.

A pity. Well, next time.

Tuesday, February 3, 2015

Considering good and evil

5:15 a.m. Good morning, Rita. I'm looking forward to today's question and response, as it is a subject on which I have pretty strong opinions, and I don't actually know what yours are, despite our having lived in the same house, if on different floors, for so many years. (Only about four and a half years, come to think of it. Seemed more.) Here's the question.

[From James Austin: "I'd appreciate hearing what Rita has to say about 'bad' guys, both here and in her nonphysical environment. 'Bad' is my generic term covering the range from 'I don't like what he/she/it does/thinks' through those who hurt and abuse others, to 'pure evil.' Rita made strong statements about 'as above so below'; since we have 'bad' people in the physical, that principle would imply there are 'bad' nonphysical beings.

["Again, if specific questions are needed:

> • are there 'bad' larger selves?
> • if so, do they create 'bad' people in 3D?
> • can 'bad' people be a part of 'good' larger selves and vice
>   versa?
> • is this sort of discussion confused by differences in what
>   'bad' means in 3D versus the nonphysical?"]

And your reaction is?—

I agree with you, this is an excellent question, because it shows that he is *thinking about* the material, not merely accepting or rejecting it. "If A be assumed to be true, wouldn't B logically follow, and if so, what about C and D?" This is the only way to make this material or any new material truly yours. You have to wrestle with it.

Like Jacob wrestling with the angel until dawn.

I don't know about that, but it is important to wrestle with it. Only when you try to apply any new idea or set of ideas do you truly come to grips with it, or them.

This particular question won't get a "yes but no." In saying that evil and good, existing in the physical, must exist in the nonphysical, he is correct. However, as usual, for this statement to be meaningful, it must be explained.

That's what we're here for.

Indeed it is. And that fact might well be kept in mind. That's what we're here for. More on that another time, perhaps.

Very well. Good and evil. The first thing to be said is that language does indeed use the same words to describe very different things. The second, that everything is about viewpoints and choices. And if more time remains today we will go beyond this, and if not, we will address it later.

Language as a problem

So, language as a problem. As James Austin accurately says, three categories of values are lumped together. But this is another of those situations where, to understand A, you need to understand B, but to understand B you need to understand A. We can't make the short, simple statements that would clarify the subject not because the subject is particularly complicated but because we have to describe one variable in terms of another variable, and the description gets tangled easily. Only when you function outside of 3D will you realize the difficulties inherent in attempting such descriptions in sequential form (language within time), given to people experiencing reality one moment at a time—a reality that includes, in a way, their own consciousness! Thus, for you it is a juggling act merely to keep your attention on one thing as you move through time. It isn't like ADD so much as attention-*diversion*-disorder, and it is inherent in life in 3D. But, to explain rather than complain—

A joke, Rita?

A joke. You'll get used to it. Tell them of your insight into the tree of the knowledge of good and evil.

All right. My friend Jim Marion, author of Putting on the Mind of Christ *and* The Death of the Mythic God, *was in town visiting one day, and I told him I'd had a sudden insight and wondered what he thought of it. (Jim is a trained theologian, a former Catholic priest, a scholar, and a trained psychologist, a student of Ken Wilbur, from which viewpoint he wrote his books. They are not books of theology but of psychology.) I said it had struck me that maybe the story in Genesis about The Tree of the Knowledge of Good and Evil was actually meaning The Tree of the Perception of (things as) Good and Evil, which would change the meaning of the story considerably. In other words, rather than saying they opened their eyes, it would say they fell into a condition of judgment based in duality. Jim thought a moment and said—I can still quote him, so many years after—"Hebrew has very few abstract words. That is a very permissible translation."*

Tastes and values

In other words, you see, my answer is that many things that are called evil or good are *in themselves* merely a matter of taste, arising from one's own values. This is the first layer of this particular onion, a matter of taste. If one person's value system is headed by truth and another's by kindness—to fashion a simple example—they will take very different views of a white lie. If one chiefly values strength and valor, and another chiefly values harmonization and mutual accommodation, the one will think the other weak, the second will think the other unfeeling. You understand. The most superficial layer of this question of good and evil may be said to be a matter of tastes.

Such tastes are rooted in values, which themselves are rooted in the general composition of elements that make up the individual soul. Thus, to some extent it could be said that *one* purpose of fashioning souls of many elements is to provide spokespeople for every possible nuance of feeling. If you have 3D strands coexisting within you, and your life is the process of coming to an accommodation with them, your view of the particulars of good and evil at this level is necessarily going to be different from everybody else's. You see? It isn't only a matter of expressing every possible shade of preference along one given line from positive through to negative—it is a matter of expressing every possible shade of preference along *many* such lines, all that are active within the individual. Hence you are going to find people whose values [on certain issues] are identical to yours, or close to them, yet very different—perhaps bewilderingly different—on other issues. Also, thus you find your own values, no less than those of others, quite inconsistent within themselves. Not that you or others fail to always live your values; not that the values you hold are mere pretense; not that they are chosen or acquired at random, but that each of you is a representative not so much of any particular strand or combination of strands within you as, you might say, the *ratio*, the final accommodation within you, of that bundle of strands.

A lot in that paragraph. More to unpack later, perhaps.

That's according to what people want. But all that refers to the superficial level of, shall we say, good or evil according to preference. From where *you* stand, certain values, actions, preferences, are undesirable because they offend your embodied values. A pacifist may condemn martial expressions *as if they were wrong*, which to that individual they will appear to be, but those same qualities when they express as heroism in saving lives will not appear evil even to the same person. A daredevil who likes to live on the edge may value risk-taking so highly as to underrate others whose prime value is nurturance or preservation—until, perhaps, an accident reveals the practical value and benefit of nursing!

You understand. At this level, it is closer to a matter of opinion arising from what you are—a matter of taste, call it—than a moral stance. But, as noted, there are deeper levels. And rather than proceed through intermediate stages, it will be most illustrative to consider the question at its other extreme—pure good, pure evil.

Pure good, and pure evil

Go right ahead. Ten words or less?

It may take a little more than that. And I see we are unlikely to finish even this much of the subject while staying within your limits.

I don't mind overdoing a little.

Well. Consider what the opposing poles of good and evil look like from the place of non-3D perception. In the first place,

Sorry.

From non-3D, even duality itself is experienced differently. It is *seen* but not *experienced*, one might say. Or, it is recognized but not as an inescapable strait-jacket but as a guide to clarity. The nature and expression and consequences of positive and negative are very different when experienced in their totality than when experienced moment to moment in slices of time one after the next.

I have heard it said that outside of the physical world there is no duality.

You have heard it said, and [have] argued against it. Rightly so, from a deeper knowing. But the argument is futile, because any argument conducted by two people who are using the same words to mean different things is going to be futile—except, perhaps in as much as the argument itself wakes one or both to the realization that the words are creating slippage.

Duality is a fact of created life, an ordering principle no less in intellectual than in physical life, no less in moral composition than in mental orientation. But duality can orient you, or it can entrap you, depending on your relationship to it, and this is where we need to begin next time. We did less than I had hoped, but well begun is half done, they used to say.

I look forward to more. I wish I could do more at a time.

Righteous persistence brings reward.

I've heard that. Till next time, then.

Wednesday, February 4, 2015

3:30 a.m. And here we go again. We seem to be working our way backward around the clock. Soon we will be starting at 10 p.m. Not that I'm complaining! Miss Rita, your move.

Very well. Funny, I'm not sleepy at all.

Yes, very funny. I wonder why that is. So—?

Duality in non-3D

I was saying that duality is in the nature of all creation, and at this point I need to remind you of something we were told when we were doing this from the same "side" of the division of 3D from non-3D, and that is that it is a mistake to think that the non-3D side of life is somehow exempt from the conditions of duality that exist as ground rules. At the time, we were thinking in terms of physical v. nonphysical and tended to think that the significant difference was whether one was in the body or not. "The guys" informed us that the nonphysical was *a part of* the physical, and I don't know that we ever understood that properly, even after we were told that the chief difference between us on our side and the guys on their side was not in our natures but in the characteristics of the terrain we respectively inhabited.

You can understand that easier now, if you remember that we are conceptualizing it not as physical v. nonphysical but as awareness of 3D v. awareness of all dimensions of which 3D is only some. Of course we are part of the same thing. We are in the same space, inhabiting the same world. How could it be otherwise? So now we move into wider ramifications by way of investigating shared duality as it manifests in the question of good and evil. And what we're about to discuss could serve as a bridge between modern exploratory metaphysics—call it that—and traditional religious teachings. As you have long insisted, those teachings contain valuable clues. It is firsthand experience and reconceptualization that brings their inner truths and descriptive insights back to life again.

The spirit of the teachings brings life, and the letter kills.

Literalism is idolatry. I believe you read that somewhere. I seem to remember your quoting it to me.

I don't remember quoting it, but I do remember reading it, though I don't know where. They could equally well have said literalism is superstition.

Any words may be made into superstition, including these, if accepted and repeated without understanding. And the greater the authority of the authors, the greater the danger of rote repetition and consequent unconscious distortion into something they were never meant to be.

I know this seems like a diversion from our topic, but it is not. It is, perhaps, a clearing of skirts before going farther.

You will want to prove these words for yourselves, at least I hope you will. One way to do so is to take the teachings you grew up with and reexamine them as if ("as if!") they were the record of people's experiences, a record that was distorted not for political reasons (though that could happen as well, after the fact) but because any experience and insight becomes distorted when seen as if [it were] a 3D experience, and the record becomes further distorted when read by those whose experience does not extend beyond 3D.

In other words, by those whose lack of additional perspective prevents them from reading back into the scriptures what translation into 3D terms took out.

Precisely. Well, as you know, Frank, I did not live in the Christian tradition I was born into, but in the modern Jungian understanding that I learned over time. But anyone who knows anything at all about Christianity or Judaism or Islam knows that they center on the heavenly war between good and evil as it plays out "here on Earth." They go about establishing the relevance to ordinary life in different ways and thus express, and create, quite different ways of seeing the world, as each one emphasizes different qualities, but what they have in common is this perception of the war between good and evil, a war that begins not in 3D but in non-3D; a war that moves into 3D because in a way it is about 3D, and is about humans in particular.

Other religions see the world—see the nature of reality—differently. Shinto, for instance, or Confucianism, while observing the existence of disharmony, do not concentrate on good v. evil so much as harmony v. disharmony, or balance v. out-of-balance conditions, which has a slightly more accurate nuance here than the word "imbalance."

This does not make one view "right" and others "wrong," any more than looking up rather makes looking down wrong. In fact, considering the fact that various valid religious traditions see the world differently helps you keep the wider view—the wider horizons of possibilities—simultaneously in mind.

So let us proceed, as good Westerners, to consider the nature of good and evil as absolutes rather than as the matter of expression of tastes that is the most superficial end of the spectrum of behavior we are considering.

Duality and scripture

Religion takes the principle of absolute good and identifies it with the creator, which it identifies with God. It takes the principle of absolute evil and identifies it with the disrupter, which it identifies with the devil. (Understand, I am simplifying and gliding over nuances, here. I was no theologian and, in fact, was not even much interested in religious matters when in 3D, and as you will learn over time, we aren't particularly different "over here" and what would make us so? So for me to connect to scriptural sources would be a farther stretch than it would be for any of you in the body, where you still have greater possibility of choice.)

This traditional religious understanding is not wrong; it is not even

I lost it, hesitating over possibilities, not sure where you wanted to go.

Any body of knowledge must be explained at the level of understanding of those who listen to it. Or put another way, you could say that any congregation—even if it is a congregation of one, reading the Bible, say—*must*, necessarily, understand whatever it is taught in the only way its level of being allows. Scripture cannot bring a leap of reconceptualization; it can only serve as illumination at the present level.

A lamp unto my feet.

Yes. And as you used to insist, it is necessarily written to give people something, no matter what level they read it from, anywhere from reading a myth as a literally true history to reading it as a coded allusion to realities to which many are blind. It is a translation designed to appeal to many levels of being—but still it is a translation susceptible to being grossly misunderstood especially if read from a level of being that assumes that its own is the only level that exists, and, therefore, whatever the scripture seems to those at that level *must be* the only "right" meaning of the words.

So, if we are to look at reality in a different way, it is important that you not jettison so much past description that will open up to you in a new way when you come to it with new eyes.

I have been telling myself for years that I should study scripture, but it doesn't seem to happen. Apparently it is not my path.

Maps and explorers

Or perhaps it is a matter of timing. Now, your hour is nearly up, and it may not seem like this discussion has brought us anywhere on the subject of good and evil, but, in fact, if it has awakened anybody to the fact, or reminded them, say, that this question of good and evil is integrally connected to the exploration of reality that is the scriptures, it will have served to anchor an abstract question in a wider context. There is no use explaining without considering the rough maps provided by earlier explorers. They may have gotten major features wrong; they may have guessed where this or that river arises; they may have put down descriptions with greater definiteness than their experiences warranted. Still, their journals should be explored, their maps perused. Why? So that you can perpetuate their errors or omissions or misunderstandings? No—so you may *profit* by them.

So, to end for now, I remind you that we really are moving to answer the question and the associated questions. Good and evil may be considered to be absolutes within our experience of duality. We in the higher dimensions (call it) who—I remind you—continue to exist in 3D even if we have no body to anchor our consciousness there, are as much in duality as you are in 3D. That is an important fact that will at first be an obstacle for some of you. Still, it is the truth, and will help explain some things as we go along. Being in duality, we experience good and evil. However, not being subject to the constraints of a limited consciousness moving from one time-slice to the next, obviously we experience it differently. As I said at the end of yesterday's discussion, it can be an orientation, rather than a trap.

However, there is much more to be said on the subject. Enough for now.

Thank you, Rita. I for one don't care how far afield you have to range in order to tie this in to our practical lives. I feel our position keenly, as being at the cusp between two ways of seeing the world. I am well aware that we can't yet see the next way of seeing it, and won't live long enough to see it triumph, but maybe we can see more of the opening stages.

And maybe each of you can help it be anchored into the world. Enough for now.

Here's your hat, what's your hurry, eh? Okay, more later.

Thursday, February 5, 2015

4:30 a.m. Good morning, Miss Rita. So—good and evil, continued.

Yes. Helpful to have the question poised for you, isn't it?

It is indeed. There's all the difference in the world. It makes me aware of how hard it can be, to try to do both ends of the process.

I again encourage all who read this to bear in mind the environment it is describing. *One* world, a shared reality, a difference in environments, but still a shared duality, experienced differently by different parts of our being. If you can remember this while we talk about the problem of good and evil (and other topics to follow) you will find your comprehension of many things gradually changing, integrating. But if you only read these words without making the effort to experience them from a new place, what effect can they have?

New wine in old wineskins.

You need an analogy suited to the times. People in the time of Jesus would have understood that analogy, so that is how he put it. He would have used a contemporary analogy today as he did then.

New software running on a previous operating system? Something like that?

Well, think about it. Notice that even trying to find a modern equivalent served to make the reality of the thing being analogized more real to you. In any case, the point remains: to absorb new mind-sets, new orientation is required—and, at the same time, new orientation facilitates absorbing new material.

Once more, to understand A, etc.

Yes. That's the sense of it.

Good and evil in non-3D

Very well, I said we would resume with some words on good and evil as it is experienced outside of 3D. The one crucial difference in the experience of the same reality is that of time experienced as a whole rather than in slices.

You can see that if you experience anything in time-slices, it is going to vary moment by moment, and whatever aspect it presents at any given moment will appear dominant. Like your experience of your lives in general, it will be always out of proportion. The present moment always far outweighs all others, in terms of its intensity and its—effective importance, call it. Your lives are never experienced in proportion until you see them from a place from which all moments have equal weight. Again, this is by design, to enable and enforce the process of successive change. Still, it is necessary to bear in mind that your judgments are necessarily biased by the disproportionate importance of any given moment.

This is what I was referring to when, at the end of our last session, I said that duality can be experienced as orientation rather than as a trap. It is all in the ability—or inability—to remember other moments while experiencing any one moment.

Thus, pain. We once asked the guys about pain and they said they know it hurts, but it is so useful. You and I, Frank, knew enough to know that this was not callousness on their part, just as they had also said that we would find them somewhat chilly, emotionally, if we could experience them in their own element. Now I know the meaning behind the statements, and I'll try to make it clearer than it was to us then.

You will bear in mind that we have moved beyond that perception of a thing as evil merely because it upholds values that may be considered a matter of taste. We are attempting now to look at pure evil, pure good, as best we can discuss them.

The first thing to be said is—from what starting point?

I can feel what you mean. I can feel where you want to go with it, but I don't have the words for it.

Merely stay with the feeling and the thought will clarify as I say more. That's all that ever happens; it's merely taking long enough here for you to experience the gap.

Combining scales

Good and evil may be considered to be on a long line, with every possible gradation between them. If there were only one line, it would be simple. *It would also be static and would offer little or no potential for choice and movement.* It is in the crosscurrents created by the coexistence of different combinations of positions that the possibilities of choice and growth and movement—and of retrogression, of course—become possible.

It is hard to get words around this.

You only experience the difficulty when you try to strategize ahead, so to speak—to structure it before it comes out. Don't fight the process, and all will be well.

That is, I will experience that it is well.

Exactly. To continue. Every line of choice may be considered a different scale.

That's awkward. It isn't going to be understood.

Rephrase it if you can.

I know. Take it by the seven deadly sins, say.

That's acceptable. Go ahead.

I take it that you are saying that anyone may be at a different position between good and evil along many different scales, and the result is different for each, because of the productive complications of a more complicated system of measurement. Or, not more complicated system, more comprehensive.

Yes, close enough.

So we may measure ourselves according to different scales and, for instance, one such set of scales are the seven deadly sins as described by the church over the years. I made an acronym to help me remember them: LEG CAPS. Lust, envy, gluttony, covetousness, anger, pride, sloth. That isn't the order of importance traditionally given to them, but it was the only acronym I could devise. (And I can imagine our readers now sitting down and industriously looking for a better acronym. I smile to think of it. Put P first, guys; pride is supposed to be the first deadly sin.)

That serves to illustrate the point. Not the question of sin—that is for another time, perhaps—but the question of measurement of different qualities of good and evil. You see? Not, how does anyone rate, how is anyone doing, in overcoming temptations, but, what different ways can good and evil be experienced?

But I can feel people's hackles rise as soon as you even mention the word sin. There's too much resistance to it.

Scaling

Well, it was *your* example! I'm smiling. Let's look at it from another direction, then, tying it to behavior. Cruelty would be one. Call the scale compassion-to-indifference. Or, a slightly different way of looking at it, identification-to-rejection. You can see that any one person—at any one time—is going to fit somewhere on that scale. They are very compassionate, very aware that "all men are brothers," and they are constitutionally unable to deliberately hurt anyone else, for just that reason. Or they are very aware that the world is divided between themselves (and anyone else they identify with) and the rest of the world, and they see no objection to doing as they wish, taking what they want or, indeed, may strongly value the sense of self-assertion they experience in subjugating others to their will. That is, this is a scale that ranges from compassion to indifference, or from identification to rejection of identity, or from kindness to cruelty.

In a life in 3D time-slices you are going to experience any given position one at a time, and it is going to be correspondingly exaggerated in your consciousness, as any moment is exaggerated in importance.

We—yourselves outside 3D—do not experience it that way. We experience good and evil, as every other duality, more as a ratio than as a once-and-for-all choice, or a situation.

And, bear in mind, any one measurement—cruelty, say—*is* only *one* measurement. Regardless where a person may be on one scale, you cannot reliably predict where that same person is going to be on another scale. What does a person's cruelty or compassion tell you about his or her—

Did you get at a loss for a concept to fill in, or did I lose the beam?

A little of both, because to continue that thought in this context would be to mislead, but you were strongly expecting a continuation, so could not feel anything but interruption.

I keep learning about the process as we go along.

Should that surprise you? A teaching is going to have many strands to it, some implicit.

Let us leave that thought unfinished for the moment and leave it that the question of good and evil has many axes, hence many positions for people to occupy simultaneously. Hence, you are unlikely to meet a person in body who is pure good or pure evil—and if you don't find one *in* body, you needn't expect to find one *outside* the body. Compound beings cannot be expected to be all one thing, regardless of what "thing" is in question. And we in the higher dimensions who have been shaped by 3D experience are, inevitably, ourselves different mixtures of good and evil.

It has been said—I forget who said it—that the line between good and evil does not run between us, but through us.

That's right. And so people who like to divide others into good or evil are merely truncating their own self-perception.

Your hour is over, and we will have to continue at another time.

Feels like we are inching along.

Slow and steady wins the race.

That sounds like a handicapping formula that would be disastrous.

It depends on the length of the race and the relative stamina of the racers. Until next time.

Next time, then.

Friday, February 6, 2015

Three forms of evil

4 a.m. Miss Rita, open for business. More, I take it, on the subject of good and evil. I doubt we have quite exhausted the subject.

Not quite. We're more likely to exhaust the reader than the subject. But, as I said, slow but steady.

Very well, bearing in mind that the nub of the underlying question is, what is the nature of good and evil when considered in the nonphysical *as well as* physical parts of reality, we come to the question not so much how we experience it but, what is it really? We have carefully differentiated between what seems to any individual to be evil but is really a matter of taste, and that which comes from the principle of pure evil that exists as the opposite of pure good. And I remind you, all creation exists as dualities, or perhaps I should say can be described and perceived as dualities, and the higher dimensions clearly (I hope it is "clearly" by now) cannot exist under different rules than the lower ones, given that they are all one thing in different terrain.

In any moral question (and for that matter in any question even of physical structure) a safe procedure is to remember that the universe is scaled. As above, so below.

Man is the measure of all things.

That, too. You don't have to stretch your imaginations to try to figure out how things might look. First imagine it as you experience it on a human level, then imagine that familiar phenomenon expanded or shrunk in scale. Because the universe repeats at different scales, this is as good a guide as any.

So, if you want to know about good and evil in the nonphysical, the place to begin (once you've reminded yourself of the facts we have been laying down as groundwork) is with your own commonplace experience. How do *you* experience good and evil in your own lives, both short-term—at any given moment—and long-term, the results of tendencies experienced over time.

And in the examination, bear in mind that at the center of the question is *you*, yourself. Your own experience of evil that seems external to you; your own experience of evil that seems to be a part of you; your own experience of evil that seems to cohabit your mind and being against your conscious will. These three overlapping contexts will lead you anywhere you want to go in the exploration of good and evil.

If this were an hour from now, I would be hearing that as a summing-up.

Which would then allow you to take a nap! :) However, not quite yet.

Yes, a summing-up, because it is all implicit in what I just said. But as always with something new, first comes the statement, then the exploration of the statement. Then the restatement.

Three ways in which you experience evil:

1. As something external

2. As a part of yourself

3. As a recalcitrant part of yourself

This statement isn't quite right—is quite wrong, in a way, as we shall see—but it will lead us to greater understanding. The process of learning is the process of replacing error with less egregious error, sidling toward the truth.

To understand A—

You must never forget it, because that is the only way the unfamiliar can be made comprehensible.

So we will begin with the easiest to see—evil as something external. And in the course of examining the three conditions of experiencing evil we will answer James Austin's specific questions.

Evil as external

It is always easiest to see evil in the actions of others and—to our eyes—in the *nature* of others. In this discussion we omit—as I said—questions of a difference in taste being seen as good or evil. I am now talking about pure evil, and its manifestations. But we are not quite ready to try to define pure evil or even relative evil. We have more ground to cover first.

Take someone who did evil deeds, of whose evil you are sure. On a political level, a Hitler or Stalin. On an economic level, anyone

No, skip that, it will bring us back into preferences, as policy decisions are always a mixture of good and evil, and it will only blur the picture. So leave it as political monsters at one end and individual criminals at the other end, and "criminals" here has nothing to do with statutes, but has to do with the doing of evil. Rapists, murderers, thieves, arsonists—fill in your own specifics, as long as they have in common the quality of willfully hurting other people either through active malice or through exaggerated selfishness.

You, yourself, have not issued orders that resulted in mass suffering. At the other end of the scale, it gets a little closer to the bone, even though (presumably) you are not a murderer or rapist, but still let us confine ourselves for the moment to instances where you observe (or even imagine) evil as something *you* did not do, did not abet, did not approve of. Evil the contemplation of which hurts you.

Considering this aspect of evil has this advantage—*it reminds you that evil actually exists.* You can't define it out of existence by finding the right formula. You can't meaningfully explain it as "merely the absence of good" unless you care to explain gravity as "merely the absence of weightlessness." That is, you can wrap the words around it so that it *seems* to make sense, but a close reading will reveal that either you aren't saying anything or you are saying what is not so.

I don't think you would have said this while you were in 3D, Rita. At least, that isn't how I remember you from our discussions.

You will find that reconnecting with the rest of you is apt to alter your view of things. I won't say you wind up outvoting yourself, but you certainly do see things differently. This is a diversion, so mark it down for future examination if you wish, but 3D is for fashioning the habit-system that is our mind; thereafter that habit-system is exercised continually, and often comes to very different conclusions than it would have on Earth where it saw things in fragments.

To return to the point: Evil *exists*. Duality is not a quality and the quality's absence, but a quality and its opposite. And points between the two extremes, of course, but the point is that the polarity exists, it can't be explained away.

Now it will be easy to lose sight of the fact that what we're calling pure evil or pure good is not *one* thing so much as it is the connected extreme of many qualities. Remember, I tried to give you the idea of many expressions of a tendency. That's why. When people allow themselves to flatten the discussion to one scale—good at one end, evil at the other—it does allow them to make compact statements, but it does not aid understanding. It would be more accurate to say there are many, many good-evil scales, all being bounded together.

I got an image of the lines of longitude on a globe, all beginning at the north or south pole, and covering the whole globe by diverging somewhat—but all beginning at one point and ending at an opposite point.

That's the visual analogy that seemed to do the trick. The poles represent concentrations of qualities that share something of the same nature.

Is this akin to the teaching that ultimately the universe is suspended between love on one end and fear on the other?

Closely akin, but the kinship may not become apparent for a while. Nor is kinship identity.

Time to wrap up for the morning. The first way you experience evil is as something external. It isn't something wrong with *you*. It isn't that you can't see straight. You didn't cause it and you aren't (necessarily) misperceiving it. It's there. But what is it, really? It will be a while before we're able to bring that to light. Meanwhile, we must look at evil as you experience it as sharing your value-system (that is, areas in which you consent to evil) and evil as you experience it as contending against you. And this is where we will resume next time.

Thank you, Rita. As you no doubt know, people are finding real value in this discussion.

And as you are aware, that is always very gratifying to a teacher.

Till next time, then.

Saturday, February 7, 2015

Evil as attractive nuisance

6 a.m. To resume—

Evil as a part of you, a touchy subject.

Is this not where we are forced into the subject of sin? And, you're right, nobody likes that subject much. Say "sin" and you get a cross-eyes, perplexed reaction from people who wonder if you can really be so simple-minded and superstitious as to believe in sin. They assume then that you must be a fundamentalist. Or another kind of person, they assume that you are wandering on your own when a good pastor could give you the word so much more professionally, competently.

Let's see if we can discuss the subject of evil as part of you without provoking either of those reactions. We looked at evil as one end of various polarities—as a South Pole to the globe that is human life—and we will look at it as an attempted infringement upon the human will. Here let's look at it as an attractive nuisance.

Hmm—like an unfenced swimming pool?

Just like that. Something that glitters in the sun but constitutes a danger for the unwary, or lies unsuspected in the dark, a danger that may be stumbled into.

Remember, human nature as we are describing it is a *compound*, not an element. That is, what you are is a mixture of diverse elements that may or may not come to function as a unit over time, but will never be the unitary being that an angel is, say, or a blade of grass. That is what separates humans from the rest of nature, the fact that they are compounds learning to function as though they are units, and therefore manifest what they are in very changeable ways. You know how astrologers say of Pisces that they may suddenly begin to "follow the other fish?" In other words, they may appear to be something quite other than they appeared previously, without changing their nature, merely following a contradictory—built-in contradictory—pattern. We're not on the subject of astrology, here; that is only an example of the kinds of complexity built into human possibility.

I see it in myself, certainly.

Well, all right. You are a compound. The other thing to remember is that nobody in form is pure evil or pure good or pure *anything*, precisely because you are compounded of so many strands that are themselves compounds. Human life in 3D is infinitely complex, no matter how appearances may be. And, remember, if it is true for beings functioning in 3D, it does not cease to be true of those beings when they cease to function in 3D; it is only that the manifestations change with the changed terrain.

So if you concede that evil, as one end of a set of polarities, has independent existence (I don't mean independent from its part of any given polarity, I mean independent in the sense that it is not mere perception, a sort of abstraction or illusion), and if you concede that humans are compounds rather than unchanging internally consistent elements, surely you must admit that no one is created who does not incorporate some good, some evil. As we said, the line between good and evil (a very tenuous line, sometimes, hard to discern) runs not *between* people—so that you have good people and bad people—but *within* people, so that you have a person's good nature and evil nature.

This is not a difficult concept to see, although it may not be agreeable to everyone's feelings. Jungians will understand it easier than most, but where is the practicing psychologist of any school who can believe that people are pure good or pure evil?

Now, Frank, you know that sin may be defined as "missing the mark"— that is, as tendencies or actions that lead a person astray. This is a more accurate (and more compassionate) view than the one that says sin is a moral failing for which the person exhibiting it must be punished. However— brief digression—both views are somewhat true. Sin may manifest because it is part of your nature and you can't help it, but it may manifest more, or less, easily according to whether your free will assents to it or resists it. If the former, then "missing the mark" applies, much as anyone practicing a skill may be less than perfect at it; if the latter, then individual culpability cannot be escaped.

You can't be blamed for having the impulses, just for giving in to them.

Not quite, more like just for *encouraging* them. You see? It is almost the difference between witnessing a bank robbery as an innocent passerby as opposed to aiding and abetting by acting as lookout for the robbers.

I see.

It gets more complicated than that, but you will learn when you begin to function from outside 3D (or rather, without a body) that if you want to discuss anything, you are going to have to ruthlessly suppress extraneous connections that occur to you.

Which implies that this is what you are doing continuously, mostly silently.

Of course, because even mentioning that the side-trail exists is enough to tempt me, or you, into pursuing it.

Evil as compulsion

All right, now we can come back to the question of sin if people want to, and you can see if anyone comes up with a better acronym than LEG CAPS for the seven major headings under which different tendencies or temptations may be categorized, but for now let us proceed to the third manifestation of evil in 3D, evil as it contends with your will as though attempting to control you and change you.

"As though"?

Like everything in life, it isn't quite as simple, but yes, as though. How you experience it is all we can address at the moment. To try to redefine causes before effects are recognized for what they are is to lead yourself astray.

So the third manifestation of evil appears as if separate—for it has an effective will of its own—yet appears as if an integral part of you—for it has a strong internal ally in part of what you are. An instructive analogy would be the behavior of an alcoholic whose awareness is acute enough to see his or her slavery, but whose will is not strong enough to overcome the compulsion to drink. Or substitute heroin or the substance or manifestation of any addictive tendency.

You see the difference? Whereas the second condition had the element of complicity, this has the element of compulsion. There is all the difference in the world between being tempted and being coerced.

So—now we may circle all the way back to the initial questions, and see them with new eyes.

Are there bad larger selves? Do they create bad people? Can larger beings be mixtures of good and bad? As you see, the questions are in error only in assuming uniformity where there are compounds. But that error in the unstated assumption makes a yes or no answer equally misleading.

It is just this kind of fundamental question, or perhaps I should say just this kind of questioning of fundamentals—that leads to productive restructuring of concepts, for surely no one who has read these paragraphs over the past couple of days can still be seeing the question as they would have had we given a yes or a no or even a yes but no.

And the answer to the question of the cause of confusion is not so much in the difference in terrain as in the fundamental misunderstanding of the compound nature of human existence, both in 3D and afterward.

And that, even though it is not quite an hour today, is a good place to stop for the moment. Next time we can begin on another question, and any follow-up questions suggested by this discussion can come later, wherever Charles thinks appropriate.

Okay, thanks, Rita. Even though we're stopping a few minutes early, we got quite a bit today. I look forward to whatever the next topic is, and I hope our readers do as well. Till then.

Sunday, February 8, 2015

Angels and humans

6 a.m. All right, Miss Rita, we have another question, which I make to be #11 unless I have lost count, and #12 if you get to it today.

[From Jim Austin: "I was struck by some of the things Rita said in the various parts of an earlier question, and surprised no one has commented yet. Her idea about thinking of angels as 'beings' who have not had and will not have the 3D experience reminded me of those who suggest angels and demons are the same type of being, differing (maybe) only in their 'regard' for humans. It also brings to mind don Juan's (Castaneda's teacher) 'inorganic beings', although they had some penetration into 3D.

[But she strongly suggests we look beyond such '3D things' in new directions. For example, at 'the relationship' between larger selves, those with 3D experience, and those without (later referred to as 'unitary beings'). She relates that larger beings are a unique factor, implying they/we (through the experiences gained in 3D life) are constantly changing.

[So how is this useful in daily life?"]

As you see, they're up to your old trick of actually thinking about your material rather than merely accepting it and allowing themselves to be unchanged by it.

Yes, and I'm very pleased to see it. Not much point in reading new material and not attempting to assimilate it, and the process of assimilation is naturally going to proceed better if underlying contradictions or vaguenesses are brought to light.

And I have little doubt that you are going to take a given question mostly as a springboard and then proceed to elucidate what you want to elucidate, like a politician at a press conference.

Any sincere question is going to pose the opportunity to discuss some area of any given topic, because after all, everything connects to everything. The big variable is a person's ability to hold and interrelate various thoughts moment by moment, so that new links may be formed that will hold them together in the future as aspects of one thing rather than, as previously, as unconnected or relatively unconnected different things.

My point about angels and humans is simple enough and is one of those things that was obvious to previous mind-sets in previous civilizations but has been blurred or disbelieved by what was called "modern" thought, which, of course, was merely a transition between stable worldviews.

"Of course"? That's a fairly large statement to throw in as an "of course." I know what you mean, but don't you think you should elaborate a bit?

Well, *you* are the historian! And after all, it's only an "of course," because a moment's thought will show that different civilizations have different ways of seeing things, and some of them are relatively stable and may continue for generations, while others are relatively dynamic and may change radically within themselves every couple of decades—or faster—and may pass away entirely when another stable worldview steps into the place the dynamic interval has cleared for it.

If you are meaning that we had, in the West, the long medieval period as one stable worldview, followed by the Renaissance and Reformation as a fast-changing solvent, that would make it—. Well, it gets tangled, when I try to apply what is a simple-sounding statement.

That's the kind of analysis best done not horseback, as you always say, but slowly, pondering it. It is a different manner of thinking, analysis as opposed to association. If you let yourself think about it, later, a scheme will suggest itself, or several alternate schemes, because, after all, to generalize is to slur over certain distinctions and emphasize others.

Now about angels and humans. Humans are compound beings shaped by one or (usually) more 3D experiences. The human soul is *created* in 3D (that is, the elements may be chosen outside of 3D, but it is in 3D that the mixture is fashioned), it *develops* in 3D as it experiences choice through limitation and shared-experiences-in-living-together, and it continues to manifest its 3D-created characteristics after the body in which it was created and nurtured is no longer required.

The human soul is thus unique, in that it alone is a compound of previous elements that has changed and has the ability to continue to change.

And this is different somehow from animals, say?

Let us deal with the distinction from angels first. Angels represent entire classes of beings, many unsuspected from 3D, that are *not* compounds, but are purely what they are. Angels do not breed and hence are not the product of past mixtures of elements. They do not experience themselves as bound by time and space, hence do not form the habit of seeing themselves in isolation from others, do not experience their lives in disproportion as humans do because any present moment exaggerates its own importance relative to the past and future; they do not, therefore, change as human beings change. They may manifest different qualities at different times (or so it will seem from a 3D view) but they do not, because they *can* not, alter their basic attitude toward the world. They cannot sin and repent and sin a different way and repent again; they cannot suppress a part of themselves and favor a different part of themselves, in other words. That is a privilege and a predicament confined to compound beings shaped in the 3D pressure-cooker, or test tube.

As I'm getting all this, a part of my mind is saying, well, this somewhat accords with the biblical story of the revolt of the angels who refused to admit the possibility that "made" beings like humans could ultimately attain a plane superior to their own. But wouldn't that story imply sin and therefore change among the angels?

Try to stay with what I'm setting out and don't tie it to what else you know or think *prematurely*. You will want to be doing just that, obviously, only don't do it too soon to get the full flavor of the new way of seeing it.

Don't fly off in the heat of the day without a blanket. Okay.

Remember when you got that humans could be looked at as the tricksters in the universe? That was referring to 3D, but it applies to the rest of it, as well. Beings deliberately constructed out of disparate materials are going to provide something different than beings whose essence is not compound, hence is unchanging.

But be careful to remember that this description is leaving out important aspects of the situation that need to be kept in mind. "Human," for instance, means "compound beings created and nurtured in 3D consciousness," so don't slip into thinking this refers only to one little neighborhood—planet Earth—and one little family—humanity as you know it. The 3D universe is filled with humans, most of which you will never experience contact with even vicariously.

3D means Earth, yes, but not *only* Earth. Humans means homo sapiens, yes, but not *only* homo sapiens. We don't need to pursue the subject, but don't let it slip entirely out of mind.

As to angels and demons being the same thing, yes in that they are two examples of unchanging beings not shaped by the 3D experience even when they participate in 3D events, for then they are *in* 3D but not *of* it. That is, they share the 3D dimensions but have not been confined to them as human consciousness more or less is or experiences itself as being.

But we could look more closely into the question of angels as they react to events. I can't think of a way to put it that is clearer than that, and maybe this is too much to get into, but let's see.

Take the story of Lucifer, the light-carrier, who refused to admit that compound beings could become of greater worth than angels. (That's one way of reading the story.) Lucifer and "the fallen angels" of the story rebelled against being placed lower in the scales. Taking that story as a given, see that they didn't choose which *part of* themselves to follow. Instead, *what they were* chose a course of action. You see the difference? It wasn't a matter of angels choosing what to be, as humans do; it was a matter of choosing how to express what they were and are and must always continue to be. The expression can change—they can change their minds and conduct, so to speak—but they cannot follow another fish, for there is no other fish to follow.

Now, the entire story of good and bad angels, and temptation and warfare over human souls, is true enough but cannot be seen correctly if forced into a 3D orientation that assumes human individuals to be integral rather than compound, for instance. But the 3D world is surrounded by non-3D beings who silently interact with it and attempt to sway humans to be more one thing and less another. In so doing, the angels are only acting as their natures dictate, and—remember this!—what is "good" and "bad" is still the fruit of the Tree of Perceiving Things as Good or Evil.

Outside of duality, this would all look different, but how do we escape duality, except conceptually, given that the non-3D and the 3D alike are existing within it? I will leave that as a rhetorical question.

I will defer consideration of the larger beings until another time.

Thank you, Rita, it continues to be most interesting. I had a thought, overnight. Did you take time to plan all this? In other words, did the time between March 2008 and December 2014 go at least partially to your planning out a course of lectures?

That isn't the simple question you think it is. Add it to the queue.

Okay. Till next time, then.

Monday, February 9, 2015

4 a.m. Rita, Jim Austin poses the following question:

Well, I had gotten thus far when, rereading the question that I had printed out for the morning, I realized that it was what we had worked on yesterday, and I had to reread the previous session in order to remember where we were. So I guess we should resume with a discussion of this much:

> [From Jim Austin: "{Rita} strongly suggests we look ... at 'the relationship' between larger selves, those with 3D experience, and those without (later referred to as 'unitary beings'). Earlier, she relates that larger beings are a unique factor, implying they/ we (through the experiences gained in 3D life) are constantly changing. So how is this useful in daily life?"]

The question is based on a partial misinterpretation of what I meant. I seem not to have made myself plain, and such questions serve a valuable function for any teacher, showing her where she has inadvertently led her students astray. Or "he," of course.

That's all right, I am not a masculinist, or whatever the equivalent of feminist would be.

Oh? I hadn't noticed.

Smiling. Touché. Anyway—

An undivided reality

I contrasted what we—following the guys' nomenclature—are calling the larger being, on the one hand, with angels. The contrast was between a compound being, that by its nature changes continually, and a unitary, or perhaps we should say, internally consistent being that does not and can not change. Each has its function, and the functioning and the nature of each can be best illustrated by comparing one to the other.

Again—I dislike being so repetitious (to the point of tedium, it seems to me), but let me remind you to bear ever in mind in these discussions the nature of reality as undivided rather than physical v. nonphysical. If you allow yourselves to slip back into the accustomed scheme dividing physical and nonphysical *as if they were different universes*, rather than different parts of the same universe, your thought will split into two, probably unknown to yourselves, and rather than a reorientation you will experience merely a playing with words.

But if you can remember that reality is undivided and that what you are experiencing in 3D is really only a localized version of a more comprehensive experience, you will remember that there can be no true division into body and spirit, only a different placing of emphasis. You in bodies nonetheless inhabit the higher dimensions you are mostly unaware of. We not in bodies nonetheless inhabit the 3D world though our consciousness is not tethered to it by bodies, and is not limited to it by the tricks of perception caused by living in time-slices and relying primarily upon sensory data for our orientation.

Thus you can see two things. First, interaction is continuous, whether perceived or not. Second, *your*, as well as *our*, field of activity is not limited to 3D. (This sort of ignores the fact that, as I have said, "we" and "you" are not separate from each other; that fact alone should demonstrate that one cannot be in one place only and the other in another place only.)

So it will be worth your while to remember that when we say "the larger being" we refer to the beings of which you, and we, are part.

Discovering unconscious assumptions

Now, this is such a simple statement that it requires considerable explanation to be sure that it is not misunderstood. And a short digression to tell you why that is so as a general rule: The shorter the statement, the greater the chance that it will be accepted without processing. You might think, "well, that's well and good," but, in fact, it allows you to create your own version of what it means, because a host of unconscious associations will arise within you, and will be attached to the words, and it will seem to you that the short statement "obviously" meant something shaped by your unconscious assumptions.

Colin Wilson used to call TGU [my acronym for The Guys Upstairs, or The Gentlemen Upstairs] "the Man Upstairs" in emails to me, which showed me that he was thinking of them as singular, and probably thought I was employing a code-word for God. There is no way that TGU can spell The Man Upstairs, so it seemed clear to me that Colin, who was way too intelligent to make such an elementary error, was seeing what I was saying through his own filters.

As everyone does, of course. The trick is to become as aware of them as possible, so as to become able to correct for the consequent (and antecedent) bias. That is the value of *thinking about* these things rather than merely accepting or rejecting them by reference to the understandings you bring to the discussion ahead of time.

So, process the question of what "the larger being" suggests to your mind. Realize that *there is no way you can trust unconscious assumptions to be correct.*

Reread that, if you will. I realize that it *seems to* contradict the very process of trusting intuition that we are engaged in (for how different is it, to trust intuition or to talk to "the other side" or to receive messages from one's own non-3D self?), but, in fact, it is very much consistent with one of the major themes you have received, Frank, from the beginning of the process of active communication in the 1980s—use *both* processes, logic and intuition. Use *both* analysis and perception. Avoid Psychic's Disease and Closed-Mind equally.

And so you can see that this is one reason why that is to be desired: Only by receptivity can you expand beyond sensory-driven logic, but only by conscious thought can you discover and correct for unconscious bias.

Defining the larger being

Bearing this in mind, among the many things "the larger being" does *not* mean are:

- God

- All humanity

- All creation

- Yourself and a few kindred souls only

- The creator of the universe (if you conceive of this as different from God)

Any of these assumptions will send you down different garden paths. For our purposes, let us define them so:

Larger beings incorporate smaller but similar consciousnesses and function in a way that is different and incomprehensible to those elements that comprise them.

Remember, you experience yourselves (usually) as if you were units, whereas it is at least equally true to say that you are communities. In fact, it might be closer to the truth to say that an individual in 3D is a community learning to function as a unit, and the unit is designed to function as one unit in a larger community functioning as a unit, and so on and so forth, all the way up and down the chain of being.

> [At first I wrote, "one unit in a larger community learning to function as a unit," but then I stopped, went back and changed it to "functioning." I note this because it felt like a correction was being insisted on, and in the process of transcribing, I see that the two versions convey very different meanings.]

But "the chain of being" doesn't include noncompound—integral—beings. It refers to compound beings.

Does this imply that our cells are themselves compound beings?

That is exactly what it implies and it is true, what you intuited, that you as an individual are the equivalent to them of their larger being, and your communications to them are equivalent (to them) of messages from TGU. That is, they experience communications from another order of intelligence whose true mode of operation is a mystery to them.

Again, as above, so below.

Yes, only bear in mind, the world is full of many things besides compound beings formed of 3D experience. And one way in which the larger beings are compound is that they may be composed of elements some of which have *not* been shaped by 3D, as well as some that have. Just because we examine any given element in isolation does not mean it may rightly be considered to be truly isolated. All things connect. It is merely that for the purpose of close examination and analysis, you can look at only so much at a time.

I was struck by something you said in passing yesterday to the effect that any generalization is a slurring of certain differences and an emphasis, perhaps an over-emphasis, on certain similarities.

Given time and attention such distortions iron out, but it *does* take time and attention.

Now, your hour is over, and a bit more. I believe we have answered the question not as posed but as it would be better posed. If not, we can come back to it.

The only loose thread I see is, "How is this useful in daily life?"

There could be two alternate answers to that. One, the answer is implied in the description of what the larger being is. (Consider the difference between our definition and the unconscious assumptions built into the term "higher self," for instance.) The second is, "that's a large topic in itself; either that, or it is the theme of this entire work." Sorry to be so cryptic, but that's enough said, at least for the moment. We can continue with question #12 next time.

Okay, Rita. Continued thanks.

Tuesday, February 10, 2015

11 a.m. Given that we didn't get to talk earlier today, and given that I'm not really hitting on all cylinders yet (but given that the alternative is packing books, getting ready

*for my move!), I thought maybe we could try this directly on the computer rather than
writing it out in longhand first. If so, that will save more than an hour of work. Rita, is
this fine with you?*

The experimentation with procedure is fine with me, provided that you
don't let yourself get overextended. Today is a good day for this experiment,
in that the questions are small and easily disposed of. Take them in any
order you wish.

Love and fear in duality

*All right, let's start with this one: "3D is not really a duality but instead a continuum
in which we look at both ends of one stick. Is this true of love and fear as well?"*

The short answer is "yes," and for once there are not caveats or crosscurrents to look at. Although people talk about living in pure love, entirely
banishing fear, that is more an ideal to be lived toward than a goal that can
actually be reached. This, despite what people claim. If you are living in
a world of duality, what makes you think you can station yourself on the
extreme end of the spectrum and not participate in the other end, or rather,
in gradations?

No reincarnation?

*Makes sense to me. All right, how about this one? "In one sense there is no reincarna-
tion. Neither Rita, Frank, nor Charles will return other than as a strand in a new
entity or soul. Is this correct?"*

Again, yes. In this case we need remind you that the question as posed
says "in one sense." Look at it another way and it looks quite different. This,
though, not for today, because we are not going to do a full session, or anything like it. Just make a note that the question could be considered in more
detail and from different starting places.

Memory

*Another, as we continue to gallop through the easy ones. Charles says, "Andrew
Bartzis says Earth is a 100 percent free will and no memory planet. No memory*

presumably means we do not recall the strands and bundles that comprise us. While in 3D wouldn't it make life easier if we could relate to the strands composing us?"

Remember, the fact that someone says something, even if with great certainty, has *nothing* to do with whether the statement is accurate. Your own experiences, and those of so many TMI participants (that is, people whose firsthand testimony you can weigh), tells you otherwise. If it is a "no memory planet," how did the field of past-life review and NDE experiencer and psychic communication across time and space come to be? And as to 100 percent free will, that is true *in a certain sense* of the words. From any given moment of time (which, of course, is always experienced as "the present"), your free will is at least theoretically large. However, it is hardly unlimited! Everything that came before that moment could be regarded as a limiting factor. This statement is at best somewhat true, but not very.

The demonstration of the fact that it is not very true is that, in fact, you can relate to the strands composing you. It is a skill that can be learned, which means it is not closed off.

Is 3D functioning correctly?

Another? "Why was the 3D world created? Is it working as it was planned? If not, is it possible to change the direction and get it back to its original formation?"

This one makes me smile. Do clouds work the way they were planned? Do the elements of any system you can name work the way they were planned? And if they did not, would 3D individuals, even working in close harmony with their non-3D components, know what to do to bring things back to balance?

This one, I'm afraid, is going to require too long an answer for today's energy level to handle. Charles asks, "I'd like to turn the conversation to the questions of why the 3D world was created, why larger beings continue to create new souls, and why the 3D experience so often feels like 'suffering.' Several people have asked questions about reincarnation with the hope they would not have to return. I think readers would like to know how to learn to make better choices, presumably in line with the reason for the creation of 3D and with the help of their larger beings."

You are quite right. Save this one for another day, and the other one as well.

Well, we did get at least something done. Are you okay with the process?

[I meant, my typing rather than writing and then transcribing.]

It doesn't matter on this end except insofar as it renders you more able or less able to do the work. Suit yourself and experiment away.

Okay, thanks. More tomorrow, I hope.

Wednesday, February 11, 2015

4:45 a.m. Well, Miss Rita, here we go again. Since I spent so much of yesterday sleeping—and woke up a while ago realizing I am well again—no reason to delay starting.

Always a pleasure to remember the feeling of being well. It's easy to take for granted, no matter how much experience we have. Possibly that's a good segue to our topic of the day, suffering. But first, a thought on yesterday's experiment. You said you don't care how I do it, handwriting or computer, but it felt different to me, perhaps not quite as connected.

You were not quite as connected. The method had nothing to do with it. You were ill, and that's going to affect your perceptions and your abilities. But if you don't mind the extra work of transcribing, handwriting has the advantage of being a little slower, a little more—well, it gives you a little time to sink into a given sentence as it is being expressed. Your defining characteristic is *speed*; therefore you experience its limitations as well as its advantages. So something that slows you down a little is not an obstacle. For others, it might be. One size does *not* fit all.

Well, while we've been off-line, so to speak, Charles has been thinking about how to proceed, absorbing other people's questions, thinking about what is most useful and most practical to try to learn. Before I ask the questions he posed for today, do you have any thoughts on the subject of what is the most useful? Or, come to think of it, would you care to point us toward the theme of the book—if it is to be a book—or of the conversations anyway?

Of course I have a theme in mind, but perhaps it is better if each person derives his or her own idea as we go along. The danger, you see, is that if I explicitly were to say, "the theme is—" then everything said after that point, not to mention *before* that point, might be *forced* into conformity with what someone assumed I meant by the theme. Fluidity in perception is much more important than consistency of thought. In fact, the effort to enforce consistency would be a great impediment. So I think I will decline to state my intentions, and you will have to figure them out as best you can, in the only way you ever absorb new material—you will have to wrestle with it, question it, question *yourself*, be alert for your own possible unconscious assumptions and be willing to question them once they happen to come to light.

I can accept that. That's my usual mode, I suppose.

Actually not, but we don't need to go into that here and now.

Cruelty and suffering

Very well. Here's Charles's question as I rephrased it and he agreed, and a follow-up he added.

[Charles: "Suffering: It's difficult trying to reconcile 'all is well' with the conditions in 3D. Some statistics: 45.2 million people are living in refugee camps, 21,000 people die of starvation each day, 500,000 people murdered in a year. Of course, I wouldn't know this if I didn't read the news on the Internet, because it's not my subjective reality. Is the 3D person choosing these circumstances? Is it true that no matter what happens, car accidents, cancer, etc., we in 3D are making the choice? Or is non-3D making the choice and we in 3D are the focal point to see how we handle it? And the question from Martha fits nicely depending on the answer you get."

[Martha: "Every day I ask what in the world can be the purpose of all of the suffering in the world? After eons of time, haven't these so called larger beings had enough of it? I'm sure their 3D strands would appreciate a break from these never-ending plotlines of pain and war, disease and poverty, pollution and cruelty. And back to yesterday's session, could she expand on the part about non-3D entities that interact with us and how much influence they have as telepathic trouble-makers or helpers?"]

As you may imagine, I see the question quite a lot differently now than I did when I was in the body. As you will remember, I was quite concerned about all these things, and I ached to be able to do something effective to stop it all, but there was so little I could do. Sending money to charities was about the practical limit to my ability, and that seemed so limited as to be almost pathetic. I kept up with the news, more so as my physical mobility became more limited and my world constricted. So it was a reorientation for me when we heard the guys first say, "All is well. All is *always* well." It took quite a while before I came to believe it. At first I took it provisionally, in the way one does, tasting it, feeling how we respond to it. And I questioned them on it, I seem to remember, but gently. I was asking the questions, and if I got answers I didn't expect or didn't immediately understand or agree with, should I quarrel with the answer, or pursue it until I was sure I understood? And, in fact, over time I came to see what they meant, and came to at least provisionally accept it.

But we did not have you "there" to explain it to us.

We did, in a way, of course. I was here then as you are here now. But I know what you mean. So I will try to give the explanation that would have helped me then.

You, Frank, will remember the explanation about childhood trauma. But others will not, so I'll mention it here. I was bemoaning its lasting effects that could persist through a person's entire life, warping their perceptions and inhibiting their choices—their *real* choices, available to them—and the guys reframed it, saying that if someone came into life wanting to experience a certain set of things, of which feelings, emotions, reactions would all be part—a childhood trauma that enabled/required them to continually call to themselves reminders, or triggers, that would lead them to experience it again would be very useful, ensuring that they would experience the same thing, from slightly different angles, until they were through with it, either in that life or when the life was ended.

Or afterwards?

They didn't say that, but it is true, in the form of unfinished business, it could continue into another life. And bookmark this statement, it is important. But to stick to the subject at hand:

It is in that sense that all is always well. *Suffering is useful.*

Now, that doesn't mean that *inflicting* suffering is justified, nor that observing it unmoved is justified. One's reaction to observing the suffering of others stems from one's value system and one's ability to feel. The fact that suffering is useful to the person suffering does not justify sadism or indifference.

However, the fact that suffering occurs in life is only to be expected in a world of duality. But this is a very tangled subject, with interrelated themes.

- Justice of the world

- Manifestation of hidden relationships

- Delusions of competence

Let's stop with just those three, for the moment.

The justice of the world

The world is *just*. However, any particular time-slice is apt to be very unbalanced, full of what looks like injustices. It is as if you were, on Tuesday, to see all the week as Tuesday and think how out of proportion it is, for it never to be Wednesday. An absurd example, but I meant to show that any judgment of a situation made from consideration only of a present moment is necessarily going to be so constricted, so short-sighted, as to be wildly inadequate.

As an example, tell the story of the man at Timelines in 2003.

Mick had been raised by parents who were abusive and allowed him no free will whatever. He was punished for the most trivial things. After one of the exercises, he relived a memory of a life in which he had done the same thing to others. The point was not to punish him, but now he knew what it felt like.

But as I'm writing that here, I'm seeing all kinds of reincarnation questions arising.

Defer them. The point is, the world never seems just, and at any given moment it probably never *is* just. But seen from a larger view, it is and must be. Again, that doesn't mean it is all right to be cruel or indifferent. It means, by all means, express your compassion, but don't think that because this person or that group of people is suffering, therefore the world is unjust. *They* in this lifetime may have done nothing to "deserve" what is done to them. But nothing happens to anyone that is not fully compensated, see it or not, believe it or not.

So, justice. But we had better stop here and continue another time.

All right. I must say, "manifestation of hidden relationships" was clear to me as I wrote it down, but now I have no idea what it means.

I guess you'll have to stay tuned, won't you?

I guess I will. Till next time, then.

Thursday, February 12, 2015

Controversy

4:30 a.m. We'll try it directly on the computer this morning, Rita. I'm too tired to think of writing and then transcribing. We'll see how it goes. If I can tell a difference, maybe I'll have to abort and start again in the journal, either today or next time.

But I was lying in bed unable to sleep—unable to turn off the thoughts—and as I expect you know, it started with the dreams I woke from an hour ago or more, particularly the one involving you. For the record, I'll record the dream. I can't help wondering if it was a communication from you, or a dramatization of my internal state, or what.

I was doing something—looking in a garage, I think—and I became aware that a car came up behind me, and paused, and moved on, going up an alley on my left. I thought to look at it, and I could recognize your head of silver hair in the back seat. So I followed, but when we were all together, there were a lot of people there. Besides you and me, there was a woman who helped take care of you who I knew [in the dream, not in real life] and her daughter that I didn't know she had, and my brother Joe, dead these 35 years, who dropped into the scene and lay there, I think unconscious. All those people are in the way of your and my communication with each other and I wondered, either in the dream or outside of it, whether all this controversy about suffering may be creating static on the line, or, alternatively, if static might be the result of doing this wire-walking in public. There were more dreams, but I don't remember them. In any case, your comments please, and then can we continue stirring people up by talking about a subject on which they have strong opinions.

It will be worth your while to look at the dream closely, but this is not the time and in public is not the way. You might say that I was prompting you—reminding you of certain preconditions—but it's always a mistake to reduce a dream to a simple message, just as it would be to reduce a novel to a description of the plot. Simplification is always distortion. Necessary distortion, sometimes, but distortion nonetheless.

Of course I am aware of the controversy about the topic of suffering. In such cases, the conclusions people come to are less important than the question of whether their thought processes were activated or not. That is, when the subject arose, did their truth-detector, as you call it, engage, or did they play old tapes of opinions previously arrived at? If the former, they had engaged with the material; if the latter, they have not. Progress may come out of engagement, regardless of conclusions and final stances (assuming there could be such a thing as a "final" stance), but what could result from refusal or inability to engage?

The potential for static on the line comes not from others but from yourself, of course. When is it ever different in life? "If only 'they' were different, or acted differently, then I wouldn't have to—" etc. That often seems true and never is, and a good thing it isn't, or your free will would be dependent on outside variables.

Viktor Frankl said the one thing no one can take from us is the ability to choose our attitude toward what happens to us.

And he learned that wisdom in a hard school. So the point is, don't let your awareness of others listening in, and don't let your concern over their possible reactions, move you off the place where you need to be, to engage in this enterprise. I on my end promise that I won't be thrown off the rails either. There is a big difference, you see, between being flexible and responsive, on the one hand, and being dependent upon external feedback, on the other.

Now, that's all I am going to say about your dream. You have the resources to explore it further, and I would advise you to use them, but not in public.

Delusions of competence

To return to the subject of suffering.

I just glanced back, to refresh my memory. You said three things— the world is just, and then you were going to talk about the manifestation of hidden relationships and delusions of competence.

Many of the difficulties people have with this and related subjects stem from the mind's persistent pattern of reverting to thinking of people as unitary individuals rather than as functioning communities. If you think in those terms—especially if you don't *think* so much as automatically (unconsciously) *assume*—you come up with logical sounding and often persuasive descriptions of the way things must be. So if you can't stand the idea of the universe being unjust, and yet you see bad things happening to good people, to quote an old book title, you invent the idea that everything that happens to you now is payback for something you did earlier, or, presumably, is an advance payment that you can use at a later time to amortize something you haven't done yet!

But even the idea of "bad" and "good" people is a distortion based on an inadequate concept of what we truly are and how we truly function. We won't follow that up at the moment, but make a note of it. The point will be obvious to some, less so to others. And in fact, the previous paragraph is full of similar distortions all caused by unconscious assumptions. That we know what a "bad" thing is, for instance. That "bad" things shouldn't happen to "good" people if this were a just world. That everything has to be repaid. (It does, actually, but not in the way that is so often assumed when people begin throwing around words like Karma.)

So let us talk about hidden relationships. Or come to think of it, let's dispose of delusions of competence, since it will require only a few words and we're halfway there.

People have strong feelings about what they see or think they see, and those feelings are rooted in their values, and so far well and good. But that doesn't mean they are competent to judge what they see. It doesn't mean they understand or that they even see clearly. Think how scientists continually see more and more deeply, the more they investigate any phenomenon. The whole field of chaos studies, invented about five seconds ago (in terms of a civilization's lifespan), suddenly demonstrated that what looked—well, chaotic—had implicit laws that it followed. Think of it! *Chaos* is rooted in *order*, and order in chaos. The more closely you look at anything, the more complex it reveals itself to be, and the more interrelated.

Yet people think themselves competent to judge and even condemn, because it offends their sense of the fitness of things.

I remember the guys telling you that just because you don't like sharks, that doesn't mean the world doesn't need predators, and also scavengers. They said without killers the world would be awash with live bodies, and without scavengers it would be awash with dead ones. As I recall, you didn't like the answer much.

No, I can't say that I did. But I respected it, and that's the difference. A scholar learns to respect the data, not quarrel with it, and to wrestle with the argument, not dismiss it. It was easier, perhaps, because Bob [Monroe] always said Earth was a system of organized predation modified by the existence of love.

The point here is that there is a very big and crucial difference between rejecting an argument because something within you feels that it is untrue, and rejecting it because something within you says, "by rights, it *shouldn't* be true." The latter amounts to pretending to know the dynamics of the system, and also sets up your own morality as presumably superior to that of the creator of the system.

It still surprises me how easily people talk about making "a better world," as if they or anyone knew how to do it. Working on our own stuff, sure; we can do that, and it's a lifetime job. But reforming others? Or putting some automatic mechanism into place that will fix things? I don't think so.

But, you see, working on yourself *is* the way to make a better world, and thank you for that deft segue.

You're welcome. Any time.

Hidden relationships

Once you stop thinking of yourselves as unitary individuals and experience yourselves as communities, you begin to realize that you extend in all directions as well as backward and forward in time. If you have uncounted strands, each of which was an "individual" comprising uncounted strands, which each—. You see? *You* change what *you* are and you impact parts of yourself that you will never experience until your consciousness centers on the non-3D and you can see yourself as you actually are rather than as you look in any one particular time-slice that you call "right now." As you have experienced, Frank, and as many others have experienced somewhat less publicly, you, in your present, can impact and therefore change other strands of yourself in *their* present [i.e., the time in which they live], which in turn will have further ramifications, again usually unsuspected by you.

That is the power to change the world. That is the *only* power to change the world. The only power you *have*, and the only power you *need*. Because, perhaps it may not have occurred to you, changing the physical world at any given moment is not the point of all this. The physical is a subset of the non-physical, created to serve a specific purpose, and doing so. *You* are the purpose of the whole exercise, not foreign relations or the elimination of poverty or a cure for cancer. All things pass away, but does the nonphysical pass away?

This is a part of what I mean by hidden relationships. Another part is that you do not know the healing effects that suffering can produce, or the growth. It is always a mistake to judge the suffering of others as if you knew. You don't, you can't, and in a sense, it isn't any of your business. To alleviate the causes of suffering is well and good. Who can argue against it? To *want to* alleviate it, however, is not necessarily any more than an emotional impulse. At worst, a self-indulgence, reassuring yourself that you are a caring individual. To condemn the world for containing what you perceive to be injustices is to arrogate to yourself the right to judge what is beyond your ability to understand, let alone to prescribe how to cure. *Actions always have unanticipated consequences.* The evil that you shut the door to here may come with redoubled force through the window there.

Now, that's enough for today, and if it is any comfort to you, I don't think that doing it on the computer costs you anything in clarity as long as you don't succumb to the temptation to go back and revise.

Okay. Well, more next time. Our thanks as always. (And I am glad not to have to type all this in again.)

Friday, February 13, 2015

Choosing your attitude

5:40 a.m. Good morning, Miss Rita. I'm going to try this on the computer again, since yesterday seemed to work out well enough. If we ever get to a patch where speed works against me, I trust you will advise me to go back to pen and paper.

I would be more likely to advise you not to change your environment but to change your stance within it. Changing your environment is all well and good, but it is a roundabout way to accomplish what may be accomplished easily and simply once you know how to do so, and you do know that. It is a matter of choosing your attitude. Just as you can choose to reject a mood that tempts you—you don't *have to* be mad, you don't *have to* be impatient, or depressed, or discouraged (nor, elated, exalted, or other

varieties of emotional experience more on the manic end of the scale)—
so you don't have to fall into any habitual behavior, once your consciousness is aware of what is happening. So now, if I were to say to you, "Frank,
slow down a little; you're moving too fast to sink into the connection," you
would know how to do it and wouldn't therefore react to the suggestion as
a criticism, but as merely a helpful suggested course-correction.

*Okay. I presume that hint was made for others as well, given that I got the gist of
it long before I finished typing out the sentences.*

Pretty much everything we're doing is for others to benefit from as
well, if they can. A distinction between what is meant for one and what is
meant for all is usually an arbitrary one anyway.

A survey cruise

*So as you know, Charles has provided quite a queue of suggested questions around the
topic of suffering and the related topic of good and evil. And as you no doubt also know,
we're perfectly happy with you proceeding wherever you wish to go. What you don't
answer today in one way will probably be answered another day, in another context.*

That's right. You might think of this as a survey cruise.

*Meaning, I take it, the peacetime cruises the U.S. Navy used to make, and perhaps
still does make, in which the ship is aimed down a specific line, and soundings are taken
every so many feet until they have a chart of depths along that line—and then they
alter course, go over the same ground at a different angle, and do it all again, until they
have a pretty accurate map of the depths beneath their keel. Thus, survey charts. Probably an obsolete procedure in this era of satellites, but of course, I don't know. In any
case, a nice analogy to what we're doing.*

If you keep to that analogy, it should ease any anxiety you might have as
to whether we will miss something important if we go left instead of right,
up instead of down.

Also, I remind you, there's no hurry. We are not having to hasten to
catch up, lest we get left. The 3D world has been going for quite a while, and

the non-3D world for quite a while longer than that, so it isn't like there's
any rush, here. Impatience, yes, and well I remember it. But rush, no.

Very well, let's look at a few of those questions and I will try to clear the
ground of misunderstandings, and we'll see where it takes us.

An assumption of separation

Okay, here's the tag end of Charles's earlier question that hasn't been addressed yet, I
think. After citing a couple of statistics on the prevalence of suffering in the world, he
asked, "Is the 3D person choosing these circumstances? Is it true that no matter what
happens, car accidents, cancer, etc., we in 3D are making the choice? Or is non-3D
making the choice and we in 3D are the focal point to see how we handle it?"

Yes, this is a good starting place, and you might as well throw in the
other question that he suggested might follow depending on what you got
about the first one.

> [Martha's question: "Every day I ask what in the world can be
> the purpose of all of the suffering in the world? After eons of
> time, haven't these so called larger beings had enough of it?
> I'm sure their 3D strands would appreciate a break from these
> never-ending plotlines of pain and war, disease and poverty,
> pollution and cruelty. And back to yesterday's session, could
> she expand on the part about non-3D entities that interact
> with us and how much influence they have as telepathic trou-
> ble makers or helpers?"]

I hardly know how to address the question, as it is so laden with hot
buttons wired to dynamite. Any given angle of approach—speaking of sur-
veys!—presents problems not so much inherent in the material, though it
will seem like that, as inherent in people's ingrained automatic responses to
approaches to the material. I mention this not as a complaint, nor really as
a description of difficulty, so much as a red flag so that readers may be aware
of their own part in their reactions. An emotional reaction usually seems
inevitable, as if any right-thinking person would naturally *have to* respond
to a given statement in a certain way. But in fact, just as I mentioned a

moment ago, it is always a choice, but the individual may or may not be *aware* that it is a choice. So reader, if you feel your hackles rising, it would be valuable for you to observe and choose your reaction. *Valuable entirely regardless of what your finally chosen attitude is.* This is not about opinions, but about consciousness.

Charles's question rests on an assumption that is not true, and so does Martha's. The assumption, all the more powerful for being unconscious, of course, is that there is a meaningful difference between you in 3D and we in non-3D. The very language asserts this to be a true distinction—the language of my previous sentence asserts it—but it is wrong, and I have been at some pains to build a picture of reality that would help overcome this linguistic bias.

This is *one* world. We all extend to all of it. There is no division between 3D and non-3D in the commonly accepted sense; no "veil" to penetrate, no bridge to cross to get to the other side; no "other side." *One* world. 3D beings are part of larger beings that may be partly in 3D and partly not in 3D, but are of the same substance, and therefore of the same nature, functioning in different terrain and therefore appearing different.

I know it can be difficult to hold that in mind, but to the extent that you can, you will avoid many complications that are *apparent* but not *real.* That is, they *seem* real, but are actually optical illusions.

If 3D and non-3D beings were units, individuals, and could be validly considered to be different in nature rather than all part of the same thing, then it would be possible to look at life as a matter of "who's responsible, here? Who is pulling the strings, and who is being made to dance to them?" but suppose you asked that of movements of your legs, dancing? Who is responsible for the movement? The brain directing? The localized intelligence executing? And what difference would the answer make? *It would be an unmeaningful answer, because it is an unmeaningful question.*

And it tempts us back into the villains-and-victims scenario.

It does. If one or the other is responsible, one or the other is to blame, or is being put upon. So, you are dancing. Is your brain to blame? Is your link to the non-3D (where your mind, rather than your brain, resides) to blame? Is it your legs? Is it your nervous system, your musculature, your acquired sense of balance? You could *decide upon* an answer, but it would be the result of a decision, rather than the necessary conclusion presented by an impartial review of the facts.

This doesn't answer Martha's initial question, "what in the world can be the purpose of all of this suffering in the world," but it does dispose of the follow-up statements posed as questions. Since you are well beyond your hour, we can stop here and continue next time with just that question, which after all is the root of all the questions on the topic—what is the purpose of suffering in the world?

All right. It seems to me the process of typing directly into the computer continues smoothly enough to warrant further continuance. Yes?

I'll let you know if I see a problem.

Till next time, then.

Saturday, February 14, 2015

7 a.m. Late start this morning, though I don't mind. Well, Miss Rita, I certainly do feel like I am riding a runaway horse, not for the first time. Performing in public like this is bringing in questions faster than we can deal with them, and now Charles is offering me several questions and saying, if not this one, try this one, or this one, etc.

So—just a note on the process as I am experiencing it—there is the pull of the continuity of your narrative (you say, "next time we could begin here") and the pull of past threads to be followed ("bookmark that and we will talk about it another time") and the pull of individual responses in the form of email and blog comments ("Rita said x and such, but it seems to me . . .") and Charles's own requests for clarification from me, and then as I say the posing of alternate questions we could ask.

None of this bothers me, and I'm delighted that enough people are taking the material seriously enough to wrestle with it and respond to it. But I'm sure glad to have that naval soundings survey analogy to reassure me that in a sense, we can't really get lost. And I'm glad to have Charles's presence as a sheet anchor to windward. I can see

that it would be easy to lose all sense of direction, exploring these things. In fact, I won-
der if that isn't more or less what I have done, all these years.

A compass

In wondering that, you are showing yourself to be a child of the age you live
in. So do many of your questioners. I mean by that, you are disregarding
the continuing presence in your life of your nonphysical self. This is a bit
of a diversion from the topic of suffering and good and evil, but it won't
take long, perhaps, and pursuing the thread because it presented itself is an
example of a way to live connected.

You have a compass.

What good is a compass to a navigator who doesn't know it exists, or
doesn't consult it? None. But the compass is there, used or unused. Why should
you or anybody fear getting lost, as long as you are consulting your compass?
And if you don't consult it—tacitly or not, that is, doing it consciously or automatically, either one—how can you expect to follow any course?

Between us, we're in a nautical mood today, I see. I take it you mean what the
church would call conscience, only in a wider sense than knowledge of whether an
action or thought or projected action or thought is good and evil.

The physical self forms what we loosely call an ego, and that ego is conscious of what the senses report to it, plus what its reactions to its environment report to it as emotions. As long as the ego's world remains bounded
by such limits, you have a very small boat in a very big sea, terrified of
storms, navigating at random, subject to course correction by emotional
reaction to any stray circumstance. But when that ego realizes that it has a
compass, everything changes, or can change, if the compass is intelligently
used. The ego's higher self (call it) not only can read the compass, it can
connect to GPS. It not only knows where the boat is, it knows how it got
there, and why, and where it set out for. And—stretching the analogy quite
a bit, but true to life—the higher self knows that it is the cause as well as the
experiencer of the circumstances the little boat finds itself in. Or, not quite.
Let's say, it recognizes that no storm or difficulty or anything that comes to
be experienced is either random or purposeless.

But let's drop the analogy at that point. You see that I mean to say that if it were up to you (as it often seems to you) to shape your lives, you would be vastly overmatched.

Always outnumbered, always outgunned, as I read somewhere.

So in this particular instance, if it were up to Charles as his ego exists or you as your ego exists and neither of you were in connection with your "higher selves," your non-3D components that have never left you nor ever could leave you, then yes, you'd be lost in moments. But it is the very connection with the non-3D that renders this possible. Renders your *lives* possible.

And in the non-3D part of ourselves, we live and move and have our being.

Well, isn't that a perfectly valid way to describe your situation?

It certainly seems so to me, and of course I find it satisfying to have a way of understanding the 2,000-year old Christian tradition without having to sign on to their contemporary understandings of it. I mean, all that knowledge and wisdom, couched in language that we find unmeaningful—I always knew it meant something, even if it didn't mean what it was explained to mean.

And where do you think that knowing came from, if not your non-3D extension, or source? You tended to think of it as past-life knowledge, I think, but in that case, why can't you read Egyptian?

I'd like to know that myself. But as you always say, let's consider that at another time. The hour is half over and we haven't gotten to the question yet.

I think you will find that we have, actually. It's all tied together. How can we discuss the question of good and evil, and of suffering, and of the question of the meaning of life, if we allow ourselves to disregard the fact that appearances are not accurate, that you are not boats afloat in an unknown sea, adrift, with no origin, no purpose, no projected port, no task, no larger purpose?

I remember Joshua Lawrence Chamberlain writing somewhere of a moment during the war when he suddenly experienced himself as part of the entire army. (He was a Union officer in the Civil War.) I don't know how to say it in few words. He had always experienced himself as an officer in the machinery, so to speak, but at this moment he had a sort of mystical sense of himself as an individual participating as part of one large thing. I suspect he was experiencing something similar to what happens when small boats realize they are part of a regatta and couldn't get lost if they wanted to. Either that, or they are fishermen as in Captains Courageous *and work alone but not lost.*

But meanwhile, I'm sure people are wondering when we're going to return more directly to the subject at hand. So let's take up where you left off, saying, "Since you are well beyond your hour, we can stop here and continue next time with just that question, which after all is the root of all the questions on the topic—what is the purpose of suffering in the world?"

Suffering as by-product

Let me suggest a slightly different way of looking at the subject that may help some people. To say, "What is the purpose of—" is to isolate something that cannot be understood in isolation. If you were to try to say, "What is the purpose of a knee in the world?" you couldn't begin to answer the question even in the simplest of ways without referring to the thigh and the calf, and even if you left it at that, it wouldn't make any sense, not really. It might, for instance, be looked at as a weakness in the leg, because obviously such a complicated joint would look like a makeshift, compared to the relative simplicity of the bones it connects. And, of course, if you want to explain about the mobility it offers, you are going to wind up talking about hips and feet and the body in general, and gravity, and musculature, and blood circulation, and the ongoing repair of cells—and there's no end to the things a simple discussion of knees would entail. And every time you tried to put it into context, somebody would be saying, "But I want to know why there have to be knees in the world, and you're telling me all these irrelevant things!"

Explaining how to make a watch.

Yes, except in this case there is no other way to do it, if the person asking the question doesn't even have the concept of time!

So rather than asking, "What is the purpose of suffering in the world?" I suggest it would be better to ask, "What is it in the nature of the world that produces suffering as a by-product?" That may sound like the same statement, but it is not. It is like explaining about exercise and how the deliberate exhaustion of the muscles' cells produces pain but also produces new growth. In this case, as so often, context is everything. If you were to decree that nothing should ever produce pain, because you have decided that pain is bad, then what have you just done to life? How many doors have you closed off? How many activities of greater interest and with greater rewards have you just foreclosed?

I agree, of course, though I don't know how it will look after I disengage and our joint mind is not shaping my perceptions!—but I predict that some will look at this as merely an apology for evil.

No doubt. But you can learn from a lesson or you can reject it—you can't really do both.

And here we are at the end of an hour, unless you want to continue.

No, I am content. I think you will find that this was a better session than you think. Right at the moment, you are thinking "we didn't even get to the question until it was half over," but when you come to look at it, you may think differently.

Well, we'll see. Till next time, then.

Sunday, February 15, 2015

Modes of operation

5 a.m. Good morning, Rita. Your rephrasing of the question as, "What is it in the nature of the world that produces suffering as a by-product?" seems to have opened doors for Charles. He suggests that you continue along that line. Or, of course, we could follow another of his suggestions.

And before you begin either, I might ask what's wrong with me this morning? I have rephrased this question several times. I don't feel particularly clear-headed, though I am not sleepy, and I feel like the temperature here is way too hot, even though I just checked the thermostat and moved it from 65 down to 64. Is there something going on that I should know about? Is this a day when I should use the journal rather than going directly to the computer?

[pause]

No answer. Maybe I should do this another time?

You were wanting an example of how you think, which amounts to an examination of your preferred mental processes. Waiting gives you a taste of what you are, by withholding what you do easiest.

Hmm. So I daydream, basically.

You don't *construct*, anyway. You don't build logically. Consciously connecting or not, you remain in receptive mode. The paradox inheres in the fact that you can work industriously while remaining in receptive mode, but after all that paradox produces a certain kinds of writers.

Pain as feedback

Now to the question. I suggested that suffering is better seen as a by-product than as a desired result, and I could continue in different directions by continuing to use physical pain as the metaphor. Thus, pain as a signal to the body that something is wrong. Pain as a signaling system, in other words. That is one very useful attribute of pain that is easily overlooked. Pain as feedback looks very different than pain as something introduced into the world for the entertainment of the non-3D.

I am still not functioning well. I had to delete the paragraph that just came out as a garble. You never answered the question. What's wrong with me today?

It isn't a question easily answered. You can feel the difference in that it feels like the top of your head is heavier.

Whatever it is, it feels oppressive.
Like a sinus headache, without the headache?

That's a good way to describe it.

And you are wanting an explanation that says for some reason your connection isn't clear, and you are asking by means of your connection to someone centered in non-3D.

I never said it isn't ridiculous.

Just sit with it for a few moments. Either your head will clear or it won't. If it doesn't, you can always do this another time.

[5:30]

5:37 a.m. I guess I'll go read for a while, or maybe go back to bed. Not accomplishing anything here.
7:30 a.m. I guess we're not going to get anything today. Finished the book, tried napping for a while, woke up suddenly, but as I sit here, I've got nothing. I think I will pass this on to the list, for their interest, but no point in putting it on the blog or Facebook. I do wonder what's going on. There was a little dizziness, too.

Monday, February 16, 2015

Unsuspected background influences

5 a.m. Beginning again, Miss Rita. I think today I'll leave it up to you where we begin, and I'll try it in the journal, the old way. Something didn't work out yesterday, and I'm wondering if it is too many variables.

Or could it be that things beyond your ability to observe them make some times propitious and others not, and some times extremely auspicious and other times particularly unsuitable. It is a mistake to underrate the powerful influence of the background influences in your lives. You aren't immune to them, and how should you expect to be? You are a part of the great beating heart of the world, or a part of the great clockwork, if that more mechanical analogy appeals to you—part of a vast undivided eco-system that extends throughout all of 3D (because, of course, there cannot be any absolute divisions) and extends throughout all *non*-3D, as well, which is going to be a different thought to you, therefore an important one.

When in 3D—I remember it well—there is a tendency to think that the nonphysical world is unchanging, somehow static. But how could that be, given that the 3D world is *part of* it, and *reflects* it, and provides part of the background for it, as the non-3D provides part of the background for 3D? It is all in one's viewpoint, one's place to stand, which is the background and which the foreground?

The non-3D world has its tides and its seasons, and they are reflected in the mental and psychic background of life in 3D. And I'm going to leave this for now—think of it as a teaser for coming attractions—and return more directly to the question of good and evil, and of suffering, and of the justice or injustice, the compassion or indifference, of life and the factors that make life. I will talk and you will respond, internally or externally, and I will continue to talk following any sense of the lack of comprehension and the nature of the mental or emotional obstacles to understanding as we go along.

This seems to be working much better, pushing the pen across the page as I have done for so many years.

Well, as I said, it slows you down a bit, and helps in that way, so oddly enough, the extra work of transcription becomes worthwhile. Continue as you prefer.

The real nature of tragedy

Now, about good and evil. Remember that anyone reading these sessions in a fixed form—a book, a printout, a collection of emails, anything—is going to receive a lot of information in a time much more compressed than what it took to express initially. So things that are already ancient history to you—said two weeks ago, and half forgotten—will come [to the reader] within minutes of this session, perhaps. So will anything remembered through the process of random rereading, which, by the way, is a process I recommend for making new connections.

So concepts that took some time to establish will be accepted easier not only because initial readers broke the trail for them, but because the sheer weight of material will lend authority, as for instance in the case of Seth's material.

One such concept is that the world is just. Any given piece of it, seen in isolation, will seem unjust or unnecessary or even downright arbitrary, but this is because it is being seen divorced from context. The ugliest fact is nonetheless part of a seamless whole *and has its place*. Wolves kill baby deer, if they get the chance and are hungry. Cruel? Well, how about the world if any one species has no natural predators to keep it in check? A herd of deer half-starved because they have outstripped [the carrying capacity of] the environment they live in is not a pretty sight either.

But this is not a lecture on ecology beyond this one statement. *Tragedy is not what it appears to be.* And if you will walk with me a bit, I can prove it to you.

Near-death experiencers have reported what they went through on their way out of life, and you will notice that in every case, as soon as they were free of the 3D-only perspective, they not only were okay with it, usually they were glad of it, and often enough were extremely reluctant to be returned to life. So much for death as a tragedy in and of itself.

Similarly, such accounts—and accounts by scientific naturalists— notice that the animating intelligence often leaves the body before the actual trauma that ends the life.

We don't feel the splat.

We don't feel the splat, exactly. When there is no need for pain, why experience it? So much for horrible traumatic deaths.

Furthermore, various reports—from NDEers, psychics, etc.—show you that sometimes people see behind the curtain and see the inter-weavings of various free wills that produce apparently random events. It cannot be proven to anyone determined not to be convinced, but then, what can? Nevertheless, it is a fact that *nothing happens to people without their consent.* And, since that flies in the face of so much experience, let's look at it.

I can hear the howls of outrage.

Yes, outrage that I am about to say that all is well. Why? Is there an emotional payoff to believing in what you call the victims-and-villains scenario? Clearly there is, or there would be no outrage at hearing good news. However, that reaction is not to be confounded with incredulity, which is a very reasonable reaction.

That is, it is one thing to think "you're going to have to convince me, on this one!" and it is something very different to think "life is unfair and only those of a lower morality can doubt it; I am not going to be seduced." For those whose self-definition is closely tied to a belief that they are more moral, more sensitive, than the creators and maintainers of the world around them, I have nothing helpful to say other than "know yourself." For those willing to be convinced—no matter how high their standards of proof—the following:

Is it fair that cells in a body sacrifice themselves for the sake of the body as a whole? Is that even a fair description of the process, given that the cell's life and death is as it was planned for cells in general?

Is it possible for a cell to have a purpose separate from the body of which it is a part? I don't mean, can it have separate (or relatively separate) awareness; I mean, can it not be part of what it is part of?

Is it unfair that some cells become part of a fingernail and share whatever happens to that fingernail while others get to be part of "something important" like heart muscle? Is it unfair that various cells are sloughed off or sacrificed while others are not?

Of course it is unfair, or at least discriminatory—*if* you look at it from the point of view that pretends the cell is a valid frame of reference rather than a close-up of one part of an interacting organism. But if you look at the larger picture, the cell's importance and its proper place in the scheme of things changes. Not that it is insignificant, for it is not a question of number, but that it is by nature a part of a whole and cannot be understood in isolation.

But 3D life tempts you—all but coerces you—into seeing 3D lives in isolation, and of course life is going to be seen as unfair, chaotic, undirected, painful, meaningless. Is that the fault of the structure of life, or of a constricted point of view?

What is it for?

So, trauma, injustice, apparently pointless suffering, and all the results of the seven deadly sins—are they only illusion?

No, not illusion. To explain something is not the same thing as explaining it away. But they are not what they seem to be, any more than your lives in general are what they seem to be when looked at from a too-constricted perspective.

Life can *hurt*. You know it; everybody knows it. The question is, though, what does it all mean: what is it all for? If the millions who die in concentration camps are not victims, what are they? If people suffering because of other people's indifference or cruelty are not victims of injustice, what are they? Do they "deserve" to suffer? If children, or adults for that matter, spend lifetimes in constricted circumstances because of physical illness, or as a result of accidents or deliberate maimings, are they victims? Do they deserve to suffer? Are they paying for past (or future) sins?

None of these questions can be resolved meaningfully without considering the widest context of life. Any smaller context is going to look like injustice. *Context is everything* in understanding life.

And we should stop here, as your hour is up and this is a natural place to pause.

While we're pausing, Rita, I have a question. Why are we sticking pretty closely to one-hour sessions? It seems to me that when I was talking to Papa, we'd go about an hour and a half. (Of course, I may not be remembering that right.)

That was a different process, though to you it looks the same. You and he were interacting more; your contribution was based more in what you knew and learned about the facts of his life, which led you to pose questions. But you can't do that here, because you don't have any 3D data on my present life, nor what we're discussing. So you are attending a lecture rather than participating in a conversation, so it requires more attention, which burns the candle faster.

That makes sense. Okay, next time then, and I guess I'll continue with pen and ink, even though it seems like an extra step.

No reason not to do what is easiest.

Tuesday, February 17, 2015

Context

4 a.m. Okay, Miss Rita, you're on—should you choose to be. Context, in judging life?

The point should be evident. Nothing seen out of context is going to make sense, and why should anyone expect it to? Logically it amounts to a tautology: Things only make sense when seen in a way that lets them make sense. If for some reason you were to have a vested interest in "proving" that life is unfair, you could do so easily, unanswerably, merely by narrowing your focus and selecting your data. But "proving" that it is *not* unfair, though it involves widening your focus and broadening your selection criteria, is not as easy as that, which is why so many theological and philosophical efforts to do so are so unsatisfactory and, often enough, forced and unconvincing.

The fact is, the context that is critical is not selection of data in time and space—historical examples—but specifically the broadening of the process to move *beyond* time and space, to move *deeper than* time and space, because it is specifically in assuming that life is what it appears that the underlying errors of interpretation sneak in and lead to outrage and despair.

Somebody wrote somewhere that if, in the Middle Ages, a man had known that he was the last man on Earth, it wouldn't necessarily have produced the despair that it would have in the 20th century. In fact, it might not have bothered him much at all, if he was working from the assumption that God knew what He was doing. The external facts would have been the same, but the assumptions and interpretations would have produced an entirely different effect.

Without glorifying the Middle Ages unduly, that's exactly right—yet even your capitalizing the word "He" in referring to God reminds you—or ought to—that that way of seeing things can not be reintroduced nor, lightly disguised, enter in the back door. I know that isn't what you're doing, Frank, but it is important that others know explicitly that this isn't what either one of us is doing.

No, and I'm not introducing Divine Providence by calling it Evolution, either.

In any case, (not to get off on a tangent) the point is, the "modern" way of seeing the world led to several dead-ends because they seemed logically incontestable but morally repugnant and practically without a way forward.

1. Life begins at birth (or conception; choose one) and ends at death, and that's the end of it.

2. There is no "supernatural" world to relate to. No God, no angels, certainly no humans-become-dwellers-in-heaven (i.e., saints). We are alone on Earth, and that's the end of *that*.

3. We are alone in a pretty meaningless universe, and any attempt to see meaning—any teleology—is self-deluding weak-mindedness.

4. Most of our surroundings are dead. We living (who, remember, are here by accident) are a few exceptions to an overwhelmingly dead universe.

5. Because of the foregoing predicaments, you must put your hope (if you insist on having hope) in the future, in science, in social evolution, in what does not exist, *because* it does not exist.

6. By reaction against this, some move to want to destroy the entire intellectual, social, economic edifice that left them stranded, and so they become glorifiers of anything primitive, even while continuing to remain dependent upon the same infrastructure derived from the worldview they reject.

7. Similarly, others (sometimes the same people at different times, confusingly enough to themselves and to others) accept the description of the world but reject it at the same time, or, anyway, reject its consequences. They accept the premise but hope to reform the effects.

Wanting to build "a better world."

No reason to mock the impulse. I felt it myself, especially before Bob Monroe turned what I thought I knew upside down! But it is true, you can't build a better world merely by wanting to. You need to know the roots of what's wrong with it.

Now look at those few underpinnings of the dead-end view of the world. Remove them and what do you have?

Eternal life. Perpetual interaction with the other dimensions, the rest of life. Inherent meaning. A *living* universe. And there is no need to invest your hope in social movements, or the inevitable "progress" that time will no doubt provide, nor some sort of mental split that will allow you to have your materialist cake and eat your nonmaterialist values, too.

That metaphor kind of fell down, there.

So it did, but the point should be clear. By considering the universe—by *re*-considering it—you have already half escaped the mental/spiritual trap set by your times. But of course it isn't possible to remain in the doorway for-ever. Either you will move out into freedom or the trap will close around you again. In short, you will let this and other material change your life, or you won't. You can't both change and nonchange, not ultimately. You can waver for a while, but sooner or later that will amount to deciding by default.

Choice and free will

I don't know if this is the time—I assume it is, since it came to mind—but somebody asked how "all is well" can square with free will. I didn't understand the question, but I imagine you will.

No need to say much about it. Find the question and quote it.

[Jude McElroy's question: "If all is well, and all is always well, does this not preclude free will? I easily see that each of us has predator threads and prey threads; it would seem if all is well, it does not matter which one we focus on and exhibit. If I can't screw things up, do I really have free will? As below . . . . one of my cells can screw up the system by becoming cancerous. As above . . . ?"]

The logical confusion lies in thinking that the free will is somehow dependent upon the *result* of the choice, rather than in the nature of the choice as affirming a set of values in the person choosing.

It is true that each version of reality stems from choices made. But—

Hmm, maybe a longer subject than it appears at first, so let's go into it a bit.

Every possible choice exists, and creates its own universe, so to speak. *This is sort of true,* though not in the way physicists think, because they are conceiving of things as proceeding in time as they imagine it, things coming into existence decision by decision.

It would be more accurate to say that all these possible universes, the fruits of infinite numbers of choices by infinite numbers of people, *inhere* in the universe and, therefore, of course, always have. That's what inherent means. You make a choice, you don't *create* a world, you *walk* a certain world. You choose and your choice provides you the next step on your path.

Doesn't that make more sense to you just intuitively? Does it *feel* right that your every choice should create a version of the answer? Or is it not more intuitively right to say your every choice is a choice among worlds already existing?

Not that I knew any of this in life. I remember being pretty thoroughly confused when the guys tried to explain it.

Some of that garble had to be from me trying to make sense of it and getting it wrong. I remember struggling with it myself, and leaving it not quite making sense, but sort of making sense. I must say, this is much clearer.

Well, if it is clear that life in 3D is merely a long (or short) walk in the hall of mirrors, or labyrinth or however you wish to see it, then it should be clear that life in 3D is not about *creating* a better world (or a worse one, either); it is about creating *you*. It is about using 3D and 3D's conditions of existence to carefully forge a mind—a soul—that will thereafter function in non-3D as a unique mirror, or touchstone, among the others already existing.

So now come back to your accustomed view of reality, whichever it is, and attempt to see the world through both, alternately, or through both in a stereo view, if you can do that. From the everyday view, pain and suffering, good and evil, still exist. We haven't defined them away. But the context for life being different, how can the meaning and the very experience of good and evil, and of suffering, not be seen differently?

So that is what I meant by context, and that's enough for the moment. You and Charles may consult and see where you wish to go next, or if you ask the right open-ended question, I'll go off on my own hook.

Okay, will do. Your work continues to meet great response, and it is a pleasure to act as your amanuensis.

You just wanted an opportunity to use the word.

I did. Till next time.

Wednesday, February 18, 2015

6:10 a.m. Well, Miss Rita, Charles has given us a choice of several questions today. What's your pleasure?

Let's start with the easiest, or perhaps I should consider it the hardest, because I can't see the difficulty.

Choice

[Charles said, "And this sentence from today's session is a mind-stopper. It turns 'free will' completely upside down from any previous understanding. 'The logical confusion lies in thinking that the free will is somehow dependent upon the *result* of the choice, rather than in the nature of the choice as affirming a set of values in the person choosing.' Can more be added to it?"]

Why would anyone consider a choice in terms of the results it produced, externally, rather than the results it produced (and, really, revealed) internally?

If free will were about negotiating a morass, then I suppose the results could be "scored" according to results, although even there, one's values would determine how one scored it. But it is about shaping your soul; continual choosing among alternative reactions to seemingly external provocations or stimuli. In such case, how can the nature of free will be in dispute?

I can remember when this free will business as the whole purpose of 3D existence wasn't nearly as clear to you. When the guys first came in with it, I'd have to look up the result, but I remember it as being a new idea to you.

It is clear enough now! If 3D is to shape a soul, and the shaping is to be done by the presentation of opportunities to see one's own characteristics as if externally seen, what would be the point of constricting the choices?

You don't need to persuade me! I'm just reminding you, you didn't always see things that way.

No, but by 2008 I certainly did, and had for some while. Do you think any more needs to be said on the subject?

I suppose we'll have to see from whatever feedback we get. That is one valuable aspect of the way we're going about this. When we lose them overboard, they can sing out so we circle back for them. Next question?

Martha on mirrors, I think.

Mirrors

[Charles: "Or . . . do you want to pose Martha's question
before we leave the topic? 'It is about using 3D and 3D's conditions of existence to carefully forge a mind—a soul—that
will thereafter function in non-3D as a unique mirror, or
touchstone, among the others already existing.' Can she please
clarify this statement, especially the part about being a unique
mirror? Mirror of what or for what purpose or to whom?"]

*Well, I remember even as I wrote it, I was wondering if mirror was the right word,
but I didn't want to stop to clarify.*

That's all right; perhaps it was a good thing, in leading us to clarify
further. What I meant is simple enough. The 3D-created mind serves as a
window, or mirror, or interpreter, call it, to the non-3D mind it connects
to. And that mind, of course, connects with others closest to it, and ultimately to all minds.

*I can see that this one is going to cause us to do some work, Rita. I see clearly what
you're wanting to convey, and it is much like the time I was acting as translator for the
guys, trying to give you the concept of spools and threads, and even as I would speak,
I would hear how every word was open to being misinterpreted by you because of the
associations each word would bring, that would tempt you off-trail—and finally they
told me to paint it, so that your eyes could see the relationships as I explained them. But I
don't know how we would paint this one. It's simple, but not so easy to describe in words
without the words themselves—like "mirror," like "window"—getting in the way.*

Perhaps we can get at it by analogy. Start with the saying you like and
see if that clarifies things.

*All right. One time I was in the emergency room of the hospital, and, as I lay there
recovering, I watched the nurses spending all their day tending to people. I thought of
a saying I had read, that "God has no hands to use but ours," and I thought, how true.
The nurses weren't necessarily all emotional over the incoming patients—how could*

they be, if they had to deal with people needing help all the time?—but they were an effective example of love in everyday manifestations.

Without going into the theological implications, perhaps it will be clear that, just as 3D hands are required if one is to deal with 3D situations, so 3D eyes—3D awareness—is required if one is to experience 3D as it appears when one is within it.

Perhaps unfortunate that "3D eyes" suggests visuals, as "seeing visions" suggests movies.

But perhaps mentioning the possibility of misunderstanding is enough to avert it.

At any rate, it is those who experience 3D reality who serve as interpreters of 3D to those who have not experienced it.

A form of telepathy, I suppose, just as you and I are doing now.

Yes, that is actually a very close analogy. But if the other person did not exist—if the person serving to mirror 3D did not exist for the non-3D person to link with—how could the transfer proceed?

Boy, we're going to pay for those loose statements!

Well, you may insert your *caveats* if you think it would help.

Nothing transfers but awareness. Nothing moves or is subtracted from one place and put into another. It is just a matter of information processing, only the information in total—not just words or concepts— in fact, not primarily words or concepts, but the whole feel of an experience. And it isn't so much being transferred from one being to another being, necessarily, as from one part of one to another part (3D to non-3D) and hence potentially anywhere.

If you think that will help, good. And you might round out the answer by adding that the purpose is the same as the purpose in shaping minds in

3D in the first place. The non-3D has a *stake* in the creation of 3D minds, and therefore a stake in 3D matters, in a way quite different than you in bodies commonly think.

The guys told us, long ago, they don't particularly care about our political or economic arrangements.

No, the list of things we don't care about from this side is extensive! How concerned are you about the results of the daily chariot races in ancient Rome? But you might very easily have an abiding interest in the mind and heart and daily life and struggles of any particular ancient Roman.

Good analogy. On to number three?

Let's take Dick's.

Cognitive impairment

[Charles: "And I think this question from Richard Werling will be of interest to a lot of people: 'Frank, here in my Continuing Care Community we have a couple of dozen folks with cognitive impairment. The impairment is a continuum ranging from annoying loss of short-term memory to loss of the awareness of Self. Some time ago, I got a flash that this has a role in the evolutionary process of our species—but that doesn't exactly compute in my 3D mind. It does seem that this 'dementia' could be a variation on Rita's 'coma' experience— when she gradually allowed her consciousness to include her 'larger self.' Could we ask Rita for some elaboration on this evolution of cognitive ability?"]

That was a flash of true insight. The situation will become clearer to you [plural] if you will remember that it is not a matter of certain states being preferred from this side and others not.

Just as we may not like sharks but that doesn't make them less necessary to an ecology, we may not like senility or coma or the results of brain damage, but that doesn't make any of them less useful to the non-3D, or rather to the sum total of things.

Yes, although "useful" slants it, a bit. Say interesting, perhaps, instead. If you were looking at a landscape, how could you appreciate it for what it is if you disliked trees? Or *only* liked trees? It is the value judgments you impose or allow that distort your "external reality" for you, thus ensuring that you never see anything as it really is, and that you never see anything in precisely the way it appears to others either.

If you start from the very natural idea that unimpaired functioning is "good" and any disruption of that functioning is "bad"—how can you see clearly what is really going on? When I first tried pot—which certainly qualifies as a disruption of functioning!—I got a quick lesson in the difference between "normal" and our idea of normal. Or—well, perhaps this is a side issue, but I mean, merely, so much of our experience of life cannot be well understood if we attempt to judge it prior to experiencing it. But we have only a few minutes left in today's conversation, and I want to finish saying a couple of things that Dick's question suggests.

Dick, suppose those patients were having *super*-normal experiences. In other words, suppose that—whether or not they could communicate them—they were experiencing something well beyond the normal range of human experience. (Understand, I am not saying that they *are;* I am saying, suppose they were.) You can see that those 3D individuals having those extraordinary experiences would be of value to the non-3D community (call it) which, of course, would be able to share the experience via first the 3D person's non-3D components, and then as general shared knowledge.

Well, remove the filter that says this abnormal condition is valuable, but this one is an unfortunate predicament, and you can see that outside of 3D the value may be the same.

Something else flickered by, but went away while I was still writing this.

There are always more connections to be made, in any direction. But this is enough for today. Only, the thought Dick had is valuable. Much that seems abnormal and even catastrophic around you—the explosion of autism, for instance—bears within it the seeds of things unsuspected but not therefore undesirable.

Undesired, but not undesirable. In the sense that people often want things to stay the same.

Yes—while they want them to improve!

So be careful what you ask for. Okay, if that's it for today, I'll start pounding the keyboard.

This choice of questions worked well, reducing the strain on you and allowing me to pick the ones that were the closest to the energy of the moment. Congratulate Charles for me, and I will see you next time.

Okay. I know I don't have to add, "be well." Comes with your territory now, right?

Actually—add it to your list of questions.

Hmm. Okay. Till next time.

Thursday, February 19, 2015

Autism

3:30 a.m. Okay, Miss Rita, since it seems I'm not going to get any more sleep anyway, we might as well start. I haven't counted the questions Charles proposes as possibilities, but there must be a dozen of them. Where would you like to begin?

Let's start with my comment about autism, or the way my comment was held to apply to autism and other situations.

[Charles: "Rita said, Much that seems abnormal and even catastrophic around you—the explosion of autism, for instance—bears within it the seeds of things unsuspected but not therefore undesirable.' I think anyone who is or knows someone who is autistic would appreciate knowing more about the 'seeds of things unsuspected but not therefore undesirable.' I'm thinking particularly of parents I know who have an autistic child having difficulty coping in 3D. What can they learn from non-3D that can help both the child and the family?"]

The response is based in a misunderstanding, perhaps. What I did *not* mean in particular was that autism, or any other physical condition that distorted a given person's relations with the 3D world, was in and of itself necessarily a precursor of a change in the conditions of life. What I *did* mean was that lives lived under such conditions produced souls with a very different experience of life, hence with a very different composition.

I think I'm getting where you're going, but it's going to have to be spelled out a bit.

Feel free.

I get that you're meaning that, again, the important thing is not the 3D experience but the non-3D soul that emerges from that experience and that such souls are different somehow from souls that have not gone through something similar.

Yes, only don't exaggerate the difference. Just as autism is in some ways similar to people's experience of life under heavy cocaine usage, so in a different way it may be similar to lives lived under permanent or persistent physical afflictions that by their persistence add a certain flavor to the life, hence to the soul.

So to answer the question as posed, I'd say don't expect that the condition will necessarily produce anything recognizable from within 3D existence. It may; it may not. But the fact that 3D is now throwing off so many autistic individuals means that the non-3D is receiving more souls shaped in such circumstances—just as it is receiving many souls shaped by lifetimes overshadowed by drug usage—and, therefore, it will have an effect. But given that the effect of anyone's addition to the non-3D mind is not obvious to you in 3D, you mustn't expect to be aware of the difference, nor is it necessarily important that you be.

"The seeds of things unsuspected" had more to do with the non-3D pool of possibilities presented by diverse minds than with anything seen in the body.

Yes, but not entirely yes. Over time this will affect 3D reality as well. However, you may or may not make the connection. But that's enough on this for the moment.

Charles's second question?

Non-3D life and the 3D world

[Charles: "Rita said, 'At any rate, it is those who experience 3D reality who serve as interpreters of 3D to those who have not experienced it.' Would Rita explain more about those beings who have not experienced 3D? How is 3D life beneficial to them? Do they use this information to serve as 'helpers' to those who are presently in 3D? Any other information about beings who have not had 3D experience would be appreciated."]

All right, but I'm going to disappoint him, I think, because mostly I'm not going to answer the question, for one good reason. Suppose I tried to paint a picture of life in the non-3D as it applied—or rather, did *not* apply—to those still in 3D? What could that be but a theoretical exercise, a speculative venture of no practical use in rearranging your notions of who you are and why you are, with all the practical results that flow from that?

You don't intend to explain the TV show the man on the top of the mountain is watching. The fish at the bottom of the sea have more pressing concerns.

Not "more pressing," even, so much as more practical. What is beneficial to the non-3D world, as I have explained before, is that the conditions of 3D life allow the creation of non-3D minds that could not have come into existence otherwise.

The creation of compound beings—souls made up of many strands that learned to live together and hence grew into a single habit-system—is unique to the 3D world. And "world," I remind you, doesn't mean Earth as one planet, but means all of 3D creation. And "3D creation," I remind you in turn, is one part of an undivided reality. Don't let yourselves step back into thinking of "our side" and "your side."

As to the part of the question about non-3D beings serving as helpers, this is a misunderstanding. What 3D beings experience as "helpers" or angels or higher selves or larger beings can only be—well, how to say it?

How about this? We can only connect to the parts of ourselves that are outside 3D, not to beings that are entirely non-3D, hence anything we get from non-3D beings has to be via our own extension.

Not quite. Not wrong, but many nuances are wrong. It would be better to say only compound beings can communicate between 3D and non-3D, but in practice since compound beings can also communicate with non-3D beings, it appears more seamless than it is. Your own non-3D portion of yourself—your larger being of which you are a part—

Sorry, lost it in that long parenthetical expression.

The point is this. You naturally relate this whole discussion to the 3D world around you. But really it centers on the non-3D world that is so vastly greater. We compound beings and products of compound beings are a specialized breed—the non-3D's hunting dogs, I suppose you might say—but most of reality is not hunting dogs.

So, life elsewhere is largely incommunicable to us, and anyway isn't very much our business?

Anything that interests you is your business, but that doesn't automatically mean you can access it. Nor does it mean an intellectual curiosity is always the most urgent item of business. Let's move on to the next question, as it is connected to this one.

Non-3D's stake

["Rita said, 'The non-3D has a *stake* in the creation of 3D
minds, and, therefore, a stake in 3D matters in a way quite
different than you in bodies commonly think.' Would Rita
explain how their 'stake in 3D matters' is different than we
think?"]

I explained that their stake is in the creation of new viewpoints *in
itself*. It has nothing to do with outcomes in 3D except insofar as they
make further development easier or harder—or rather, insofar as they
point things in one certain direction rather than another. But Earth is not
the only game in town, so it is a mistake to think that everything hinges
on what happens in the next presidential election, or in the course of
changes in present civilization, or in the rise and fall of races or cultures.

*Understood—though I think that statement would have startled you, while you
were in the body.*

Oh yes! But you know, they do say travel is broadening. Number four
next.

What non-3D cares about

[Charles: "Rita said, 'No, the list of things we don't care about
from this side is extensive!' What would the list of things non-
3D cares about include?"]

[I misread this as "the list of things non-3D *doesn't* care
about," and Rita answered it that way, apparently responding
to what was in my mind rather than what was written and
misread. Interesting.]

Pretty much everything you care about other than the composition of
your character and the nurturance of your soul. Politics, ideology, econom-
ics, technology, religion, science, —you name it. I suppose I should add,
"except insofar as they cause or reflect changes in what and who you are." In
other words, we don't care about the results of the latest elections, but if you

participated in some way, directly or vicariously, we would care about how that experience *changed you.*

You have to understand, everything is upside down from the way you think of it. The individual is *everything,* and the abstract mass—be it class or nation or race or anything—is just a shadow. Do you think the Democratic Party means anything in non-3D? If it did, then what of the Czarist Party in Russia, or the *populares* in ancient Rome, and so forth? But any given soul is of unchallenged worth, because it is *real,* it is a *creation,* and it is *unique.*

One more?

One more, and your hour will be up, and probably a little more than up.

Fishing

[In an earlier session, Rita said, "The whole point of creating a soul in a given time and place, comprising certain traits and predispositions, is to create an enduring resource; so, when successful, there would be no point in throwing the elements back in the soup!" What would constitute a "success" that would "create an enduring resource"?]

This is simpler than it seems, in concept, but may not be so easy to grasp in detail. The short answer is, to the extent that a lifetime created a unique new window on 3D, it is valuable. But it if did not, not.

That sounds awfully cold.

I know, it sounds like we are saying "that life wasn't really worth anybody's time, forget about it."

That is exactly what it sounds like.

And that is both an accurate and an inaccurate summary of our position. The closest analogy I can think of offhand is fishing. If any particular

cast doesn't catch a fish, we pull the line back and cast again. Would there
be any point in leaving the line in the water so we wouldn't "waste" the cast?
Do we hurt the line by pulling it back? The apparent callousness stems from
your viewing it from the 3D, which tends to make illusions seem real and
reality seem illusory.

And that's enough for the day,

Pretty nearly an hour exactly. Okay, our thanks as always, and we'll see you next time.

Friday, February 20, 2015

3:30 a.m. A choice of several, Miss Rita. What's your pleasure?

Let's do as we did before, starting at the top and proceeding more or
less in order.

What would I ask?

*Okay, take it away. First question in Charles's list is, "What questions does she wish
she had asked but didn't when she was in 3D?"*

I understand the sense of the question. Literally, the answer would be
"none," because I am well content with where we went, what I recovered,
how it went. But in the sense Charles meant it—more or less, what in retro-
spect might have been a productive approach that, in fact, we didn't think
to try—I think it would have to be an extension of your basic question.

What would I ask if I had enough sense to know what I ought to ask?

Yes, that one. Because that amounts to saying, "I know that my perspective is limited to the extent that I allow my time-slice-delimited consciousness to try to run the show, and I know that my non-3D consciousness has
a perspective that is wider and undistorted by this limitation of the moving
present—so slip me a clue, and I'll gladly listen." But it isn't any tragedy that
I didn't think to do that—and, in a way, any time spent listening to Guidance amounts to doing just that, in any case.

So to put it in terms of the lives we in 3D are leading at the moment—

Guidance is always there, always willing. Connect to it by your *intent* to be guided, and it is the equivalent of asking the question you would ask if you had sense enough to know on your own. *You,* as a 3D-bounded intelligence, may not know; but you, as a 3D-bounded intelligence connected insepara-bly to a non-3D part of yourself, *will* know, *do* know. Clarify the channel and you will have all you need, all you can handle, at any given moment.

Higher dimensions?

Charles's second question may be answered in a line—that is the purpose and the scope of this entire series of communications.

*His second was, "**Which questions did she ask when in 3D that remained con-fusing or unanswered but have been clarified or answered in non-3D?**" So how about, "**Is her larger being communicating with the dimension 'above' hers in the same way she is communicating with you?**"*

I see I have not yet communicated this clearly. I am tempted to skip on, because this requires some work on your part—that is, it isn't short and sweet—but the next items aren't any easier, so we might as well plow into this one.

The confusion is partly inherent in language, partly a matter of confu-sion of background. Let's see how we can go about this.

First, remember that there is one big difference between 3D and non-3D, and that is the set of conditions 3D was created to have so that it could create and nourish compound beings. 3D has:

- perception of separation in space and time

- delayed consequences

- a "moving present moment" that makes choice a continuing necessity / possibility.

These conditions do not apply outside of 3D. In non-3D it is clear that connections are as real as separations; manifestation is instant (that is, there is no perception of external v. internal); and although we experience separation of events, or of states of being, in the way produced by time in 3D, we are not helplessly carried along as in a river, and we do not lose our perspective (thinking "the present moment" more important than the others). In a sense, we live continually in the present; in another sense, we live continually in all time. We may pursue that later, if you wish—I rather expect that *Charles* will wish! (said with a smile)—but the present point is that 3D and non-3D are different experiences in a way that is unique. It is a mistake to think that, therefore, we in non-3D are distinguished from another "layer" in the same way that you in 3D experience yourselves separated from non-3D.

And, anyway, we aren't really separated from non-3D at all.

Well, your experience is separate, unless and until and to the extent that you broaden your awareness to encompass dimensions that are often blurred by the intensity and narrowness of focus of 3D experience.

So to paraphrase, the 3D/non-3D frontier is not a model for another such frontier above or beyond our own non-3D components.

Compound and unitary beings

That's right. But that is only half the question, or anyway half the answer. Because the question implies this question: Do we in non-3D—*as part of compound beings*—interface with other, noncompound, beings in non-3D. And *that* is a different story.

Yes, I can see that it is posed a little clearer that way.

Remember, the guys began with us by telling us that the difference between them and us was not a difference in essence but in circumstance.

The same thing, expressing in different terrain, they said.

But now that we have refined that understanding, we see that it isn't exactly different terrain—non-3D is the same as 3D *physically*, but our perception here has been freed of the limitations that made us (to varying extents) perceive higher dimensions as if they were aspects of time, as I said. So, while it is convenient to speak of 3D and non-3D, it remains important to realize that this is *convenience*, not literal distinction. We are where you are; you are where we are; the reason you are not constantly aware of it has to do with limitations on your consciousness, not from your "moving" or not moving here or there. It's all here.

So, bearing that in mind, the true distinction is between compound beings and unitary beings. There isn't some additional dimension we must climb into in order to deal with noncompound beings, and there isn't some tangible distinction in terrain as there is between 3D and non-3D. What remains is a difference in essential nature. *There* is the frontier, or the challenge, or the opportunity for interaction and growth.

Looking back at the question, I'm not sure Charles or anyone will feel you quite answered it.

I *began* an answer to it. Clearing away shrubbery—as you say—is an important part of moving to new understanding. Unlearning what you thought you know, or, mostly, realizing what you had been taking for granted, and ceasing to do so, is as important a step as emptying a glass so you can fill it with something different.

Are you now in a position to fill it with something different?

I am. *You* are not. By which I mean, not that you are necessarily unprepared for more (some are, some are not, but it will always be so as people come to this material), but that there is an educational value in the pause after one step and before another.

Letting it marinate.

That's right. Time spent pondering is always time well spent, regardless of whether or not you come up with new insights as a result. It is always good to live with new material, for the continuous slowly boiling mixture that you are will send different elements to the surface as time moves, and so the material will be folded in more thoroughly.

Material for more questions in that last paragraph.

Of course. But not right now.

Limitations on communication

It is 4:15, we have another ten or fifteen minutes. Shall we begin on the next one?

Well, let's see. The questions with their context are longer perhaps than the answer need be. Go ahead.

Question four for the day, posted on my blog by someone using the name "cat's paw":

[*Cat's paw*: "Let's say the 'limitations' imposed by 3D conditions vary wildly from individual to individual, but still obtain across a wide spectrum. Based on your work (and Rita's help here) and Monroe's and countless others, of course, we have some sense of the benefit of these 'limitations' for non-3D and beyond. Now . . . let's say a significant 'limitation' for 3D humans here and now is a constraint on perception based upon 3D conditions generally, but also the specific historical conditions operating at present. This constraint on our perception presumably prohibits (some of, most of?) us from readily perceiving and interacting with the non-human intelligences all around us ('aliens' may come to mind, but I am thinking more of Earth-related intelligences: plants and animals for sure, but also cryptid beings for which there is lots of anecdotal evidence but little physical evidence like Sasquatch, 'faeries,' and other apparently even stranger beings).

["So, keep in mind for the questions that follow the pre-supposition I'm working from: it is incumbent upon humans to widen both their sense of 'community' and 'intelligence' to include nonhumans in those perceptions and definitions; that it will make us more 'human' not less to do so.

["1. Through what effort or process can we learn to perceive and interact with nonhuman intelligences more consciously?

["2. Why do nonhuman intelligences (allegedly) seem to be less 'constrained' by 3D limitations than humans? Is this a matter of historical-developmental conditions (modernity) into which we are born? Are non-3D factors also determining these constraints on us from the 'outside' as it were?

["3. Does Rita interact with some of the intelligences I'm alluding to in non-3D?

["4. Are there 'risks' or potential 'dangers' we should be aware of?

["5. Is (over-) reliance on thinking linguistically a specific constraint that limits perception on this front?"]

I agree that there is much more for humans to become aware of. I agree that to do so makes you—not more human perhaps, but more fully developed as a human (always bearing in mind that you as a human are inherently and inextricably connected to your non-3D component—that you are therefore no less connected to anything you connect to via 3D). In fact, to add to that parenthesis, you never know whether you are functioning "via 3D" or "via non-3D" for the very simple reason that it is a matter of interpretation, or viewpoint, which way you see it.

As to the specific questions—

1. Increased awareness is always the same process regardless of what it aims toward. The effort to live more in the present moment, getting out from behind filters and scripts, clarifies the screen and makes it easier to see.

2. That *is* mostly a "seems." Nonhuman intelligence of any kind—be it plant or ET—has its own inherent possibilities and limitations. You cannot expect the intelligence that governs your body's autonomic systems to study astronomy, remember. Don't envy others their abilities if you are unwilling to envy them their limitations.

3. Yes, and so do all of you. But it is one thing to interact, and a different thing to recognize the nature of the interaction. See #1, above.

4. No.

5. Hmm. This deserves a larger answer than we can give here, so let's begin next time with this one, and we can move on from here. It won't take an inordinately long time to answer, but it offers the chance to say a couple of things, and I shouldn't like to miss that opportunity.

Okay, we can close up shop for the moment. Thanks as always, Rita. Many people in your classroom, and we're thanking you as we go.

Till next time. Nice apples you're leaving on my desk.

Smiling.

Saturday, February 21, 2015

Words and the non-3D

5:30 a.m. You had said you would continue on from where you left off, and there are a bunch of questions more that Charles posed, that I printed out and have ready to go, Rita. But it is a weird uneasy feeling, doing this, knowing that I don't quite have a handle on the questions and hoping you do.

You should put it on the record, so that others doing the same work will recognize that their difficulties are not unique to them.

Yes, I've sort of been doing that right along, and for that reason. Also, it's a more honest way of proceeding than it would be if I were pretending I could just waltz along, in control of the process.

Many times, I understand the question and could answer it myself (not that I'm always sure where "myself" leaves off and "Rita" comes in). But other times, I read the question, realize that I don't really understand it, or where it is coming from—and I proceed to put pen to paper and answer it, and all I can hope is that whatever comes out is truly you, or anyway someone "over there," and not just gibberish. It never has come out as nonsense—that is, it comes out in comprehensible sentences—but often enough all I can do is keep up with the flow and hope it's making sense. I often do this with the uneasy feeling that a close examination of the material would show that it is full of inconsistencies and contradictions.

But you continue to do the work.

I do. There's nothing equally interesting to me, and it feels like I have spent so many years honing my abilities that I have to proceed on trust that it all adds up to something. And, of course, when we see response from people indicating that what they read resonates with them, that helps. It's just that the work always, or mostly, or anyway often enough, comes with that uneasiness attached.

And now we have covered two journal pages and haven't begun today's work.

Not true. The process, the encouragement of others by example and by stories about your experience of the process, is an inherent part of the process of encouraging people to redefine themselves so that they can move out of their old outgrown shell and into another, larger one.

If you say so. All right, you said you wanted to say a couple of things about the final question posed by "cat's paw."

["Is (over-) reliance on thinking linguistically a specific constraint that limits perception on this front?"]

Well, as I said, I could have answered, simply, "sometimes it is." But it will be more useful to explain a little more.

Bob [Monroe] stressed that NVC—nonverbal communication—was an essential skill if people were to communicate with what he thought of as the nonphysical world. This is because of just this problem of sequential versus intuitive perception.

May I rephrase?

You have the pen.

I take it to mean, thoughts, words, are sequentially processed and can only be sequentially processed. Nonphysical reality is, by definition, outside 3D and therefore is, by definition, not easily even described, let alone experienced, as a sequential 3D-time-slice-limited process. Therefore, the habit of communicating in non-3D helps develop the ability to experience non-3D with fewer filters because it doesn't involve silently and unconsciously translating everything into 3D terms, which, of course, is a process that involves a certain distortion.

I thought you were worried about not understanding the material.

Very funny. Sometimes I get it, sometimes I don't, but what I just said seems clear enough in light of what you've said before this.

Don't forget—and this is for everybody, Frank, not just for you—what you get while you are linked to other minds always seems obvious, always seems yours, except when you are groping for new material. It may not seem as obvious when you are processing it on your own afterward.

In any case, your summary is good enough. Any sequential process is going to impede *perception* of the non-3D. But it is important to remember that you will make sense of that experience only by integrating it with the rest of your life, and that will be done through 3D means of processing; in other words, sequential processing usually involving language. The whole point of 3D existence, as Bob used to stress, is the simultaneous balanced employment of intuition *and* logic; perception *and* interpretation.

First wallow in the sensation, then use the worm of thought to understand it, he told our Guidelines program.

That's right. And that's enough on this very important question.

Okay, onwards. In order?

Why not?

Living in communication

[Charles: {in the 35th session} Rita said, "This should be a tremendously encouraging fact! You aren't in charge of the agenda; you don't have to figure out what to do; you aren't in any way lost; and nothing you became is lost or unemployed. It is a state the very opposite of stagnation."]

I shouldn't need to say much about this. It is only when the 3D-formed ego, thinking it is on its own, unaware of its integral connection to non-3D (through its extension in that direction) and to other past 3D experiences, other 3D-shaped minds (through the strands that comprise it).

Sort of lost control of the sentence, though I know where it's going.

The only time you feel lost and alone is when you don't feel your connection to more than the 3D-defined self that the senses report. As long as you remain in connection—or, and this is important, as long as *you live in faith that the connection has not ceased to exist*—you don't have to worry that you don't know what to do, you don't know where you're going to end up, you don't know if you're safe, you don't know if "external" events are going to overwhelm you. If you remain aware of your connections, you recognize that the hardest challenges have meaning and that it is very true that "all is well, all is always well," regardless of whether you see it or not, feel it or not, approve of conditions or not, feel adequate to circumstances or not.

You don't need to do anything, any time, but your best, and in this context "doing your best" refers not primarily to external efforts but to your

attitude, your concentration on the underlying point to all of life's challenges, which is, how do I respond to this? What are my values and how do
I express them? How will my response to circumstances show me who and
what I am to date?

Can't get lost, can't get hurt.

Well—
You know full well you *can* get lost, *can* get hurt, judging in 3D terms.
I don't mean to explain away difficulties any more than to explain away evil
or suffering in general. But it is true that from your non-3D perspective you
can see that the 3D drama doesn't mean what it seems to mean from within
the drama. Life is *meant to be* convincing, after all. How much would it
accomplish for you to be going through the motions saying, "I know I just
broke my arm, but it really doesn't mean anything"? No, when you break
your arm you can't define your arm into an unbroken state. (The question
of miracles is a side-trail at the moment.) It is in non-3D that we experience things that way—instant manifestation, instant change. The point of
3D circumstances is delayed consequences so you *don't* have to experience
everything as ephemeral. I realize—I well remember—that often enough
you would like nothing better, but all that would happen is that you would
define away anything you didn't like or didn't approve of, and therefore
couldn't profit from the play.

*Which bears on the topic of why there is so much pain and suffering in the world. It
is because we can't escape the consequences of our actions merely by wishing them away.*

You wouldn't accept that if *I* said it! Try it again, more carefully (which
by the way will give you a sense of the difficulty of trying to teach from a
distance).

*Well, pain and suffering are the results of decisions and actions in 3D. Some are
our own decisions and actions, and some are not. Therefore we experience results both
firsthand and secondhand. Come to think of it, this sounds like the old "Earth school"*

concept I have so much resistance to. So I suppose that aspect of it must be true, or true enough in context.

That's a little better. 3D experience is always *real* in the way that anything is real that does not yield to contrary desire. And, as I say, it is the persistence of external conditions that is a prime value in 3D. But it is the fact that such perceived conditions are only *relatively* true (i.e., true only while in 3D) that is your Ariadne's thread out of the 3D labyrinth.

I guess we aren't going to get to the next item on the agenda. Anything more to say about this one?

You aren't in charge of the agenda—therefore, you can relax about it. You aren't lost or perplexed at the non-3D level, and if you can learn to trust that—the easiest way to do so being "all is well"—you will find your own way easier not because "external" circumstances ease (they may, they may not) but because you don't waste so much energy in anxiety.

Okay, Rita, thanks and we'll see you next time.

Sunday, February 22, 2015

5:30 a.m. Miss Rita, it occurs to me, maybe you would rather lecture than answer questions at some point. I assume you will let me know.

Of course. But for now this serves. It is always good to know where your students' understanding is. And questions will reveal that.

Okay, shall we continue down the list?

We might as well. Charles may substitute questions as he sees fit, since the burden of shaping the material is going to fall on him. But at any given time, it is safe enough, easy enough, to see what has been given previously.

Okay, here's the next on the present list.

Unique windows

[From Charles. {In the 17th session, Rita says} "This is simpler than it seems, in concept, but may not be so easy to grasp in detail. The short answer is, to the extent that a lifetime created a unique new window on 3D, it is valuable. But it if did not, not." Just for clarification, a 3D life that did not create a "unique new window" isn't lost but isn't used again to create a new soul. Is this correct? For example, Hitler certainly created something unique, so would his 3D life be part of a "bundle" to create a new soul? I realize I'm using 3D judgment in my question.]

I think this isn't coming from a clear understanding (and I realize that his level of understanding now has surpassed that that existed when the question was formed, but it will be useful to others to see the divergence and the course-correction, so to speak).

You mustn't let the "individual" concept sneak back into your thinking when you are thinking of the progression of strands through 3D experience. That is true *in a way*, but is not true in a way.

You're going to need to do some "splaining," Lucy.

Oh, I know it. (And bear in mind, most of your readers will never have seen *I Love Lucy*, ultimately. You're dating yourself.)

You mean "Lucy, you've got some 'splainin' to do" isn't going to pass into immortality?

That's exactly where it is going! As opposed to remaining current! But to return to the question—

I remind you, reincarnation as commonly understood and described obviously is not false, or you wouldn't have so many reports over so many centuries from so many people. But it isn't to be seen only one way, either, or you wouldn't see so many sincere searchers after truth rejecting the idea for good and sufficient reasons. When someone poses a question in the way this one is posed, it falls into just the assumptions that divide human opinion on reincarnation. It is hidden in the language, you see, and the language shapes perception in the same way that it [i.e., language] has been shaped by past perception.

Yes, you've said that more than once, and the guys before you.

And we'll need to say it again, I have no doubt, because the habits that arise out of language are persistent.

"Hitler's 3D life" certainly could be a strand in other bundles—not just *one* bundle, notice—it isn't as if that life were a physical commodity that could only be transferred, hence could go only to one place or another, or even one place at a time. Any given life, once lived, is a resource from which other lives may be created. Those lives may incorporate that life (that strand) in greater or less importance. That is, the entire new package may include Hitler's life to a small degree, or a larger degree, and with that, may emphasize this or that aspect of his personality. It isn't a unit in the way language tempts you to think of it.

Let me see if I can rephrase that, so we know if I'm getting it right. Hitler comes into existence. He incorporates 100 strands, say, and who knows who they were? After he dies—whether in 1945 in Berlin or afterward in Argentina or the moon—the mind that he formed during life may be used as one strand of other lives, and each of those lives will, of course, be different combinations of minds, and so will be dominated by different ratios of characteristics (that's one way to put it) not only among the different strands, but within the different strands. But in any case, the use of a strand in one person does not in any way affect its availability for use in others.

That's right. And that is one reason why particularly effective combinations may echo through history—not, exactly, that a person's reputation leads others to emulate him or her; closer to the opposite way around—that person's characteristics are used repeatedly for reasons of the larger being's, and therefore many people in 3D find themselves drawn to accounts of the original life. And so you see Caesar and Napoleon echo down through the centuries—and Jesus and St. Francis and Muhammad.

As in David Hawkins's Power vs. Force?

He is reporting results rather than causes, but he's worth looking into with this explanation in mind.

But how about Peter Novak's The Division of Consciousness?

A valuable springboard for thought, but again proceeding from a very different idea of how things work.

Finished with the question?

Not quite. "A 3D life that did not create a 'unique new window' isn't lost but isn't used again to create a new soul" makes the mistake again of regarding as a unit what is not a unit. The point here is that when a particular mixture of elements proves not to be valuable as a window onto 3D, it is not necessarily used in the creation of others. But the elements of which it was put together obviously do not cease to exist; it is the particular creation that may be, essentially, disused. And once more I caution you not to assume that you or anyone can judge the uniqueness or value of any one window on the world. Most of what you are is hidden from all others, not by reluctance or stealth but by the nature of things. Judge not.

Lest we be judged?

No, just, judge not, because as the guys always told us, you never have the data. Most of anyone is always inaccessible and incommunicable.

Still waters run deep.

Yes, but so do rapidly running waters, and no one can plumb another's depths. *Now* we may move on.

All right, the next one seems to be closely related to it.

The purpose of creation

[Charles: "Rita said yesterday, 'What is beneficial to the non-3D world, as I have explained before, is that the conditions of 3D life allow the creation of non-3D minds that could not have come into existence otherwise.' So a 3D life is 'successful,' adds a new perspective to non-3D and is therefore retained as a thread for a new soul. And this process continues on and on for what purpose? (I know . . . another fish question.) But, doesn't everyone in 3D have an insatiable quest to know what all (3D, non-3D, unitary beings, etc.) this is for? Is it for 'curiosity' as Bruce Moen suggests, 'play' as Joseph Chilton Pearce suggests, or as Edgar Cayce said in a reading, 'God's desire for companionship and expression'?"]

The purpose may be simply stated as the cooperative construction of ever-more-intricate and versatile windows on 3D through the creation of ever-more-intricate actors in 3D.

Now, you may look at one or another aspect of this and come down with very different ideas about it. If you trace the larger beings' purposes, life in 3D is seen as one thread in a tapestry. If you trace any particular thread's "progress" through the weaving, life is seen as a journey, a progression, a rising or sinking in development.

The latter is closer to what people typically think of as reincarnation, I think.

Yes, because it is what it looks like when you proceed from that point of view. That's why I am laying much more emphasis on the view from the larger being's end, as balance.

Now as to the purpose beyond this immediate purpose, that may have to wait until the fish develop better TV reception. I'd prefer to stick to topics that actually bear on your lives as you live them. What use is it to allow yourselves to be distracted from what you can do (and, one might say, are responsible to do)?

Well, as Charles says, there is a certain natural curiosity.

Yes, there is—and I would prefer that it stays focused on what it can learn to understand and (in the positive sense of the term) manipulate, rather than be dissipated in idle speculation.

And that will do for today.

All right, Miss Rita. Thanks as always.

Monday, February 23, 2015

4:10 a.m. All right, Miss Rita. We can proceed with the previous list or start on Charles's updated list. Let me reread them, and then we can go where you please.

You felt my preference as you read them. My preference / your preference—*in this context* it is hard for you to sort out which is which.

Very true.

That's a confusing thing when you first start doing this and a confirming one after a while. Wasn't it?

Yes indeed. If I had let my doubts about "maybe I'm just making this up" stop me, it would have been largely because the information was so readily there that it seemed too good to be true, so maybe was wishful thinking.

Always good to note for the record, as a part of the experience. Very well, copy Charles's note and the first set of questions.

Manifesting the non-3D being

[From Charles, "quoting Rita's answer to Cat's Paw: '...I would prefer that it stays focused on what it can learn to understand and (in the positive sense of the term) manipulate, rather than be dissipated in idle speculation.' I think that's well put, Rita (and Frank). With that in mind, could Rita speak to this: She emphasizes repeatedly there is no separation of 3D and non-3D, but from our limited perspective that often does not seem to be the case. I also get that 'information,' ideas, hunches, even events or situations may originate, as it were, in non-3D though we mostly remain unaware of the fact.

[1. "Is it the case that the more we are able to bring (or allow, or manifest?) our non-3D (larger) being into everyday 3D life the better or richer the experience?"]

Answering (1), no, there is no such rule. People are formed for many different reasons, of different components, which in effect gives them different missions, different priorities and possibilities. But this answer must itself be seen in context, the context of "who is likely to read it?"

Yes, I get that, all right. Those whose "path"—whose composition—makes them interested in the material are no doubt interested for a reason. Those who are not interested, are not interested for the simple reason that it doesn't interest them—that is, it doesn't concern them, they aren't going this way.

Yes, it is pretty nearly that simple. If you have no interest in woodworking, you are unlikely to spend a lot of time on woodworking websites, let alone pick up a chisel and hammer, or drawknife, or whatever.

So it amounts to "listen to guidance [to know] whether you should listen to guidance."

In practice, I think you will find that this is what people do. No one is bereft of a pole star, no matter how it may look to others or even to themselves. But that doesn't at all mean that they will or should therefore conceptualize it the same way or even be aware of it as such. You may be a woodsman or a mechanic or—make it as 3D-oriented as you please—the access to guidance is there, recognized or not, conceptualized or not.

Everybody has a guardian angel.

Yes, except that the angel is concerned less with abstract questions of good and evil as if it were a hall monitor, and more with questions of good or evil *for the mixture that the individual person is.* If you concentrate on an abstract set of rules, as the church did, you will see it as an innate source of knowledge of whether you are transgressing or not, and this is not a mistake, but it is limited. A wider view sees that that guardian angel may be equally well seen as a person's perception of his or her non-3D component, there to offer advice when requested (or, sometimes, urgently required), and of course it will always proceed from the point of view that what the person *is*, is right, regardless of whether what the person specifically *does* in any given circumstance is right or not.

Hmm. Long disquisition possible here. You want to proceed along this line, or continue with the second question?

Let's say a few words more. You have the sense of it, you begin it.

The defect of the Catholic upbringing for many people—certainly including me—is the sense of guilt that accompanies one's inability to live up to an abstract inflexible set of rules of conduct. Granted, there was [the sacrament of] Confession to give one a sense of relief, of release, of a fresh start—but it would be a fresh start to again attempt to live up to an ideal, which by definition can never be lived, but only lived toward.

And now you can see that the support of the moral code could have been given without the pervading sense of guilt and failure, had the nature of the challenge and the opportunities been given differently. If *what you are* is taken as given, then the difference between what you are and what you naturally aspire to be or to become may be more of a route-indicator and less of a reproach.

Yes, and all this without reference to heaven or hell, which are mostly exaggerations of incentive.

In this context.

In this context, yes. I mean, the conflict between what we are and what we want to be exists without the promised reward or punishment.

For you it did. For some it did. But the world contains a world of different types of people, who respond to different sets of incentives. But this is all in answer to the first question: Different strokes for different folks, and each will know his or her own way. So I would rephrase it somewhat to say, the more you are able to stay in touch with your non-3D component, the more likely you are to stay on the beam—*but this predicts nothing about how this will manifest.* In some it will be a mystical bent, in others an intellectual abstract curiosity, in others a severe allergy to the mention of anything metaphysical, etc. The variations are as numerous as the types of people, and, of course, everyone who exists is right! That is, people are not created defective, no matter how it may seem to you. Their values may be antithetical to yours (and to each other's); their beliefs may be contradictory; they may manifest many evil traits; they may seem blind to reality. It doesn't matter: they were no more created "wrong" than you were. Everybody is a perfect expression of what they were created of, and nobody is perfect measured from any abstract table of values or attributes.

So heaven and hell are useful concepts for some people.

You might say they are *true* concepts for some kinds of people, and [objectively] as true as any other description of what is called the afterlife, including this one. In this case, the yardstick is shaped to the thing being measured.

Not sure I understand that last sentence.

Let it marinate, and let's proceed to question #2, which, as you see, should require little discussion.

Openness to guidance

["2. If so, what techniques, practices, or attitudes are conducive for doing this?"]

Discard the "if so" insofar as it implies that I agree that this is for every-body, for the reasons just stated. With that understood, I decline to pre-scribe specifics, as everyone's circumstances, opportunities, and limitations are different, and a specific answer would have too much weight for some people, leading them either to feel that their own guidance is wrong or to rebel against what does not resonate. The simple answer is, you will know what is right for you. Just—ask guidance! Where else is the knowing going to come from?

That said, of course there are generalities I can give you without the risk of discouraging people. Openness to your own guidance is the key to all of it. The only thing external guidance (such as this) can do is to remind you "from the outside," as it will seem, and get your attention.

On to #3?

Yes.

["3. How important or relevant is being conscious or aware of this process—keeping in mind that we are presumably always "in touch" with non-3D yet mostly unaware of it?"]

This question has been answered above, you see. For those to whom it is important, it is important. For those to whom it is nonexistent, it is nonexistent! And every gradation between the two. It is a tautology. One size does *not* fit all.

We still have another ten minutes or so. Shall we continue or stop here?

We can at least begin on the next question.

Soulmates and resonance

[Charles quotes a question from Suzanne: "I wonder if Rita could comment on the idea of soulmates. I think of it not nec-essarily as 'that person you were destined to marry,' but as a particularly strong feeling you get, when you meet someone, that you have known them all along and/or have been waiting to find them. What is going on when that happens? Are we recognizing 'strands' that we have been part of before? (If the topic has already been addressed, disregard. I did a search for soulmate and saw nothing come up.)"]

The guys talked to us of soulmates and explained that the concept arises from the mistaken view that individuals are unitary rather than compound, though they didn't put it that way. Like most concepts, it can have a utility, but like most concepts, it is easily overemphasized and mistaken for a rule or an invariant or inflexible description of reality.

Clearly the *phenomenon* exists, or there would be no concept seeking to explain it. But the fact that an inexplicable resonance between people exists does not mean that a given concept is the best way, let alone the only way, to explain it. In this context the explanation you offer—that it is recognition of a strand that you have been part of before—is close, but it might be better to see it as recognition of a strand *that you share.* No past tense about it.

But more to the point, why the question? That is, why is the question arising within you, and why now, and what is the answer going to affect? Understand, I am not criticizing the question. I am saying that introspection into the genesis of the question and its importance to you may be worthwhile.

And that's about it for the day. We may begin again wherever Charles prefers.

This seems to be working well. Thanks as always, and we'll see you next time.

Tuesday, February 24, 2015

Spirits contend

4:30 a.m. All right, Miss Rita, ready if you are. Shall we begin with Suzanne's question?

All right with me.

[Suzanne: "A few sessions ago, you closed by saying Be Well, and Rita said to add it to your list of questions. Interested in hearing more, so wanted to make sure that question was added to the list."]

I was merely noting that life outside 3D is not unvarying bliss the way some people imagine it. True, we don't get colds and our limbs and joints don't ache, but still there are stresses, and the results of stresses.

I take it you don't mean physical stresses left over from 3D life—that is, the non-3D equivalent of phantom-limb pains.

An interesting analogy, that, actually. Let me think if I should pursue it.

[pause]

Let me say it straight, and then we'll see if I want to pursue the analogy. What I intended to make note of is that we are still compound beings, even after we have dropped the body. As a matter of fact, the tensions between various components may sometimes be stronger, more evident, without the body's buffering intervention.

Is that what Yeats meant when he wrote of being thankful for "the body and its stupidity"?

I can't answer for Mr. Yeats, but it may have been at least a glimmer of the truth that *spirits contend*, both in the body and no less outside the body. Don't think of eternity as a place of eternal rest, necessarily! That is as much failure of imagination as anything. Hence, harps and clouds and all that, that discredits the idea of a nonphysical world among the nonreligious.

An angel—a unitary being of any sort—is incapable of being self-divided, for the very good reason that there is no diversity of internal content to form sides.

But compound beings—and by that I mean anything created in 3D by sexual reproduction uniting different strains, incorporating in one body

different strands each of which may itself have been a life lived as an individual by what had been a community—compound beings are not only
capable of being self-divided; they can scarcely escape it. And this is a function we have not yet touched on. Compound beings, by their nature, are
both battleground and reconciling force for opposing forces. They live a
battle (and perhaps a reconciling) and they become a potential way forward. In short, they not only complicate the non-3D world by presenting
new possibilities, they also help hold it together by sometimes reconciling
the polar opposites they may learn to live.

*I sometimes wonder if this or that that we get in these sessions is merely me echoing
something I've read—but not in this case! I don't know that I've ever heard anybody
describe us or our function in the larger scheme of things in just that way.*

Remember, "3D," "the world"—even "people," many times—does not
mean only Earth. You may tend to think that humans on Earth are radically
different from beings also in 3D who live elsewhere, but perhaps you tend
to exaggerate the differences and underrate the commonalities. The same
non-3D being may very easily incorporate elements from various parts of
3D, just as humans may have ancestors from different genetic strands, or
different ethnic groups, or different races. Depending on the extent of difference, the internal diversity—and perhaps the internal stress—will be
that much the greater. But this is a side trail.

The central point here is that 3D life is integrally connected with non-
3D life, and if you can keep that in mind as you examine *anything*, it will
gradually reorient your thinking in new and productive directions. Trust
your guidance as you consider ideas. Entertain fanciful connections as they
arise, and consider that they may be arising not at random, as they appear
to be, but in some sequence not apparent to you, but aimed at assisting you
to new integrations.

*So when I said "be well" as a sort of generalized sign-off gesture, and you in effect
said, "not necessarily," it was to provide an entry-point for you to point out that on the
other side not all is beer and skittles—and as soon as I wrote "the other side," I went,
"oops!"*

It is hard to reorient your thinking all at once, and I recognize that three months is still pretty much "all at once." But you caught it, that's the point. And you see, perhaps, why I began with that point that it is *one* reality, not two. There is a casual utility in thinking of "this side" and "the other side," but it too easily tempts you into disregarding all the unbreakable links that are more obvious when you remember that you are observing *one* being functioning partly in, partly out of, the 3D environment.

Passion

"Spirits" as you often think of them, have passions no less than "physical beings" do. How could they not? They have self-division, values, motives. No, they don't commute to work or mow the lawn or clerk at a store, but they share human life in its essentials, and what is essential about human life is not the externals but the internals. However, naturally these things express differently in different surroundings.

Meaning, I take it, in surroundings where consciousness is not led to exaggerate the always-moving present moment.

That, and the continual sense of separation, and the ability to go for long periods of time not recognizing the results of a given thought or attitude.

But *values* remain; *passions* remain; one should say, I suppose, *life* remains. The guys told us we would find them emotionally chilly next to us in 3D. True, but not the whole story. We "here" are *seemingly* more chilly because of not riding that exaggerated present moment. But, in essence, we are *more* passionate, actually, because we are not distracted by the innumerable crosscurrents of human existence.

I'm getting more than has been said so far.

Go ahead, if you want to try. You know the limitations of language and the starting-point of visualization.

What I hear between the lines is that our non-3D component shares our emotional makeup to a larger degree than I would have thought because I would have thought that the larger being would be more neutral, as it incorporates more than one of us. ("Incorporates" is the wrong word literally, but I mean it includes many 3D beings.)

Yes, but there is a difference between the larger being and any individual's non-3D components; that's the point.

I see it clearly now, but I think I was hazy on it till now. So our non-3D component is our representation in non-3D of what we in 3D are, including whatever moves us.

Yes, but it is a two-way street, and the 3D world represents the non-3D in a way and to an intense degree that I did not suspect while still in the body.

That's because you weren't raised Catholic.

Well, maybe so. I can see there is far more in Christianity than I was willing to concede. And I admit to suspecting that you were still in the thrall of that early training.

I don't think so, but how would I know? I know that it seems to me to have had explanatory value that is usually underrated in this formerly Protestant and now functionally atheist culture.

Q&A

I thought you'd waltz right through Suzanne's question and get to the three Charles posed to come after that. But we're running short on time today.

Take it as a good lesson on the value of people asking the questions that occur to them. There may be a reason why they are prompted to ask them!

In fact, a word on that. This question-and-answer format has the advantage of what I might call multiple entry-points. Since you are not a trance medium, it might be very difficult for me to introduce a surprising topic, or a surprising twist on what seems a familiar topic, without questions providing an entry-point.

Because questions do not have to be justified as the logical continuation of a chain of thought.

That's right. They can serve very easily as points of departure.

And that's why "the better the question, the better the answer"!

Yes. A really good question—I don't mean, necessarily, a particularly clever question, or a well-thought-out question, but a question emerging from someone's sincere wanting to know—will provide more entry points for material that otherwise might have to await on some on-ramp.

Well, well. You've joined the information superhighway. I still remember your struggling with computers.

That's one thing we don't have to contend with here, fortunately—technology. And I'm very glad of it.

Well, I think you've provided us with an entry point to a host of entry points, Miss Rita. Anything else before we close up shop?

Only this. Everyone who reads, everyone who thinks about, everyone who contributes questions to or objections to the material, contributes. I hope you will all realize, there is no way for you to know whether a given question is "only you" or is being prompted by another part of yourself. It is, in fact, nearly a meaningless distinction. So don't underrate your participation.

Thanks, Rita, and we'll see you next time.

Wednesday, February 25, 2015

Living our values

3:20 a.m. Okay, Miss Rita, you're on. The questions keep getting more interesting, I think, including ones we probably won't get to for a while. What a nice sense of community!

Where would you like to start?

We may as well go down the new list in order.

> [*Charles*: "Stephen Hawking was quoted yesterday as saying
> that our most immediate threat is human behavior. 'The human
> failing I would most like to correct is aggression. . . . It may have
> had survival advantage in caveman days, to get more food, terri-
> tory, or a partner with whom to reproduce, but now it threatens
> to destroy us all.' Would Rita please comment on this?"]

*I think that is a slander on caveman, myself, but I'll be interested in your take on it.
I remember so well your down-the-line liberal views when you were in the body.*

Without getting into ideology, and certainly not into politics, let me
say that of course everything looks different from here. How could it not?
Context is all, or nearly all. Our 3D lives are a long effort to express what is
within us, which requires and presupposes a decision—a continuing decision, you might say—as to what we *want* to express, what we want to be.
You may have contradictory values included in your 3D soul—well, your
task is to judge which ones you wish to express and encourage, and which
you wish to repress and discourage. And, of course, there are productive
and destructive ways of going about all this, but if you don't realize that
we are *by nature* compound beings, the task is going to be misunderstood.

Aggression

To answer the question succinctly, let me say this. Hawking is correct and
also not.

Yes but no. Seems like we've heard that before.

And it is quite possible you'll hear it again. The only alternative is over-
simplification, sometimes.

Hawking is right that aggression as a trait threatens destruction,
although I would now judge that the danger is substantially less in 2015

than it was fifty years before. But he is making an unnoticed error in attrib-
uting it to *human* nature. It would be closer to the truth to say that humans
are *living with* aggression (as with all values and the behaviors arising from
them) that are brought forth from the non-3D and are expressed more
clearly in 3D circumstances. Life is a conflict of values, both in 3D and in
non-3D. Behavior is a little different in different terrain, but the originating
forces are, of course, the same.

*I'm torn between wanting you to go on with this and wanting you to go on to the
next question.*

There isn't any point in hurrying through things to get to tomorrow.
Tomorrow will always be tomorrow. The time is always now, as Ram Dass
reminded us.

*All right. That has always been a fault of mine, hurrying forward. So pray,
continue.*

Hawking says the *human failing* he would like to *correct*. Is it specifically human, though? Is it a failing? And even if either or both, is it meaningful to talk of *correcting* it?
The statement could be rephrased several ways. One would be: "I don't
like aggression and would like to see it eliminated." Another would be:
"There is something defective in human nature, and I would like to see it
altered and therefore cured." Another would be: "I'm tired of war and the
causes of war and I dream of a world without them." And yet another would
be—

Lost it.

Well, even this many is enough not to invalidate the statement but to
illuminate the tacit assumptions it incorporates. The additional rephrasing
dealt with the assumption of individuals acting in mutual isolation, but you
have enough to see my point here.

I would argue that it is not *aggression* but *selfishness* that threatens life as you are living it. That is, most people are not malign or even hostile, particularly; but a civilization that fosters a sense of isolation, of lack of mutual interdependence, is not only profoundly inhuman, it is also profoundly unscientific, because interdependence is perhaps the first law of nature, recognized or not. What is the much-quoted "survival of the fittest" but a statement that the most successful species is the one that best *fits in* to the existing order of things? It is not who is the most ruthless. Anything that overreaches risks pulling the temple down around his ears.

That last sentence sounds more like me than like you!

Well, it *is* a joint mind, you know. No reason your own flavor wouldn't get into the teacup. It often does.

Here is my point. Aggression flows from a sense of isolation, which may result in fear, in ruthlessness, in a sense that it is dog-eat-dog, *sauve' qui peut*. But without that sense of isolation—in non-3D, in other words—the values still exist, and still have their vigorous proponents. It is just that we in non-3D do not experience the world as you do, so of course everything expresses differently. So I'd say it isn't *aggression* that threatens you; it is the belief that you each exist in isolation—in isolation from non-3D, from each other, from your pasts and futures. But that is not what Hawking is saying, because he is concentrating on effects and not causes. This is not to criticize his work, only to clarify. Now, I suggest that we move on to something else until questions and comments proceed from this, for we have not begun to exhaust the subject.

If I hear you right, you're saying, again, let this marinate for a while.

Too big a chunk of unfamiliar material may prove indigestible, for two reasons. One, the temptation will be to embrace it but then move on, leaving it as a cyst rather than incorporating it. Two, the implications of new material only reveal themselves in connection with various facets of reality. Look at life through new lenses and each day illumines different things, as happened to us in 2001 and 2002 when we lived with the material the guys provided us week by week.

Yes, I well remember, and it's true, the continuing nature of the tutorial, combined with the somewhat random barrage of questions from the Voyagers mailing list and others, did result in our being presented new aspects of what might have been glossed over otherwise.

Glossed over, encapsulated, and in essence disregarded. Okay, next question.

Being and doing

[Charles: "I'm wrestling with 'what the person *is*, is right, regardless of whether what the person specifically does in any given circumstance is right or not.' I understand that no being is 'created' wrong, but from this comment it seems to indicate there is a 'right' choice. Would Rita please comment?"]

Charles has the first part, which is more difficult for many people than you might suspect. Not only do people criticize what others (and they themselves) *do,* they often criticize what others (and they themselves) *are.* Perhaps they do not think of it that way, but that's the effect. When you say, "I love x"—whether friend, lover, or only someone you have read about or seen—"but I only wish he or she weren't so [whatever]"—you are, in effect, saying, "that person is imperfect as is."

Well, there are two ways of saying the same thing. Either everybody is imperfect, because everybody has the defect of their qualities, or everybody is perfect, because they are as they were created and they are living that problem as best they can. *This isn't even two statements,* both true, but *one* statement.

As I say, Charles has that part, or seems to, by this question. Now let us look at the second part of this, thinking as we do.

A right choice? There are so many ways to examine this. Right absolutely? Right for the individual? And, if the latter, what does that mean? Right as in, best expressing the person's qualities at the moment? Or, as offering the most productive path forward (however that would be defined, and whoever would be the ones to define it)?

Given that, one way or another, all choices are taken *from the view of the absolute,* it still remains true that on any one pathway, only one choice is made. You don't come to a crossroads and take every fork in the road. You take *one,* regardless what happens in other versions of reality. And often enough the various options are, shall we say, ethically neutral. That is, taking one path or another won't affect, or won't much affect, your ongoing process of living your values. Whether you go east or west may make no difference ethically though it may make a huge difference (or may not, but may) in the future choices you will be faced with. But whether you can call a given choice "right" or not depends on where you stand relative to the person choosing.

You see? My point was that a person *is* as he or she was created; they *do* as they are moved to do, and the results of their choices can be argued, but the nature of the community that is functioning as an individual cannot.

Pole stars

And, as to pole stars, do we have time enough to squeeze in question three?

> [Charles: "Further, if everyone has a 'pole star,' is that referring to a preference of choices that would be beneficial to the person in 3D, meaning some choices have better 3D results; i.e., maybe less suffering? Or, if that is misunderstood, what does Rita mean by a 'pole star'?"]

When I say pole star, here, I mean the constant unvarying orientation that any 3D life cannot avoid having, consciously or (usually) not. What you *are* is hugely determinative of what you *believe,* what you *value,* what you *choose.* That's all.

And enough for today?

Enough for today. Allow me to extend my thanks for the questions, which assist greatly in elucidating the material.

And, of course, our thanks to you. Till next time, then.

Thursday, February 26, 2015

Almost 4 a.m. Good morning, Rita. Am I right that I ought to take a break from this? If so, why, and do you mean (or do I mean) a day here and there, or a longer span? This, given that there will be a matter of a week or more soon enough, when I go to [The Monroe Institute's weeklong Professional Division meeting] and then move [to the house I was in the process of buying].

There isn't any "ought" about it, but there certainly is a "feel free" about it. That much is up to you. The material will wait, and our connection isn't likely to evaporate.

Communication

Plus perhaps we'll have at least a couple of others on the line. I find the prospect exciting, but I don't know how discreet I should be about names in public. Suffice it to say for public consumption that I know of two of my friends who are talking to you, and I am encouraging them to post transcripts, and I have hopes that this public record will encourage others to try their hand.

This is material enough to fill a session.

Let's do it. The questions won't go away.

Very well—and said with a twinkle in my very-non-3D eye.

Because who's to say what's my idea and what's yours.

And what is neither or both, correct.

Here is the hope and the intent that I have. It is one thing to communicate more fully. It is another to release the results of such communication to close friends. A third, to release it to the winds, so to speak—to the world. A fourth to encourage others to do the same, and it is yet another step to encourage them to practice together—which is what this could become.

Such practice would have its difficulties and its opportunities and would be the difference between a controlled laboratory experiment and uncontrolled everyday practice, which could become everyday behavior.

Suppose you and—well, I would name them, but I feel your resistance and I have to respect it—suppose you and your three close friends, one of them *very* close—all begin to talk to me, first in private, then sharing the results among you (as you have already done), then—next—putting such communication on the public record. You all met me, and only one in-the-flesh meeting is required to set up an extremely powerful link if the link already exists in the non-3D.

You mean, I take it, that a physical meeting helps us to recognize a link that already exists but might not otherwise be recognized.

That's right. So, even though you know one another and know me, the act of bringing forth information supposedly from the same non-3D source is going to have its tensions. Fear lest you are fooling yourself, of course. Fear that the material will be distorted by your expectations. Fear that what you bring in will not jibe with what another is getting—or, far worse, with what *more than one other* is getting. All these, over and above the usual concern lest you mislead others inadvertently (since you know you won't do so deliberately).

But the overcoming of these obstacles is precisely what is going to make a further step possible.

In fact, you could almost make that a law of 3D life—it is the overcoming of obstacles that makes for change. Then it is up to you to determine the nature of the change, which you do by your chosen attitude as you address the challenge, the obstacle.

Such a controlled small-group experiment will illustrate the obstacles that will present themselves to a world of people routinely communicating with the non-3D in one way or another—and will, in its working-out, point toward helpful practices and attitudes that will arise from recognition of the obstacles.

For instance, authority.

Authority

There will be a tremendous temptation to oneself and to others to settle upon one or another person as "the authority on (in this case) Rita." That is as natural as breathing and couldn't be less helpful to the process. Because, if Frank, say, is the authority on communications with Rita (or with Hemingway, or anyone else Frank develops a non-3D relationship with), then what of everybody else, very much including people who knew Rita (or Hemingway, or whomever) much better than Frank did?

You see? Who is to say who has a better connection at any one time?

Who is to say whose internal mechanism is unconsciously distorting which part of which message?

Who is to say that *their* connection, *their* overall sense of the person, *their* messages, are right, and others' are wrong?

And—following from this and actually more important, but not always as obvious—who is to say that one's own message is wrong, one's own ability or authority is less valid, one's own contribution is unneeded or unwanted or "only" one talking to oneself?

It is in the friction of multiple messages from (and to) the same source that you will find a new freedom, the freedom that comes with true sharing in an attitude of one among equals, where the only judgment is—because it is what you will have to come to—"does it resonate?"

Do you see what I am saying? In common 3D interaction, you may accept another person as an authority on this or that, but you accept no one as an authority over *everything*. (Or, if you do, you are in for a real disappointment at some point.) You should be grateful that this is so, or you would be perpetually in a subordinate role, the student to others' teaching. But what true teacher wants his or her students to remain students all their lives? Far better for them to move out on their own, hopefully to surpass the teacher.

Consistency

Another issue will be consistency of information. Weigh consistency to some extent. Indeed, you will scarcely be able to avoid doing so. But recognize that not consistency but resonance is the touchstone. If you wish to set up a religion, then yes, consistency will be, or will anyway *seem* to be, the most important thing, as any deviation from the words of the master, as recorded in scripture, will be an assault on the fabric. But if instead of preserving a monument to the truth as found previously, you wish to continue to progress toward an ever-greater truth, consistency will serve only as a very rough guide. You don't abandon your compass, your GPS—that is, your inner certainty expressed as resonance with a given message—in order to remain faithful to a map someone else drew. To do so would amount to an implicit declaration that someone else's connection, experience, and descriptive ability is automatically better than your own. And even if that were objectively true, where would living by that idea leave you? It wouldn't help you pioneer new territory, that's for sure. New territory (new to you, that is) may be marked on the map; it isn't known to you until you traverse it.

Yet another issue will be the silent jockeying among individuals for recognition or precedence or status. The more you are aware of this as a *potential* problem, the less of an *actual* problem this will be. But it is complicated by the fact that valid information may come by means of an ego-driven individual. In other words, you will find yourselves separating the message from the messenger—and this is as it should be, indeed must be.

It has been forty-five minutes. Do you want to stop here, to make one distinct message, or start on a question, or—come to think of it—do you have more you want to say about this? I sensed completion, but maybe I was wrong.

We can end here. It is true, I do want this to stand alone, because I want everybody who reads it to engage in the great experiment. I think you will find that some have been doing it already but have been loathe to announce it, lest they be accused of delusions of grandeur.

Just as they would be if we caught them talking on the telephone.

Just remember back to your own tentative first steps. It didn't always seem so natural and obvious!

No, it certainly did not. Very well, Miss Rita, a very interesting session, not at all what I expected. Not that that is anything new! See you next time.

Friday, February 27, 2015

3:30 a.m. Good morning, Rita. Big day, yesterday. Your suggestion met response. [Two people had reported on the TMI Explorers list on their contacts with her.] Back to questions, today, or do you have more you would like to say?

Preventive maintenance

I want to second the motion about your taking care of your health as we do this. Your correspondent issued a warning that this could take an emotional toll as you proceed. Well, it doesn't *need* to, but it could. A little preventive maintenance would be just as well.

For others, I take it, not just for me.

Of course.

And such maintenance would be?

Nothing you haven't been told in the past, but that isn't to say that you have paid much attention. You needn't establish protective rituals unless ritual itself appeals to you, but you should remain aware that your mind belongs to *you*; that you in the physical have the right to make decisions and no one else does (for yourself, that is, of course); that you will need to remember to keep to a middle course, opening to the unknown but not losing touch with mundane reality.

In short, establish your *intent* firmly; you wish to explore, you wish to be of service, you wish to grow in a healthy direction, you wish to preserve your autonomy without either retreating into isolation or losing your protective boundaries. Those who prefer ritual should invent a ritual expressing this. Those who do not prefer ritual should still find a way not to forget that these are the boundaries within which your explorations proceed. Now we may start on questions.

Just in order?

Sure. Just as Charles stacks them up.

Okay, here goes.

Paths

[Chey's question: "At other times the Guys and Rita have talked about the completed being after we drop the body. I believe the guys said that the completed being is a compilation of our 3D life as 'experienced' by the 3D individual AND the experiences of that same being having lived all those other possible paths. In other words, while we were in the body, we could choose among all possible paths, and only choose one to consciously shine our little 5% (or whatever) flashlight on, but all paths are actually taken. Is the combination of all those possible paths taken compile [sic] the completed being? Or is it something different? I assume that if this or something like it is accurate, that completed being would also have memories of all those other paths.

[If so, we are actually so very much more than we could ever even begin to dream!

[And, do all those other paths that were lived but not chosen also affect our lives as we experience it with our flashlight every day, now?"]

Initially, you will remember, the guys groped for a way to explain to us the reason you (or anyone, of course) might reach another life in its state of awareness at that moment (the life in process, they called it) or might reach it after the storm of everyday life was passed and it had a vantage-point over the entire life as lived, the completed being. This was a necessary but insufficient step toward continuing to redefine our ideas so that we could become able to learn more.

To understand A, etc.

Exactly. Had you and I begun from a different place, the explanations that would have led forward would necessarily have been different. That's why different explorers bring home different maps of the same territory.

What you see depends partly upon what you are *capable of* seeing, and that depends partly upon where you were when you set out. Thus, it is good not to try to judge different schemes of things in terms of "which is more correct," and better to judge them in terms of "where did the mapmaker start from, to produce these differences between this map and mine?" It does no good to abandon the maps you have made yourself in favor of another's maps merely because that other has prestige in some form or another. The only reason to change is that you have found something that feels more correct than what you already had come to.

So, to return more closely to the question—today I would express it this way. The consciousness you are living at any given moment is aware of *one* path, even if that awareness is aware of multiple paths within the path, if that is not too confusing. In other words, no matter how complicated or rich your path is, complete with jumps to other timelines, awareness of multiple versions coexisting, etc., still you will experience your life as *one* path, not as several *different* paths even if that awareness shifts on you either slowly or rapidly. To be aware of—or, let's put it this way, you are aware of just as much complexity as you can handle, and anything more is only theoretical [to you].

So, any given life experience, no matter how complicated, is one path chosen among the many that might have been chosen. Looking at it from the path chosen, the completed-life-awareness sees only what *it* lived. It sees the results of *its* choices in that lifetime. It, itself, is the stable result of the experiment that that life was.

But looking at it from the point of view of the larger being from which the individual was formed, each completed-life-awareness is only *one* iteration, no more valuable, no less; no realer, no less, than all the others. So really we might refine our model from two to three. We still have (from the point of view of contact from 3D, which is all you have) the in-process awareness—Joseph on July 4, 1863. We have the completed-life representation—Joseph looking back on his life in the nineteenth century. But we also have—if we can get to it, which mostly depends on the level of awareness of the 3D questioner—another layer that I suppose we might call the larger being's experience of Joseph in all iterations.

Not too snappy a label.

You are welcome to improve on it. But you see the point.

Oh yes. And I feel a little better about our stumbling around sometimes. It means we don't have to get it right the first time.

And don't have to stick to superseded ways of understanding, and don't have to wonder if you're making it all up. Given sincerity and openness and an intelligently critical attitude, you'll get there. It is only when you begin to defend what you have already gotten that you will lose sight of greater understandings that might have followed.

So—again to return closely to the question at hand—we should say that the *larger being* has memories of all the paths any one consciousness created, or trod, whichever way you want to look at it. And you have access to the larger being by way of your direct connection, of course—your own non-3D component. Or, you can access any one iteration in detail; it depends on what you want, which depends partly on what you *are*.

Yes, you are more than you think. And you can learn to perceive more of what you are; it's up to you.

As to the final part of the question—yes, everything you connect to affects your lives to greater or lesser extent, dependent upon many variables. The rule of thumb I would propose is, you will experience more connection or less connection depending mostly upon your willingness to do so and also upon the appropriateness of such understanding to the path you are on, which are two categories that largely overlap but not always, and not necessarily. If you follow what *feels* right for you, you aren't likely to go too far wrong.

Next question?

Yes. You will notice that this proceeds nicely from the previous question, though Charles presumably did not line them up that way, given that he did not know how my answer would proceed.

Well, the two do have a relationship. He may have figured they were a logical progression.

You might ask him. I don't think he did, consciously. At any rate, pose the second question.

Bees and hives

[Cat's Paw's question: "I'm curious about one's relationship to one's strands in non-3D. Do you interact 'externally' with some or all of the strands that compose you as individual beings in their own right? Do you mostly know them as a part of your own being?

["I guess what I'm groping for is presumably one's strands are living their own 'lives,' —yes? Their changes and transformations would affect you as yours affects them. . . ? Now the image just popped into my head of strands/beings which, like family in the 3D world, don't get on so well, but are stuck with one another because they are 'family,' after all."]

The short answer is that outside of 3D, there *is* no perception of something being "external." Once the conditions of 3D are transcended, it becomes clear that "external" merely meant, beyond the limits of the conscious awareness as it was bounded by 3D conditions—perception of separation, binding to the continuously moving present moment, delayed consequences, etc. Remove those conditions and you return to life as it really is. (But those conditions were imposed for a constructive reason, remember. 3D is not a punishment nor a school nor a feverish illusion, but an artificially devised greenhouse for growing compound beings in the only way they can be produced. At least, that's one way of looking at it.)

So, yes, the image of family is a good one in that it suggests an ongoing unbreakable relationship. Perhaps a better image would be the bees in a hive, all living as individuals, all living as individual cells in a larger being that is less physical than metaphysical almost, a "hive." The hive—meaning, the sum total of the bees operating as part of one unit—is as real as the individual bees, yet could not exist without them. The bees are as individual as any 3D body that maintains itself, but, without the organizing principle that we are calling the hive, could not long exist and in any case would have no meaningful existence.

And that's another hour.

So it is. Our thanks as always, and next time we will continue down the list or will again follow you down the rabbit hole, whichever you prefer.

"I'm late, I'm late, for a very important date."

Don't think we don't all feel like the white rabbit sometimes, or the March Hare.

Better connections will help you feel less so.

If you say so. Okay, next time.

Saturday, February 28, 2015

3:45 a.m. All right, Miss Rita, ready for action. Your plan seems to be catching fire.

You will find that everything moves faster now. Not like the 1970s.

Thank God! Okay, questions, or do you have a theme?

Questions will do. It isn't hard to use a given question as an entry point for anything I have in mind. It isn't as if we were likely to stray beyond the bounds of the question of "what is?"

Question I've been asking all my life. All right, here's the first of the day, from John Wolf.

Sexual reproduction

[John Wolf's question: "I am confused by the apparent mixing of the body (DNA) heritage and the spiritual strand heritage or the implication that the spiritual heritage is affected or even made via the sexual reproduction process. Please clarify.

The second part of this paragraph, 'Compound beings, by their nature, are both battleground and reconciling force for opposing forces. They live a battle (and perhaps a reconciling) and they become a potential way forward. In short, they not only complicate the non-3D world by presenting new possibilities, they also help hold it together by sometimes reconciling the polar opposites they may learn to live.' has interesting implications. Does this 'reconciling' within non-3D go on among the parts of the greater being beyond the non-3D extension of ourselves? Does this 'reconciling' in the non-3D show itself as conflict in the 3D world?"]

That should lead to some clarification without requiring a good deal of explanation. Remember that this model stresses the unity of 3D and non-3D, rather than stressing differences. So it is an invitation to you (plural) to redefine your ideas of life, stressing that you extend into the non-3D (because the non-3D consists of additional dimensions usually unperceived or misperceived by those minds focused on 3D) and, therefore, the non-3D world may be said to extend into you. It is merely a matter of definition.

Well, if you are (whether or not known to yourselves) non-3D beings *as well as* 3D beings, should it surprise you that the affairs of "one side of the veil" and of the other side should not merely overlap but be an extension of each other? It is in the misrepresentation of life beyond the 3D that so much angst and disorientation originates. Once you remember that you have an understandable part in the nature of things—that you are not an accident, not contingent, not a meaningless spectator of incomprehensible activities—then you begin again to live without disorientation and anxiety.

To focus specifically on the first part of the question: It is true that physical and spiritual are intricately and necessarily linked, but the process is easily explained yet easily misunderstood.

The sexual reproduction of physical beings is a means of continually producing new mixtures of physical characteristics, so that a new soul may have a new home with new possibilities.

Probably as well to remind people that you are using 'soul' to mean the specific mind created in any given incarnation, as opposed to 'spirit,' which is the underlying unchanging breath of life that animates the soul.

Yes, although the second half of that statement is not quite that simple. But yes, "soul" means a specific incarnation, regardless of the antecedents or afterlife of that soul. The mating of different physical heredities produces continually new combinations of physical heredities for the incarnating spirit, the soul.

Perhaps an analogy will help you to understand the relationship between spiritual heritage and physical heritage. Consider each of these to be one parent.

Not so new an analogy. The spirit is masculine, matter is feminine. Father God and Mother Earth.

But if older ways of expressing things spoke to modern humans, there wouldn't be any need for new translations, would there? Once the relative polarities became entangled with physical gender, not only did the analogy become confused, but sexual politics entered in and caused needless additional confusion because of all the side issues raised by implication, as if analogy were anatomy.

In any case, consider that the physical confluence of different genetic inheritances is one factor in the new soul's environment. The other factor is what you may call the spiritual heritage but—as I try to express what to me seems very clear and obvious—I see is fraught with more potential misunderstanding than I had realized. The new soul is a new vessel, but what fills it is not created out of nothing, any more than the new body's material substance is created out of nothing. How could it be? It is just that the reassembly of cells into a new organization may *look like* it sprang from nothing if the observer concentrates only on the emerging organism forgetting the energy stream that enters and is incorporated.

May I?

Try, anyway.

The body begins as sperm and egg, then zygote, then continually dividing and multiplying cells, and as the cells continually multiply, they begin to assume their specialized form and function according to the underlying pattern of their blueprint. If you don't realize that the cells do not come out of nowhere, but are the result of the mother's nutrition and continual feed of new material into the developing fetus, it will look like magic—something out of nothing. (And indeed, the reality is magical enough!) But, once you do remember that the new being has its genesis and maintenance in an already existing being, from which, at the proper point in its development, it separates to begin a separate existence, the magic is in the overall arrangement, not in any hocus-pocus.

Yes, and although the new being's limits and characteristics are not determined by the genetics of its parents, the limits of choice are. That is, you may choose among a vast array of possibilities, but "vast" is not "unlimited."

3D and non-3D

Now, the second part of the question could be answered, simply but probably misleadingly, by reminding you that 3D and non-3D are part of the same thing. Although local weather conditions may vary, they are each part of the same climate, or say, the same ecosystem.

Yes, the non-3D forces battle within 3D. Yes, 3D battles both represent and affect non-3D. If they [that is, 3D and non-3D] are the same thing, how could they not? Just because compound beings may exist without noticeable extension into 3D, that does not mean—

I can always tell when you lead me beyond accustomed material. I tend to go wool-gathering and come back and find I have no idea how to finish something I left while I went wandering.

You will notice that it is only very rarely that I attempt to resume a sentence exactly where it was interrupted. Why pursue a dead-end when it is so easily gone around?

Now that you mention it, I do see that. So—

Anything you can feel in 3D exists as well in non-3D, except that the expression of the underlying forces may be different because of terrain. That is, in 3D you may experience isolation and the—desperation, let's call it—of struggle moment by moment to have your values prevail. Outside of 3D, we cannot very well feel either of those things, for our environment—the relative freedom in non-3D of 3D constraints—prevents us from seeing life in that blinkered focused fashion. Nonetheless, we compound beings have our values, and we do not cease to maintain and represent them. If you are kind in 3D, you will not cease to value kindness beyond the body. If you are iron, you will not soften. And if you are cruel or vindictive, you will not cease to be so. You *are* what you *are*. You represent and extend what you are made of. The major difference is that within 3D you have greater freedom of choice as to what you will become, and outside 3D you have greater awareness of your own place in the greater scheme of things.

John Wolf's question does not express the relationship between battles and reconciliation in the way that I would like to express it. Put it this way: every new compound being is a new opportunity for the expression of the potential contained within the larger being. (For the moment, I am concentrating on creation out of any one larger being, but it is not that simple, or you would be back to creation from God, end of story. But, one thing at a time.) The nature of each compound being is a bag of possibilities that each 3D life sorts and chooses among and brings together into an enduring pattern. Thus, by your work at reconciling opposing or anyway diverging forces, you help create new possibilities for reconciliation on the non-3D side as well. By your expression and choice of one or another set of values, you create an exponent of those values on the other side, in the non-3D, among the enduring archetypes, however you wish to say it.

Thus, the forces of heaven are at war, and Earth is the battleground. Or, the world is a place of creation in which 3D beings created from non-3D elements create in their turn, thus returning, to the non-3D part of the world, the elements of which they were formed, transformed. Or, values precede form as blueprints precede construction, and in the incarnation and interplay of the 3D representation of these values—particularly in that the 3D representatives are inherently *mixtures* of values, never pure representatives—is the continuous redevelopment and re-creation of logical development of tendencies.

That was quite a paragraph. I was holding on to the buckboard, hoping not to get thrown off before the horses slowed down. That is, I'm writing and not at all sure what I'm writing makes sense, because I have no time to absorb it, even though (paradoxically) it is obvious enough as it comes through.

And, as you see, it is an hour and a little more, and this is a good place to pause.

Yes, I'll stagger out of the buckboard and head for the saloon, toss back a couple of hard whiskeys, and see what the day looks like. Till next time, then.

Afterword

The end of February did not mark the end of these conversations. All through March and April, and into May, we continued, nearly always early in the morning, nearly always for an hour, plus or minus a few minutes. As I had begun, so I continued, posting the day's conversation on the TMI Explorers list and then on my blog (www.hologrambooks.com/hologrambooksblog) and Facebook page (frank.demarco.10). And the conversations met response. People continued to pose questions, objections, counter-statements, logical extensions, and Rita responded in turn.

But six months' conversations boiled up to too many pages, so Bob Friedman, as publisher, decided to split the material into two volumes, scheduling volume two for publication in 2016. Bob and I thought it important to present the material in the way it came through, but there would be value, as well, in having it digested and presented in a more logical order. So, I live in hope that my friend Charles Sides will be able to deliver his analytical synopsis of the material, which I know will prove helpful to many.

This enterprise has involved many people—not only Rita, me, Charles, and Bob, but also everyone who supplied questions or comments. In fact, as Rita pointed out (and "the guys upstairs" before her) it involves as well all who *will* read it and respond to it. In other words, not only us, but you. Our hope is that you will not accept this material or reject it, but will *wrestle* with it, to see how much is true for you and how much you cannot accept. Only by wrestling with the material will you make it yours.

Best wishes.

Additional Titles from Rainbow Ridge

Read more about them at *www.rainbowridgebooks.com*

*Consciousness: Bridging the Gap between Conventional Science
and the New Super Science of Quantum Mechanics*
by Eva Herr

Dying to Know You: Proof of God in the Near-Death Experience
by P. M. H. Atwater

The Cosmic Internet: Explanations from the Other Side
by Frank DeMarco

Dance of the Electric Hummingbird
by Patricia Walker

Messiah's Handbook: Reminders for the Advanced Soul
by Richard Bach

When the Horses Whisper
by Rosalyn Berne

Channeling Harrison
by David Young

Rainbow Ridge Books publishes spiritual, metaphysical, and
self-help titles and is distributed by Square One Publishers in
Garden City Park, New York.

To contact authors and editors, peruse our titles, and see submission
guidelines, please visit our website at *www.rainbowridgebooks.com*.

For orders and catalogs, please call toll-free: (877) 900-BOOK.